THE PSYCHOLOGY OF PRAYER

ALSO FROM BERNARD SPILKA

The Psychology of Religion, Fourth Edition:
An Empirical Approach
*Ralph W. Hood, Jr., Peter C. Hill,
and Bernard Spilka*

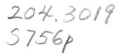

The Psychology *of* Prayer

A SCIENTIFIC APPROACH

Bernard Spilka
Kevin L. Ladd

THE GUILFORD PRESS
New York   London

© 2013 The Guilford Press
A Division of Guilford Publications, Inc.
72 Spring Street, New York, NY 10012
www.guilford.com

Printed in the United States of America

This book is printed on acid-free paper.

Last digit is print number: 9   8   7   6   5   4   3   2   1

Library of Congress Cataloging-in-Publication Data

Spilka, Bernard, 1926–
  The psychology of prayer : a scientific approach / Bernard Spilka,
Kevin L. Ladd.
      p. cm.
  Includes bibliographical references and index.
  ISBN 978-1-4625-0695-8 (hardcover)
  1. Prayer—Psychology.   I. Ladd, Kevin L.   II. Title.
  BV225.S65 2013
  204′.3019—dc23

                                                    2012010301

*To Blanka and Hugo Scharlack, my in-laws, for whom prayer
was an indispensable part of life*

And to their daughter Ellen, my wife of 58 years
—B. S.

*To my parents, Kay and Kenneth Ladd, who provided
the combination of structure and freedom necessary
to develop a love of learning*
—K. L. L.

About the Authors

Bernard Spilka, PhD, is Professor Emeritus of Psychology at the University of Denver. He has been president of the Colorado Psychological Association, the Rocky Mountain Psychological Association, and Division 36 (Society for the Psychology of Religion and Spirituality) of the American Psychological Association, and vice president of the Society for the Scientific Study of Religion. Dr. Spilka is a recipient of the Scholar/Teacher Award from the United Methodist Church; the William James Award, Mentoring Award, and Distinguished Service Award from Division 36; and Distinguished Service Awards from the Colorado and Rocky Mountain Psychological Associations. Continuing to write professionally, he is author, coauthor, editor, or coeditor of nine books, one monograph, and two major federal reports.

Kevin L. Ladd, PhD, is Associate Professor of Psychology at Indiana University South Bend and former pastor of United Methodist and Presbyterian (PCUSA) congregations. A consulting editor for journals including the *Journal of Social Psychology*, *Archive for the Psychology of Religion*, and *Psychology of Religion and Spirituality*, he also serves on the Board of Directors of the International Association for the Psychology of Religion. Dr. Ladd's research on the psychology of prayer has involved collaborations, publications, and lectures in Africa, China, Europe, India, and South America.

Preface

This is a book on psychology, the psychology of religion, and not religion per se. We discuss people and focus on the psychology of prayer, as we believe it is one of the important, if not the most important, personal religious activities in which one may engage. Prayer is behavior that is intimately associated with the central concerns of mainstream psychology: motivation, cognition, personality, and social psychology. It is therefore of prime interest to psychologists.

To the extent that we address theology and institutional religion, it is in the context of how they influence the beliefs, experiences, thinking, and actions of people. We thus emphasize the prayerful responses that people employ in their desire to identify with, contact, and influence themselves, others, and their God. Some 97% of Americans claim that they pray at least once a week; even some atheists are willing to admit that they too pray (General Social Survey, 2008). Another recent source utilizing earlier Gallup Poll data places the number praying at least once annually at 90% (Delany, Miller, & Bisono, 2007). Something this prevalent obviously possesses great individual and cultural significance.

Psychologists have written about prayer for well over a century. However, it wasn't until the 1980s that we have witnessed a significant amount of systematic objective research in the area. This seems to have increased with each succeeding decade. The one classic effort, by Brown (1994), to provide an overview of this topic has rapidly become outdated because of the remarkable outpouring of published work on the subject.

Our desire is to introduce a scientific psychological approach to what some regard as an inherently unscientific activity. Although we stress the "psychological" and "scientific," it is not possible to embrace a wholly denatured, devalued approach to prayer. Still, our effort accepts theological or inspirational ideas only if they contribute to psychological theory that results in empirical research.

In sum, we aim primarily to show how the study of prayer is integral to the key themes of modern psychology and how crucial it is for scholars to appreciate the multidimensional aspects of prayer and the act of praying. This approach leads to proper recognition of the lifelong developmental expressions of prayer and its significant roles in coping with life's problems. Controversy is ever present in this endeavor, within both the field of psychology and science in general, and we confront the controversial issues head-on. Given this perspective, we readily identify with Dostoyevsky's view, expressed in *The Brothers Karamazov*, that "prayer is an education."

Acknowledgments

I cannot ever forget Ellen, my wonderful wife of 58 years, whose "nudging" kept me working on this book every possible moment. I am especially grateful for the skillful help and wonderful attitude of Erin Meyer and her excellent staff at the Penrose Library at the University of Denver. Their ability to locate and obtain references seemed limitless. Michael Nielsen and Michael Donahue were extremely helpful in finding certain source materials that I desperately needed. In sum, aid was available whenever I needed it. Who can ask for more? —B. S.

A fair amount of the newest research reported here emanates from the Social Psychology of Religion Laboratory at Indiana University South Bend. This was generously funded by the John Templeton Foundation (Grant No. 12282). I am particularly appreciative of the dedicated efforts of a wonderful research team consisting of Katelyn Andrysiak, Briana Becker, Wanakee Brown, Cara Cook, Jaime Cora, Alyssa Dibley, Kaitlyn Foreman, Melissa Lentine, Angie Meador, Sarah Mertes, Kyle Messick, Alison Niemi, Brice Petgen, Erik Ritter, Carolyn Sherma, Amelia Sinnott, Andrea Stevenson, Erin Tracey, Sheri Vreugdenhil, Kevin Weber, and John Younas. Meleah L. Ladd developed and coauthored many of the presentations. She simultaneously kept project finances well organized. The youngest unofficial members of the team—Arryngton, Alisdair, and Aurelia Ladd—helped us keep the rest of life in balance. —K. L. L.

Contents

CHAPTER 1

Introduction to the Scientific Study of Prayer

Prayer is the very soul of religion.
—AUGUSTE SABATIER (1897, p. 109)

A history and psychology of prayer would almost be equivalent
to a history and psychology of religion.
—GEORGE A. COE (1916, p. 302)

A history of prayer would be the best history of the religious
development of mankind.
—AUGUSTE SABATIER (1897, p. 28)

*P*eople interested in prayer have literally hundreds of books from which to choose. Some are "how-to" manuals, while others reflect the authors' personal experiences. Even more tomes are dedicated to theological conceptions of prayer. In this book we take none of those approaches, though we do occasionally draw upon their insights. Rather, we undertake to explore what is known about prayer based on years of research applications of the scientific method to the subject.

Our approach is obviously just one closely circumscribed way of understanding prayer, that does not permit us to grapple with the central metaphysical assumptions underlying prayer (e.g., Does God hear and answer prayers?). Rather, in this slim volume we offer a review of scientific efforts and observations that should encourage thinking about how science and other disciplines interested in prayer

1

(e.g., religious studies, theology) can suggest and pose mutually respectful and informed questions. If, together, we are able to arrive at new answers and fresh outlooks, consider it a bonus!

Why study prayer? At first, the answer appears simple. People pray because it is appropriate in certain settings or is the only resource left for those in need. A scientific orientation, however, tells us that prayer is central to the psychology of religion and calls upon the essence of psychology itself. The scientific framework seeks to explain the issues of "appropriateness" and "need" by turning to our knowledge of cognition (how people think), motivation (what is wanted or needed), and emotion (feelings and desires). As succeeding chapters attest, scientific perspectives make us consider matters of individual development, coping, adjustment, well-being, social life, and health. Prayer is thus the psychology of religion in action and literally reflects virtually every facet of behavioral scientific psychology, from its neural roots to complex social responsivity. In this volume, we hope to demonstrate these ideas.

The quotations that open this chapter typify the views of early psychologists of religion on prayer. Many of the field's earliest scholars combined their interest in psychology with deeply held religious convictions (Spilka & McIntosh, 1999). As psychology gradually became a science, it increasingly separated itself from traditional faith. Many psychologists simultaneously embraced the perspectives and methods of science to better understand religious belief, behavior, and experience in more quantifiable terms. This gradualistic approach resulted in the early acceptance of the psychology of religion in mainline journals of the American Psychological Association (APA).

As noted in the Preface, this is a book about the psychology of prayer, not the theology of prayer. We do not deal with the validity or consistency of theological statements but, rather, explore some of the psychological ramifications of such ideas and actions (Spilka, 1976). This attempt to understand prayer by using the tools of social science should not be misconstrued as deliberately downplaying its spiritual dimension. The scientific method does, however, restrict itself to a domain of theory that generates testable hypotheses, and we strive to remain securely within these boundaries.

On one level, prayer is commonly taken for granted. The popular belief is that "everyone knows what prayer is." Closer scrutiny, however, reveals a complexity that demands further analysis. As of

December 2011, the Internet search engine Google listed some 226 million entries related to the search term "pray." Even though some of these entries cited the same source, obviously the subject is a significant topic within the public discourse.

There are few matters of greater personal importance than the prayers people offer to their God. The individual prayer and its sought-for objectives, no matter how serious and intimate the prayer is, often appear modest in manner and aspiration. As the quintessential religious activity, prayer possesses a quality that circumscribes virtually all human enterprises and hopes. Comparable to the aural adorations in Beethoven's *Missa Solemnis,* the visual message implicit in Dürer's *Hands of an Apostle,* or the fervent appeals of those in pain to a Higher Power, prayer resonates with an impressive psychological punch.

The General Social Survey's analysis of national data from 1972 to 2006 suggests that as many as 97% of Americans pray, and some 57% indicate that they pray one or more times each day (General Social Survey, 2008). Laird (1991) reported on a Princeton University survey that found "74% of men and 86% of women rely on prayer when faced with a problem" (p. 22). If we accept Clark's (1958) positing of secret religion as one we keep to ourselves, numerous prayers probably go unreported. The central place of prayer in life, personally and socially, conveys clearly why there is a need to understand theory and research in this area. Wuthnow (2008a) further asserts that "far more Americans pray than engage in other religious activities" (p. 334), including any other private or public religious behavior.

A full treatment of prayer requires a wide-ranging perspective. We see it as primarily relevant to both personal and social psychology; it is complex behavior of fundamental importance to the lives of most people, encompassing a broad spectrum of attitudes, beliefs, experiences, and knowledge. Since we cannot cover fully all aspects of prayer in its myriad cultural contexts, our intention is to emphasize the American and European milieus, for these are where most of the quantitative research has been conducted. In a few instances studies are reported from the Jewish and Muslim traditions. It is our hope that others with experience in alternative settings will in time join the dialogue.

Prayer is only one aspect of the ways in which religion is understood and practiced. No one, however, would question its centrality and its elaborate network of social-psychological and possibly even biological embodiments. Faith is expressed in many ways, and prayer is part of a larger framework of beliefs, experiences, and observances.

In the chapters to come we convey an appreciation of how complex prayer is. Simply put, prayer has many facets that can be measured. Most basically, it is embedded in the rich and involved structure of mainstream psychology. Second, praying begins early and in part reflects how one perceives the world throughout life. Its place in childhood, adolescence, adulthood, and old age is integral to coping with the problems of living. Third, prayer reflects the perceptions, cognitions, and motivations of those who pray. In recent years, these psychological realms have been supplemented by a neuropsychology that attempts to describe how the brain and nervous system operate during prayer. Fourth, if there is one major function of prayer, it is the key role it plays in helping people cope with the problems encountered in social living. For example, prayer is significant in marriage and family life, especially when confronting such personal issues as one's children, health, illness, or death. Virtually every aspect of clinical, social, and experimental psychology has a place in our efforts to comprehend this most basic of human activities. Prayer is truly critical to the way most people conduct their lives. It is an important feature not simply of the psychology of religion but of psychology in toto. A full treatment of prayer requires a wide-ranging perspective (Zaleski & Zaleski, 2005). We hope our handling of this domain will stimulate new ideas and research that will enhance both scientific and personal dealings with the world.

Finally, prayer does not exist in a psychological or religious vacuum. We should not lose sight of its place within the broad framework of religious and spiritual actions that include those not only of psychological interest but also of sociological and anthropological concern.

SOME BASICS

An understanding of prayer offers the potential to achieve insight into a variety of fundamental psychological processes (cognition, motivation, etc.). These processes are inseparable from the broader historical, cultural, and social settings in which people congregate. Here one must keep in mind the religious practices and their meanings that are taught by religious bodies, parents, and peers. For instance, what is the appropriate physical posture to adopt while praying, and should one face the East or another direction? What happens psychologically if I am physically unable to follow these guidelines? Finally, as recent work implies, prayer as a core religious element might even have biological links (Gazzaniga, 1985; Hardy, 1976; Waller, Kojetin, Bouchard, Lykken, & Tellegen, 1990).

Even passing familiarity with the history of the psychology of religion tells us that, after an initially strong reception, religion and prayer were largely ignored or rejected by mainstream psychologists. Some have viewed the relationship as a war on religion (Cummings, O'Donohue, & Cummings, 2009), but slowly over the past half-century interest in the psychology of religion has grown to the extent that research and discussion of psychoreligious issues may be found in first-line journals of the APA (Wade, 2010). In addition, Division 36 of the APA deals exclusively with the psychology of religion and publishes its own journal, *Psychology of Religion and Spirituality.* Other noteworthy publications are the *International Journal for the Psychology of Religion*, the *Journal for the Scientific Study of Religion*, and the *Review of Religious Research*. One can easily cite other journals that tie the psychology of religion to various religious bodies, all of which have included research on the theory and practice of prayer.

Unfortunately, the position enunciated by Pratt (1910) a century ago remains valid. He declared: "It is not a little surprising that in an age when so much emphasis is laid upon empiricism and the value of "facts" so little attempt should have been made to study empirically what is perhaps the most important and vital fact of religion . . . prayer" (p. 48). We may not fully remedy this shortcoming, but we hope to contribute meaningfully toward its resolution. In 1985 Finney and Malony (1985b) offered a review of the empirical work undertaken on prayer, noting a paucity of solid research in the area. We are pleased to have witnessed during the past 25 years a remarkable turnaround in that regard, with literally hundreds of studies undertaken on the subject. And yet, as we will see, too many of these studies fall short on both their design and analysis.

Finally, the scientific study of prayer invariably involves measurement. Many means are employed to assess religiousness, including the subjectively judged importance of religion, scales that deal with the structure of belief systems, and such behavioral indices as the frequency of attendance at services, among other possibilities. Sometimes questionnaire items inquire how often one prays. These indicators invariably correlate substantially with one another, and references to research that treats attendance rates are worth citing whenever appropriate. Prayer has long been considered an element of religiosity that correlates strongly with collective worship and institutional rituals and protocols.

Public and Private Prayer: The Issue of Worship

Sharply distinguishing between "worship" and "prayer" has some legitimate appeal. The term "worship" has been applied to virtually all religious activities. Most authors, however, reserve the concept of worship for collective religious activity in which large numbers of people participate in orderly structured public services, usually within an institutional (i.e., church) setting (Clark, 1958). Some authors also apply it to rites that involve relatively few individuals, such as reciting grace at a home meal or observances by small groups at funerals or memorial services. The hallmark of worship appears to be public formal ceremony and ritual. In a sense, "worship" refers to the sanctioned actions of people as prescribed by institutional doctrine and practice.

Prayer, as a personal–private devotional activity, may or may not be viewed as a form of worship, though varying degrees of overlap have been suggested (see, e.g., Smart, 1972). No criteria have been established to distinguish sharply between prayer and worship. Despite the formal use of the *Te Deum* or a well-established hymn, people always bring their own unique meanings to their church, mosque, synagogue, or temple services. These interpretations and practices may include many things, from simple habits to personally intense and complex religious mystical experiences. There is always room for personally prayerful expression within a structured service, even during those portions that specify the engagement of all participants in a single corporate prayer. Being in the "House of God" may stimulate a great deal of individual expressive variation. The conventional public worship setting may also introduce important social-psychological factors into the process of prayer. One has to consider the influence of others who are engaged in similar activities as well as the meaning of particular social settings, the role of ritualized ceremony, the degree of one's personal involvement, and other factors.

In sum, prayer is commonly submerged within the complex concept we label as "personal faith." Specifically, questions relating to the role and significance of prayer often include other actions and practices such as Bible reading, saying grace, or employing such physical accoutrements as spinning wheels or beads that are systematically passed through one's fingers.

In recent years, the increasingly popular term used to describe personal faith is "spirituality," which overlaps with religion. Distinctions between "religion" and "spirituality" are controversial. A recent source states that it is "an open question whether the practice of spirituality outside religion can be adequately defined" (Hood, Hill, & Spilka, 2009, p. 9). These authors, however, include prayer and meditation as spiritual disciplines. Zinnbauer and Pargament (2005) call spirituality a search for the sacred and consider it of broader personal utility than religion. At present, the dominant position among psychology researchers treats spirituality as the personalization of religion. We cannot readily resolve this issue. For the purposes of the discussion in this volume, prayer conceptualized as personal communication between an individual and his or her God may include both personal and institutional elements of religion.

RELATIONS BETWEEN RELIGION AND PSYCHOLOGY

The Issue of Personal Involvement

Prayer is rarely viewed dispassionately. It is an activity that elicits the deepest of human feelings. However, religious inclinations for predispositions do not necessarily compromise an objective psychological view of prayer. In fact, theology might even properly serve as a guide to developing valid psychological theory (Spilka, 1976; Vaux, 1990).

The Influence of Culture

The psychological study of prayer is subject to myriad social forces that subtly influence all members of society, including scientists. Historically conditioned cultural values structure not only our language but also our thought processes. So, we must remain well aware of our potential biases and make every effort to be objective even if we cannot be totally detached.

Questions of Bias: Mixing Religion, Science, and Psychology

When controversial topics are studied, one's assumptions and biases are often masked or disguised. Language and one's choice of particular phraseologies may subtly disguise values that violate scientific objectivity. The fact that religion was formerly long regarded as a "taboo topic" in psychology testifies to psychologists' sensitivity to studying the role of faith (Farberow, 1963). Although this hands-off orientation has been changing for some time, a persisting difficulty concerns social scientists who are religiously affiliated. When they write about religion and prayer, it is exceptionally difficult to avoid theological biases (Hinnebusch, 1969; Moore, 1959; Tyrrell, 1985). Their writings abound with judgments about the soul and spirit in prayer, "higher" and "lower" or "mature" and "immature" forms of prayer, "proper" ways of praying, descriptions of "true" prayer, discussions of the objective "effectiveness" of prayer, and getting one's prayers "answered." Some of these issues are appropriate for research, while others are not.

Among early scholars, Strickland (1924) expressed doubts about psychological approaches to prayer because he believed that the "traditional empirical method shuts off all reference to divine agency in human experience" (p. 216). Dresser (1929) declared that the "essence of prayer may be a divine–human give and take" (p. 58). Based on these perspectives, religion is inherently mixed with psychology, thus raising valid questions about the objective observation and classification of the characteristics of human religious/spiritual behavior. In this book, our task is to observe and psychologically infer, not to convert anyone to any particular point of view.

PSYCHOLOGY AS A SCIENCE: AN UNDERSTANDING

Many people like the term "science" because it conveys a rigorous, no-nonsense image that embraces everything from the atomic to the astrophysical realm. Unfortunately, the term is also occasionally appropriated to justify activities and beliefs that stray way beyond the limits of the scientific method. Thus, we too often hear of parascience, astrological science, occult science, spiritual science, divine science, metascience, various forms of mental science, paranormality, parapsychology, and similar appelations. In relation to the study of prayer, there is a strong desire to obtain evidence that it "works," as we further demonstrate later in this chapter. Indeed, we show that research supports the hypothesis that prayer assists people in coping with the trials of life. On the other hand, there are assertions that praying can bring about specific tangible outcomes. As scientists, we accept such claims as hypotheses to be evaluated. Later in this book, we examine both sides of this controversy scientifically, carefully noting precisely how the operationalization of "works" can differ greatly from practitioner to scientist.

Science and the Need for Theory

In science, theories must be *explicit*. Noted psychologist Kurt Lewin (1951, p. 169) stated, "There is nothing so practical as a good theory." A theory tells us what findings should be regarded as important and what is truly irrelevant. It provides guidance and direction for our work, and it must eventuate in hypotheses, explanatory statements that are testable. Theories are never fully proved scientifically, only disproved (or, perhaps more often, they are simply abandoned for lack of sustained interest owing to conflicting results). Exceptions never prove rules, only *disprove* them. Hypothesis testing has a high probability of resulting in modifications to existing views or the creation of new theory, which is then subjected to the same assessment process all over again.

Being Sensitive to All Sources of Information

Theological and inspirational writing on prayer is prodigious, and some of it is relevant to a psychology of prayer. Religionists write about perceptions, cognitions, and motivations for prayer and speak of individual hopes and aspirations as part of the process of prayer. Additionally, they offer their assessments of the efficacy of prayer. In other words, they allude to a psychology of expectations and attributions about the praying person and the deity that is the object of prayer. We may find some interesting psychological insights and observations offered by religionists that are not usually considered by psychologists. In the following section, we select and expand upon ideas from this literature for our psychology of prayer.

THE DEFINITION OF PRAYER

In our discussion thus far, we have relied on the general understanding of prayer that most people in our society hold. A specifically scientific approach requires greater focus. Therefore, we need to define prayer more precisely. Some 21 years after the publication of William James's noteworthy *Varieties of Religious Experience*, K. R. Stolz (1923) stated emphatically that "prayer may be simply and comprehensively defined as man's intercourse with God" (p. 18). This view posits a specific relationship between two beings. Clearly the relationship is not between equals, involving as it does the human being seeking an ideal connection with a deity. Such an effort implies that the weaker member of this paired duo turns to the stronger for help, and indeed this is the chief feature of most kinds of prayer. Given this perspective, Buttrick (1942) ascribes a certain degree of "lowliness" (p. 33) to the one doing the praying.

Moving closer to the present, Dubois-Dumee (1989) endorses this view of prayer by declaring that "prayers are ways to God" (p. 6). Similarly, Beckman (1995), for whom prayers are channels for the purpose of communication, describes "prayer as the name we give to the experience of being in communication with God" (p. 8). This definition directs us to focus on prayer's experiential nature and its communicative essence, which we shortly detail. Buttrick (1970) stressed the interpersonal conversational quality of man–God interaction, which he adapted from Buber's I–thou format. He saw God speaking for the first time through his act of creating human beings. This issue of the Deity initiating prayer and then the individual's responses possibly is a common theological interpretation, not a psychological insight.

Contemporary definitions generally emphasize that prayer is an act of communication, often employing such terms as "address" or "request," with "need" constituting the most frequent motivation for initiating prayer (Janssen, De Hart, & Den Draak, 1990). The same emphasis is found in current dictionaries, where we encounter such phrases as "reverent petition," "fervent request," and "earnest request." The classic Merriam-Webster dictionary definition stresses entreaty, appeal, and supplication. Such other terms as "adoration," "communion," and "devotion" also appear. In the next chapter we further explore how some of these popular notions can suggest surprisingly diverse psychological conceptions, understandings, and behavior.[1]

Directions Offered by Definitions

Attempts to define prayer, especially in inspirational writing, focus on the personal–theological significance of the process. Why pray? Why communicate in this particular way with God? Harkness (1948) cites the shorter Westminster Catechism to the effect that "prayer is an offering up of our desires unto God for things agreeable to His will" (p. 26). This theological assertion enriches our understanding of prayer as a behavior by bringing personal needs and wants into the picture. Prayer is thus responsive communicative behavior colored by individual motives (i.e., wants or cravings) that are inherent in simply being human.

The issue of "needs" requires additional specification. A need implies a shortcoming, deficiency, or weakness that must be corrected. As Hallesby (1975) put it, "Prayer has been ordained only for the helpless. . . . Prayer and helplessness are inseparable" (p. 17). Most motivational theorists posit wants and inadequacies that produce stress and tension when they go unsatisfied. Many commentators broaden the concept further beyond merely meeting one's needs. In part, they see prayer as offering a potential for individual growth, not just a means of overcoming some shortfall or failing.

Prayer as Communication

Prayer is communication. Through it, one relates to and even identifies with the Divine. The inspirational literature on prayer and praying emphasizes "loving God," "union with God," and a host of similar terms such as "praise," "adoration" and the like. A relationship exists between one who prays (i.e., the *pray-er*) and the Entity prayed to, with the pray-er bringing to this interaction various understandings and expectations. Clearly, pray-ers attribute power to God and in most instances anticipate benevolence on the part of the Deity. This anticipation easily translates into a belief that one has gained additional protection and safety, which results in greater peace of mind. In this instance, a sense of helplessness has been countered by an increase in one's sense of control, even if that control is only vicariously experienced. This key role for prayer, giving one a greater sense of control, is of course part of the larger realms of religion and spirituality, which appear to correlate positively with psychological and physical well-being (McCullough & Willoughby, 2009). Almost everyone prays at one time or another. Each of us has been exposed to ideas that overwhelmingly depict worship and prayer in positive terms. Images of hope, promise, reward, and desired potential are part of what motivates prayer and other religious activities. In essence, someone who prays is likely to have been well conditioned culturally to expect a positive outcome to his or her prayer.

Prayer as Conversation

The social-communicative aspect of prayer may be its most evident feature (Baesler, 2003). Whether it is psychologically conceived as occurring between friends or between a child and her father (Barclay, 1962; Herman, 1921), the relationship involved in prayer rapidly increases in complexity. Clearly, to practitioners prayer is no ordinary conversation (Ladd, Vreugdenhil, Ladd, & Cook, in press). As we noted, it is certainly not regarded as transpiring between equals, either by those who pray or by researchers. Phillips (1981) appropriately states that "it is the status of the object addressed which determines the grammar of the talk; it is no longer people's daily discourse" (p. 41). Most religious writers expend a great deal of energy defining what that "right relationship" between a Deity and a supplicant should be, and though it is not always openly acknowledged, factors such as ingratiation are commonly observed. The one who prays frequently thus opens his prayer by acknowledging the high status, power, special concerns, and mercy of God. Feelings are invariably expressed about when and where one should pray, the state of mind of the pray-er, the methods of prayer, the motives for prayer, the forms of prayer, and a host of other considerations. Simply put, prayer constitutes a highly significant "conversation," with important implications for future occurrences.

We can define prayer as an appeal to a higher power, invariably a deity conceptualized in a relational sense. It can be formal or conversational, enunciated or silent, utilizing written words, song lyrics, or contemporaneous utterances; it can be carefully circumscribed or spontaneous, public or private, involving gestures, body postures, oral formulas, repetition, concentration on particular topics, meditation, and various emotions; it can also stimulate or be stimulated by our emotions. Prayers are most commonly individual creations largely shaped by the doctrines and practices of our religious institutions. They may be premised on various customs and given at set times or during particular functions—for example, on arising, at meals, or before retiring for the night.

A Brief Note on Definition and Purpose

As we suggested earlier, there is an aspect of making an appeal through prayer, not only for things one lacks or for one's shortcomings but also for personal betterment, progress, and growth. Such appeals need not be solely for oneself, but can be for others, communities, nations, humanity, or those who have died or will shortly be born; they can focus on past behavior or future possibilities. In sum, efforts to encapsulate prayer in a few pithy words are likely to shortchange its potential scientific richness. We suggest that the best definition of "prayer" envisages a direction—in fact, many directions—into the pray-er's cognitions, motivations, personality, and social behavior. Let us now introduce the psychological underpinnings these terms imply.

THE CONTENT AND EXPRESSION OF PRAYER

Prayer and Religious Experience

One goal of prayer may be to stimulate religious experience, to enter into a state where one "encounters" God, experiences nirvana, or has an ethereal feeling that conveys a sense of unity and completeness, along with new knowledge and positive emotions such as joy and bliss (Greeley, 1974). Lewis (1959) thus identifies "prayer with all religious experience . . . the live moments of religious awareness" (p. 244). He further states that "an enlivened awareness of God is induced and maintained" (p. 177) through prayer. From a psychodynamic perspective, Pruyser (1968) suggests that the way one prays is designed "to enhance an imaginative form of thought" (p. 72), which in turn results in religious experience. In other words, prayer likely activates unconscious factors that then stimulate one to produce conscious ideas.

Associating religious experience with prayer implies the "true" goal of prayer. Even though some kind of experience is present in virtually every human activity, including prayer, much of what we experience in our daily lives is far from what the true religionist desires from prayer. And yet, often there may be little more to praying than habitual responses or mechanical petitionary appeals.

The Efficacy of Prayer

People may pray for a variety of reasons, but if for any reason they thought prayer was ineffective, the chances are great that they would cease praying or at least offer fewer prayers. Of course, the question largely hinges upon what "effective" means. Does it imply that the laws of nature must be overturned—that objective reality needs to be changed—to satisfy our desires? Or, in contrast, might the significance of "efficacy" be found in what happens to the one who prays? Established religion suggests that both possibilities pertain here.

Even in earlier times, most people believed that the effects of prayer were largely focused on the praying individual. In one of the first empirical surveys, Beck (1906) reported that 98% of his sample "regularly feel the need for prayer" (p. 118) and that 83% "believed the results of prayer to be wholly subjective" (p. 119). What we may be observing in these studies is the seemingly ever-present practical streak in most all Americans. Nowadays we might say, "If it isn't broken, don't fix it." James (1907), who stated the pragmatic principle for religion, asserted that "if the hypothesis of God works satisfactorily in the widest sense of the word, it is true" (p. 299). That "widest sense" motivationally presupposes that prayer is a major component of God's felt presence.

We are interested in the psychosocial mechanisms underlying these self-reflective experiential effects of prayer. Most of the early psychologists of religion adopted the terms "suggestion" and "auto-suggestion" to explain such mechanisms (Buttrick, 1942; Raymond, 1907; Stolz, 1913). The implication was that we could be "suggesting" to ourselves the beneficial effects of prayer and thereby be triggering a kind of placebo mechanism. This idea was extended by Festinger, Riecken, and Schachter (1956) and others who observe that when people engage in an activity they often justify it to themselves to prove the utility and significance of their actions. Though the placebo and justification effects may constitute a part of prayer's effects, they are far from a totally sufficient explanation for prayer's manifold effects.

THE NEED FOR THEORY

Science demands a framework featuring theories for whatever is being studied. Of course, one theory cannot cover all that we desire to explain. Although we primarily focus on an approach that emphasizes prayer as a complex of coping responses, we must not forget that certain theories restrict their consideration of prayer to specific behavioral and social contexts. We deal with these specific contexts in succeeding chapters. For example, in Chapter 4 we concern ourselves with developmental research, focusing on theories that explain growth and change over time. In Chapters 5–7, we address how to cope with particular problems and stresses. Quite different theoretical perspectives are called upon to help us understand prayer in relation to mental health and physical health. In addition, prayer serves a number of roles within relationships, especially those involving marriage and family. What follows in the next session is a general theoretical scheme, versions and aspects of which appear throughout this book. This general scheme provides a malleable but basic theoretical structure that undergirds our argument throughout this volume.

Concern with Petition

McCullough and Larson (1999) and Pargament (1987, 1992, 1995, 1997) propose models for understanding prayer that are both petitional and not petitional, and in Chapter 2 we discuss them both in detail. Here, though, we focus on prayer that is intended to meet unfulfilled needs, that is, petitional ones. In most instances a person prays to gain something he believes cannot be gained by means other than through appeal to the Deity. God has the power, while the supplicant clearly does not. The specific goals of petitional, or petitionary, prayer can be quite diverse (Capps, 1982). Whether the object of such appeals is minor or serious, the pray-er feels relatively incapable of independently achieving what she desires. The gap between what is wanted and what can be attained by oneself likely causes stress.

The Presence and Meaning of Stress

In simple terms, stress most usually arises in circumstances in which psychological, social, or physical pressure requires a coping response. Although there are situations where stress aids one's adaptation and is beneficial, in most instances stress adversely affects one's well-being (Lazarus & Folkman, 1984). A coping reaction may, in turn, be psychological, social, or physiological—or all three, and *prayer may function as a significant coping mechanism.*

Stress, which is virtually ever present, constitutes a serious problem, both psychologically and physically. In addition, its effects frequently persist long after the stress is first produced. The effects of Hurricane Katrina, for example, apparently increased the incidence of heart attacks some threefold during the 4 years following the storm's devastating incursion into the Gulf Coast states in August 2005 (Grayson, 2009; McConnaughy, 2009).

Daily stresses that are usually taken for granted may be consciously ignored, and yet they can become chronic and have serious repercussions. For example, automobile traffic is commonly regarded as an annoying but tolerable aspect of modern life; however, whether one is a driver or passenger, the probability of having a heart attack triples during the first hour following exposure to traffic congestion (Ballantyne, 2009; DeNoon, 2009; Mozes, 2009). This stress reaction may be further compounded by the inhalation of exhaust fumes (Tonne et al., 2007).

Recent nationwide data suggest that 37% of respondents utilize prayer to manage stress. Among the possible means employed to deal with stress, prayer ranked in eighth place in frequency of use; however, in terms of its perceived helpfulness, it ranked first, with 77% of the sample considering it their most effective stress management practice (American Psychological Association, 2008).

We should be highly cautious in claiming that prayer effectively counters stress. Pargament and Park (1995) note that prayer may function in two ways, as an active coping strategy or as "escapist and diversionary" (p. 22). It appears that both roles are useful in reducing stress.

The Issue of Control

There is a massive literature on the sense of control felt by individuals. Most of this research focuses on whether one personally feels in control in general but also in specific situations, with the studies usually exploring whether the control is vested in oneself, others, is a chance phenomenon, or rather lies in the hands of God (Kopplin, 1976; Levenson, 1973; Rotter, 1966). Thus, researchers commonly reference "locus of control." Ever since Rotter (1966) first conceptualized this variable as either internal or external, it has occupied a central role in the study of personality, coping, and adjustment. Control has also been regarded as a significant preoccupation in the existing research on religion and prayer. Stress occurs whenever one's personal abilities and defenses are relatively unsuccessful in responding to the challenges one faces. Prayer is often a "best" attempt to impose vicarious control, which indirectly enhances one's sense of internal control.

Stress and Control

Control and power are basic life issues (Lazarus & Folkman, 1984; Rotter, 1966). Generally, a person experiences lower levels of stress when she feels some degree of control in stressful situations (Haan, 1982; Lazarus, 1966; Seligman, 1975; Siegel, Anderman, & Schrimshaw, 2001).

Control viewed as a matter of coping and adjustment was initially defined in terms of whether a person has internal control, versus its being vested in some external source (Rotter, 1966). Shortly thereafter, Levenson (1973) extended external control to include references to chance and powerful others. Kopplin (1976) soon added God's control. Pargament and colleagues (1988) then posited three distinct types of prayerful appeals to God:

1. The *deferring* approach, in which the person makes an appeal and concludes that "now the problem is in the hands of God."
2. The *collaborative* style, which assumes that the individual and the Deity work together to resolve the difficulty.
3. The *self-directed* orientation, which recognizes the role and place of God but primarily regards the problem as resolvable by the pray-er. In this type of prayer, the supplicant "talks to" or "discusses the problem" with the Deity. Joris (2008) points out that this approach is reassuring, validating the pray-er's beliefs, with God serving as a "therapist" that enhances one's sense of control, thereby alleviating one's stress.

A sense of personal control may be equivalent to belief in a benevolent controlling God (Gloss, 2009; Kay, Whitson, Gaucher, & Galinsky, 2009). Being religious and utilizing prayer signify a close relationship with one's God that negates powerlessness.

Navrot and colleagues (1995) undertook an initial study of relationships between prayer and seven types of control: Levenson's (1973) three control scales (Internal, Chance, and Powerful Others), Kopplin's (1976) God control measure, and the instruments of Pargament and colleagues (1988). Collaborative, self-directive, and deferring modes were related to forms of prayer defined as Confession, Petition, Thanksgiving, Ritual, Meditation, Self-improvement, Intercessory, and Habitual (Navrot et al., 1995). Although this work should be confirmed and its implications further explored, 37 of the 56 correlations examined attained significance at the .05 level. These numbers indicate a very complex pattern of relationships among the forms of prayer and control. Generally, an internal locus of control correlated negatively with the prayer measures, suggesting that when people pray they may be relinquishing a sense of control and personal efficacy to their God. In its place, they attain a form of vicarious control by aligning themselves with God's power. When one's internal locus of control is associated with praying, prayer's effects are perceived as primarily related to the individual, whereas an external locus of control conceives of prayer as more globally influential. In other words, in the latter situation God is perceived as in charge of the larger picture—the world. In their analysis, Pargament and colleagues' control scales revealed positive ties among all prayer forms and collaborative control, the idea that the individual collaborates with, or works along with, God. The results with Self-directive control, where the person acts independently of God, paralleled the findings for internal control. The judgment that prayer was objectively efficacious was closely associated with collaborative control, again suggesting that the joint efforts of both the pray-er and her Deity normally result in objective change.

Prayer, Stress, and Control

Among the many possible reactions a person may have to stress, Pargament (1997) asserts that "when people are stressed, the religious reservoir is often tapped" (p. 5). A study of more than 1,700 young people by Ross (1950) found that the two most common reasons given for praying were that "God listens to and answers your prayers" and "it helps you in times of stress" (p. 63). Pargament further notes that "people have looked as much to religion in their search for health as they have to medicine" (p. 54). This view is objectively confirmed in this volume's Chapter 7, where we show that prayer is a common recourse when illness and disability strike. A representative example is the mental status of renal transplant patients who must confront a wide variety of stressors such as fear of kidney rejection, high costs, undesirable physical symptoms, and anxiety about social acceptance (among other possibilities). Again, the most common coping mechanism employed was prayer (Sutton & Murphy, 1989). In a specific nonhealth illustration, Kirkpatrick (2005) cites Argyle and Beit-Hallahmi (1975) to the effect that prayer helps men in battle cope with stress and fear more than any other resource.

As noted earlier, recent data available on a national sample of almost 1,800 respondents indicated what people do to counter stress. Prayer was in eighth place, with 37%. In this survey, individuals reported more than one, and often many, techniques. Of those mentioning prayer, about three-quarters (77%) regarded it as their most effective stress-management activity. Seventy-five percent of these same people placed going to church and attending religious services in second place (American Psychological Association, 2008).

Religious coping is a complex phenomenon. Pargament, Koenig, and Perez (2000) consider its key facets to be: (1) the search for meaning; (2) the search for control; (3) comfort/spirituality; (4) intimacy/spirituality; and (5) life transformation. We hold that petitionary prayer is primarily a coping strategy. Even though this theoretical discussion is presented solely for prayer as petition, it may be equally relevant to other forms of prayer.

Social Meaning and Social Context

Although we usually think of prayer as an individual, usually solitary, activity, theologically, sociologically, and psychologically prayers frequently relate pray-ers to others in a variety of ways. Theologically, *The HarperCollins Encyclopedia of Catholicism* (McBrien, 1995) observes that prayer should deepen one's awareness of others. Helminiak (personal communication, November 20, 2009) additionally points out that Catholic theology embraces a variety of social factors in prayer.

These social themes are extensively observed in worship liturgies where social responsibilities to others and fellow worshippers are stressed (Buttrick, 1942; Heiler, 1932/1958). The social nature of congregations articulating such prayers probably contributes to the creation of mutually supportive social communities (Pargament, 1997). Research suggests that such sociality is also a powerful stress reducer (Uchino, 2004).

On the sociological front, Pruyser (1968) detailed how socio-cultural influences affect the pray-er through how her prayers are offered. He pointed out how the expectations of one's religious tradition cause the pray-er to select certain words and how these are specifically patterned. One classic example of this revolves around the issue of to whom the prayer is addressed. While some traditions use a wide variety of names, others use only a few, and still others contend that the Deity's name should not be spoken at all during the prayer. This overall pattern of faith and prayer is learned early in life from others in settings ranging from the home to religious institutions. Ladd and McIntosh (2008) similarly have asserted that "prayer's role as a provider of contextual meaning and social inter-actions (tangible or otherwise) keeps a person's perceptions of inter-nal or external stress well under control" (p. 34). Understanding this interplay of personal and social factors also provides insight into how prayer helps people experience control in pursuing personal stress reduction for themselves.

Prayer and Relaxation

Both the act of praying and the content of prayers are likely to be gratifying to the person praying. As Chapter 3 makes clear, there are many types of prayer, and while they may have different effects, they also have a few things in common. One effect common to all forms of prayer is relaxation.

Traditionally, psychology has associated prayer with relaxation (Benson, 1975; Buttrick, 1942; Goldberger & Breznitz, 1982).[2] Some of the research in this area has confirmed the potential of prayer to induce a relaxation response. We see later in this volume that the ramifications of meditation are considerable. One can consciously attempt to relax; however, the induction of relaxation via prayer may signify heightened feelings of personal security and a reduction of anxiety plus a sense of growth, enhancement, and self-actualization.

What is distinctly lacking in the literature is recognition that praying also has the capacity to *increase* tension. For instance, prayers that relate to painful confessions or that highlight the disjunction between the practitioner's actual self and ideal spiritual self may result in increased anxiety. Depending on other factors, the escalation of distress may be either temporary (as in momentary catharsis) or more persistent. In addition, prayers emphasizing personal concerns are, in some instances, commonly associated with narcissism (Ladd, Ladd, Ashbaugh, et al., 2007). We also have seen (Ladd & Ladd, 2012) that, while prayers are most often thought of as linked to the development of virtuous lives (e.g., loving, joyful, peaceful, patient, kind, generous, faithful, gentle, self-controlled), prayers with an overriding emphasis on the self are potentially tied to spiritual vices (e.g., impure, grudge-holding, jealous, angry, quarrelsome, envious, morally loose, conceited, divisive issues). In other words, prayer too often is conceptualized as a purely positive endeavor. It is difficult, if not impossible, to name any behavior in which humans engage that—when taken to an extreme or under some specific set of circumstances—does not also have the potential for negative as well as positive outcomes. Prayer is certainly no exception, and investigations that explore the full range of possibilities are critical.

SUMMARY

Prayer, as part of a large religious and spiritual complex, is highly enmeshed in the vast matrix of beliefs and experiences that constitute personal faith and religiosity. As behavior, praying occupies a special position as volitional action that reflects and contributes to an individual's orientation toward life in general.

Prayer has always been a complex phenomenon from the vantage point of both religion and theology. Once psychologists decided to examine it, new and different aspects of this complexity became evident, and further examination continued to reveal additional correlates and roles for both prayer and the pray-er.

We have introduced various aspects of psychology to illustrate their pertinence to prayer. These areas are much more complex than we have discussed thus far and therefore will be further detailed in Chapter 2. In addition, such constructs as motivation, cognition, emotion, and social psychology are often intertwined. In fact, the individual is an integrated totality, and our parsing that totality into specific elements merely enables us to create convenient abstractions that make it possible to discuss and form hypotheses about human behavior as it relates to prayer.

In succeeding pages, we investigate the multiform character of prayer and some possible reasons for its diverse incarnations in different situations. We discuss what prayer portends psychologically for the pray-er. We scrutinize specifically how the concept and practice of prayer develop throughout one's lifespan. And we note that efforts have been made to study the various interrelationships among prayer, personality, and difficult life issues. Some of this work is highly pertinent to better appreciating prayer's contribution to both physical and mental health and healing. That prayer helps one better cope and adjust to life's challenges has become increasingly evident over time. Thus, understanding prayer is central to our evolving psychology of religion.

NOTES

1. These definitions resulted from an Internet search of the following sites: *http://dictionary.die.net/prayer*,   *www.Yourdictionary.com/prayer*, *http://mw1.merriam-webs.com/dictionary/prayer*, and *www.thefree dictionary.com/p/prayer*.
2. Andresen's (2000) excellent review of the immense literature in this area provides a helpful entrée into this domain.

CHAPTER 2

Prayer in
Psychological Perspective

Prayer has functional value for the individual.
—HORATIO W. DRESSER (1929, p. 54)

Prayer is an act or state of mind and is therefore subject
to the laws that govern the mind.
—ELWOOD WORCESTER AND SAMUEL McCOMB (1931, p. 319)

*I*ncreasingly, the psychology of religion is being integrated into the overall discipline of psychology itself (Hood et al., 2009). As we noted in the preceding chapter, the objective study of prayer is part of a psychology of religion that is committed to the principles of a rigorously scientific psychology. Imposing this rigor is far from simple. Researchers may construct measures of religiosity and spirituality that inadvertently support or deny the religious positions or theologies of particular churches or denominations. Kirkpatrick and Hood (1990), terming these efforts "good" and "bad" religion, show how such ideas have been insinuated into research and theory in the psychology of religion. Simply stated, prayer is behavior with a purpose. This behavior may have a variety of meanings that call into play diverse facets of experience and cognition. Calling prayer "purposive" does not mean that the pray-er is necessarily aware of all aspects of the prayer process, including his own intentions. Activating a need or desire to pray brings to the fore motivational issues that illustrate the many features of prayer and worship. To study prayer, we have to examine motivation (i.e., what is driving it—the pray-er's desires or the purpose of it) and cognition (i.e., what the pray-er understands prayer to mean, what is going on when she prays, and what she expects to result from it). Distinguishing motivation from cognition is not easy in that interpretation and intention are inter-twined and both imply action. Understanding prayer requires that we not only examine its ties to motivation and cognition but also explore it from the vantage point of both social psychology and the relatively new field of neuropsychology.

THE COGNITIVE PERSPECTIVE

During the first half of the 20th century, mainstream psychol-ogy embraced various forms of classical learning theory that were advanced in the writings of such behaviorists as John Watson and B. F. Skinner (Bower & Hilgard, 1981). The past few decades, how-ever, have witnessed a cognitive revolution that shifted the empha-sis to higher mental functions such as thinking, reasoning, problem solving, and information processing. When prayer is studied cogni-tively, attention is directed toward its meaning and interpretation, and such factors as beliefs also enter the picture. McIntosh (1995) suggests that "one way to conceptualize how these beliefs function and are organized is to consider religion to be a cognitive schema" (p. 1). He further defines schema as "a cognitive structure or mental representation containing organized knowledge about a particular domain" (p. 2). Relative to religion, prayer is a subordinate activity, suggesting that the idea of a "subschema" might be more appropriate terminology.

We must consider cognition if we wish to gain a true and com-prehensive understanding of the psychology of prayer. Definitions of prayer are invariably provided by professionals who represent a very small percentage of those who actually pray. But to consider it from a cognitive perspective, prayer should be examined from the perspec-tive of those who pray most frequently, namely, the laypeople. This task of defining prayer was undertaken in a series of studies by Lam-bert, Fincham, and Graham (2011). Examining issues such as the centrality and characteristics of various aspects of prayer, one must recognize a considerable complexity in questions of definition and perspective.

Unfortunately, relatively little solid research has been done on cognition and prayer, although a number of impressive theoretical efforts involving cognition and motivation have been developed (Lawson & McCauley, 1990, 2002; Watts & Williams, 1988). Another cognitive approach is the general attribution theory of Spilka, Shaver, and Kirkpatrick (1985), which is also concerned with motives that might activate thinking about prayer.

An interesting illustration may be seen in developmental psychologist J. L. Barrett's (2001) treatment of cognition in relation to petitionary prayer. He methodically conducted four experiments dealing with problem-solving methods by God-reference, specifically dealing with action at a distance and counterintuitive divine function within the world. He ended up formally concluding what has usually been assumed, namely, that pray-ers conceive of God as acting like a human being with extra-special powers who prefers psychological solutions to problems. In addition, respondents paradoxically think of God as existing in a divine realm and yet nevertheless as being close to the petitioner. Barrett may be the foremost scholar to develop and apply cognitive theory to the study of ritual, prayer, and worship as well as other aspects of religion.

Even earlier, Brown (1966) had undertaken a cross-cultural study of petitionary prayer among adolescents (more accurately, there was probably less cultural than simply geographic variation among his samples). Focusing on respondents' egocentric cognitions and beliefs in causal efficacy, he observed a lessening of both factors with increased age.

Employing what they termed a "cognitive-behavioral framework," Maltby, Lewis, and Day (2008) studied prayer experience and meditative prayer as they affect subjective well-being. This approach emphasized, first, a religious interpretive framework for one's personal existence and its importance and purpose. Second, this interpretive framework provided a basis for a program of stress reduction that promised to enhance subjective well-being. Specifically, Maltby and colleagues found that seven prayer measures were correlated with negative health signs and somatic symptoms, anxiety, and depression. Generally, low-to-moderate associations with the prayer indices suggest possible beneficial effects for ritual and meditative prayer forms, praying with others, and reporting favorable prayer experiences. The specific reasons for favoring certain prayer forms over others require further explication.

The fine theoretical frameworks offered by Barrett and his coworkers (Barrett, 2001; Barrett & Keil, 1996; Barrett & Lawson, 2001; Barrett & Malley, 2007; Barrett & Van Orman, 2009) are proving useful in research. However, the conceptualizations of Lawson and McCauley (2002), Watts and Williams (1988), and Wuthnow (2008a), while well thought out, still have a way to go before they really come to grips with the cognitive aspects of prayer in actual research.

Much of this work concerns the nature of the God to whom the prayers are directed. Cognition, control, and God roles are implied in the three ways of praying that Pargament and his associates (1988) delineated in the person–God relationship that we discussed earlier (in Chapter 1): basically, deferring to God, collaborating with Him, or self-directing oneself. Clearly, how one prays must be placed within a general cognitive pattern that describes how one relates personally to a hypothesized Deity.

A cognitive approach to faith frequently highlights what is supposed to be special about religious experience, since it is primarily concerned with how we think and believe. Watts and Williams (1988) assert that prayer is the way through which people come to understand how they relate to their God. Stated differently, these authors maintain that individuals connect to God through cognitive means or understandings that also have strong emotional and experiential components. Drawing on a different cognitive conceptualization, Wuthnow (2008b) emphasizes a theme that has relevance to both anthropology and psychology. He asks what makes prayers memorable and pertinent to pray-ers and introduces the notion of domain violations. The latter are defined as "categories or schemas through which information is simplified and organized" (p. 495). Wuthnow then directs attention to the nature of the language used and the specific ideas that "cross" the boundary between the human realm and the nonhuman, or divine, domain. Various contrasts accentuate the differences between the two realms, making the supplicant particularly aware of the advantages of certain prayers over others. In this way, one's memorable prayers are readily distinguished from more ritualistic and less emotionally involved ones. Wuthnow provides examples of such elements in prayers concerned with life and death, domains that themselves have boundaries that are susceptible to frequent violations. The ideas that Wuthnow explores are alien to psychologists of religion; hence, there is a need to explore this cognitive avenue further.

Conceptualizing Prayer Cognitively: Foster's Perspective

In an impressive cognitive exercise, Richard Foster (1992) analyzed 21 types of prayers mainly from a religious/theological/spiritual point of view. He divided the types into three major "directional" categories, which he termed "inward, "outward," and "upward." Inward prayers are basically concerned with self-understanding and self-change. Improving ourselves and expressing such needs constitute the core of prayers that turn us toward self-evaluation and growth. Outward prayers direct us into the world to enhance our relationships with others and external reality. Lastly, upward prayers focus our attention on the Deity, that is, adoring, appreciating, and experiencing the Divine. Objective analysis of these categories was subsequently undertaken by Ladd and Spilka (2002, 2006), who constructed objective scales to assess them and essentially ended up verifying Foster's framework through their use of factor-analytic methods. Breslin, Lewis, and Shevlin (2010) repeated this work with confirmatory factor analysis but were unable to confirm Ladd and Spilka's findings. Differences in samples, among other possibilities, suggest the need for further scale development and additional follow-up analyses. There is, however, an even more basic need to understand how variations in prayer types can significantly affect one's religious orientation and personal life.

Since praying is conceptualized by the pray-er as between oneself and a supernatural being, social cognitions are necessarily part of this interaction. The individual brings to the prayer images of both the self and the Deity. In other words, God and the self are cognitively assigned particular characteristics. Several studies showing how people think about God reveal a variety of complex images (Gorsuch, 1968; Pargament & Hahn, 1986; Spilka, Armatas, & Nussbaum, 1964). In prayer, these appear to depend on the nature of the situation and the kinds of prayers the person offers (Fairchild et al., 1993; Pargament & Hahn, 1986). For example, when prayers of thanksgiving are given, a deity involved in human affairs is posited, one who is further regarded as omniscient, omnipotent, and omnipresent. Petitionary prayers (i.e., ones that ask for something) stress the omni-image that God knows and can do everything, not the deistic conception in which a kingly God is currently inactive in the world. Codified or structured prayer has largely been studied in relation to the traditional conservative Christian perspective rather than those favoring omni- or deistic images (Fairchild et al., 1993), and no similar research has been carried out among non-Christians.

A common cognition shared by petitioners is the idea of a God in a just world, a view not only held by highly religious people but also one largely pervasive in our society. If something good or bad happens to a person, the usual assumption is that the individual probably deserved what he got (Lerner, 1980; Rubin & Peplau, 1973). In fact, belief in an ordered, just world may be largely, though not exclusively, premised on the presumed existence of a deity or deities. This notion is well expressed by Robert Browning's sentiment "God's in His heaven—all's right with the world!" (1841/1895, p. 869).

One may argue that the "just world" perspective relies on a God with ideal human qualities. In fact, people seem to possess a cognitive readiness to apply anthropomorphism to God concepts and, as Barrett and Keil (1996, p. 219) put it, to other "nonnatural entities." Consider, for example, angels, demons, devils, and the like. Though at odds with modern theologies, these ideas gain support from Scripture, religious child training, and, according to Freud (1928), from children's early life experience with fathers.

Guthrie's (1993) cognitive-anthropological approach to religion stresses the communicative aspect of prayer to a deity. Guthrie traces this theme back to David Hume, noting that those who pray may not see themselves as the object of prayer. They are in a relationship with a higher power that is responsive to them. Obviously this position can be challenged, but from their vantage point anthropomorphic symbolism largely suffuses the cognitive system of the believer and the pray-er.

Loveland, Sikkink, Myers and Radcliff (2005) employ a cognitive-social perspective that is based on Foster's (1992) outward form of prayer as operationalized by Ladd and Spilka (2002, 2006). They perceive this orientation as a "cognitive expression of concern for others" (p. 3) that ideally results in heightened participation in voluntary organizations and enhanced civic involvement. This improved civic support is even independent of greater political involvement. The respondents' frequency of prayer apparently parallels their association with groups that "focus on meeting individual needs directly" (p. 11).

The study of cognition is central to our comprehension of the human condition. Whether we are concerned with religious beliefs, experience, or behavior, cognitive processes are clearly involved.

THE MOTIVATIONAL PERSPECTIVE

Cognition implies action that is premised upon motivation; however, as we have observed, distinguishing between the cognitive foundations of behavior and what stimulates that behavior is frequently difficult. Our approach begins with the basic question "Why pray?" As we have already indicated, people pray for many reasons, not the least of which is because they want something. They need help in attaining their goals, and their Deity becomes their ally. Maslow's (1954) celebrated hierarchy of needs offers a framework of reasons for prayer in terms of human deficiencies and growth motives. Most often one prays because some unfulfilled desire or threat exists or because one has encountered danger, tragedy, or crisis. Under such circumstances, one feels a need to resolve ambiguity, fear, anxiety, and helplessness, and normally, for people who pray, prayer is the prime resource to resolve these concerns. Even if one feels she can handle the situation independently, the assumption of God's unlimited capability and potential aid may activate prayerful behavior that one hopes will elicit additional assistance.

Another motivation for prayer is personal growth; that is, prayer is regarded as having the potential to enhance one's maturity and improve oneself. Additionally, it may become an avenue to broader life perspectives, to bettering the lives of others, correcting undesirable behaviors, rectifying personal errors, and developing new insights into personal and social life. All of these possibilities can result from prayer experiences similar to what Maslow (1964) termed "peak experiences" that arise even in the absence of prior intention. Maslow explicitly identifies these as "religious happenings" (p. 59) that are, at heart, religious mystical experiences. Despite considerable discussion that relates prayer to desirable outcomes (Godin, 1985; Watts & Williams, 1988), solid, objective data evidencing this connection has been difficult to obtain (VandeCreek, 2001). Among other possibilities, prayer and positive experience may be mediated through religious orientation (Hood, Morris, & Watson, 1989).

THE NEUROPSYCHOLOGICAL PERSPECTIVE

Neuropsychology is probably the most significant major development in mainstream psychology over the past 50 years. A variety of technological advances in the assessment of brain function (e.g., functional magnetic resonance imaging, positron emission tomography, single photon emission computed tomography) have stimulated efforts to measure brain activity—even down to the activation of single neurons (Garbarini, 2005). Newer refinements of these techniques keep appearing. It did not take long for religious cognition, belief, experience, and behavior that includes prayer to become the object of such study (Hood et al., 2009). All of these efforts and findings apply only to those identified with Judeo-Christian faiths in Europe and the United States, and we are certainly not ready to generalize them to religions throughout the world.

An excellent recent review of this research work has been provided by Schjoedt (2009). He points out that relatively few neuropsychological research studies deal specifically with religion, with most, instead, relating to meditation and consciousness. Intending to broaden both the perspective and the work in this area, his program is both extensive and rigorous. In two different papers, Schjoedt (2009; Schjoedt, Stodkilde-Jorgensen, Geertz, & Roepstorff, 2008) did brain scans of participants either reciting *The Lord's Prayer* or improvising a prayer, with control comparisons also made. Neural activity was greatest in the caudate nucleus when *The Lord's Prayer* was recited and somewhat less when improvising prayer. In allied work with highly religious persons and using the same procedures, the temporal and frontal brain regions were activated, and there were also indications of individual variations in other brain areas that were energized. Viewing this field as primarily concerned with identifying brain regions and structures associated with religious experience and behavioral expression, Persinger (1987) and D'Aquili and Newberg (D'Aquili, 1978; D'Aquili & Newberg, 1999) pioneered efforts in this difficult research domain. Prayer was also dealt with in their work.

Scholars who discuss the relationship of brain function to faith and prayer vary in their approach from what might be termed "the inspirational level" to the technical minutiae of neurology. We thus read of, respectively, neurotheology and neuroscience (Clayton, 2000; McKinney, 1994). Wherein the former discipline we try to understand neural responses associated with religion and spirituality, in the latter field we attempt to stay within the bounds of traditional scientific biology and psychology. A common phenomenon is to mix subjective theoretical statements with others based on data. Some recent popular works often take this tack, confusing correlation with causation to an extreme degree (Newberg, D'Aquili, & Rause, 2001; Newberg & Waldman, 2001). As Ladd and Ladd (2010) observe, such offerings appeal mostly to readers seeking confirmation of their already well-established beliefs. Since we prefer to stay strictly within the boundaries of behavioral science, we choose to focus on replicated neural correlates of prayer and avoid what might be best termed "neo-devotional" literature (Newberg & Waldman, 2001).

Some religionists and parapsychologists believe that the neural patterns within the brain ultimately leave the skull and reach a Deity. Citing the weakness of associated electrical and magnetic fields, Haas (2007) explicitly rejects this possibility. (We discuss this line of research in greater detail in Chapter 7 on intercessory prayer.) Of course, many religious thinkers would reject the idea of reducing prayer to a neural pattern, but the unique lens we bring to this subject matter is psychological rather than theological.

In an early study, Surwillo and Hobson (1978) measured the electroencephalographic (EEG) brain activity of six highly religious Protestants. The object was to assess the rate of electrocortical rhythms (cycles per second) during pre-prayer, prayer, and post-prayer periods. The EEGs tended to be faster during the prayer sessions. Considerable individual variation was, however, observed. Given the small sample, all the authors could offer were a variety of speculations for their tenuous results. No one seems to have translated these potential hypotheses into further research.

Much more representative of the current mode of investigation is the study by Schjoedt and his colleagues (2008). Although the number of participants was still relatively small ($N = 20$), both institutionalized and personal forms of prayer were studied. The former utilized *The Lord's Prayer,* while the latter were prayers individually improvised by the respondents. Secular verbal activities were present as controls. Neural assessment utilized functional magnetic resonance imaging with echo planar imaging. Data collection and analysis were quite sophisticated. The main effects assessed were brain responses to the secular and religious content. The brain regions sampled were the temporo-parietal junction, the temporo-polar area, the anterior aspect of the medial prefrontal cortex, and the precuneous. These were chosen because of their involvement in previous cognitive research. Note that the actual test was between well-memorized text and spontaneous language generation, thus raising the question of confounds at a basic level.

While no significant main effects were found between the prayers and the secular controls, some noteworthy interactions were observed. As is common in these studies, a number of other statistically meaningful indications were evidenced in the various regions; these the researchers discussed hypothetically rather than suggesting definitive brain responses.

This last work clearly reflects the great increase in research measurement sophistication during the 30 years since the Surwillo and Hobson (1978) effort. Although not directly focusing on prayer, other scholars have undertaken work that appears closely related to that just discussed.

Experiencing one's belief in a deity is the most common precursor to undertaking actual prayer. Saver and Rabin (1997) summarized earlier work by Hay (1994) and Hardy (1976, 1979) that explicitly emphasized the importance of God ideation and prayer in religious experience. Focusing on epileptic seizures, they discussed a number of brain structures that overlap with those studied by Schjoedt and colleagues (2008; Schjoedt, Stodkilde-Jorgensen, Geertz, & Roepstorff, 2009).

Schjoedt (2009), noting the complexity of prayer, distinguishes between its formalized expression in worship and its less structured private individualized expressions. Treating prayer as an interaction between the pray-er and God that substitutes ideation for the Diety, he believes it is in some ways equivalent to "normal personal interaction" (p. 329). This comparison is questionable on a number of levels, such as the linguistic differences between prayer and conversation. Schjoedt identifies and discusses a number of neural structures that are involved in personal prayerful activity. Psychologically, trust in God plus the potential for heightened expectations of tangible actions and possible rewards are central motivators to engaging in private prayer. Rather than viewing such behavior as simple, Schjoedt recognizes it as involving complex reaction patterns. Clearly, Schjoedt's approach appears to be systematic, sophisticated, and productive.

In Chapter 7, we refer to work by Schjoedt, Stodkilde-Jorgensen, Geertz, Lund, and Roepstorff (2010) that functional magnetic resonance imaging utilizes in studying respondents' thinking about intercessory prayer as reflected in the frontal cortex regions that mediate executive and social cognitive processes. In what might be termed "charisma–trust circumstances implying God," Christian believers seem to deactivate these higher-level functions. One possible interpretation could be that the respondents suspend their critical thinking faculties. Additional research to assess such a potential for prayer appears to be warranted.

This attempt to review neuropsychological research relating to prayer is thought-provoking but far from definitive. Unfortunately, there is relatively little agreement among those conducting such work. This means the findings of the studies undertaken cannot be easily summarized or even understood in relation to one another. In addition, the findings in functional magnetic resonance imaging studies of emotion, personality, and social cognition have yielded conclusions that many scholars question (Lindquist & Gelman, 2009; Nichols & Poline, 2009; Vul, Harris, Winkielman, & Pashler, 2009). If ever there was an area crying out for new studies and the cross-validation of research, it is neuropsychology as applied to the psychology of religion and more specifically to prayer (Harris et al., 2009).

THE SOCIAL-PSYCHOLOGICAL PERSPECTIVE

According to James Dittes (1969) in the *Handbook of Social Psychology*, the psychology of religion is a subfield of social psychology. Since contemporary social psychology is highly cognitive in nature (Berkowitz, 1978; Fiske & Taylor, 1991), these issues have become central to the psychology of religion. This emphasis is implied in the title of Watts and Williams's volume *The Psychology of Religious Knowing* (1988). Discussing religious experience at length, these authors state as an aim the "conceptual mapping" (p. 2) of the religious mind. Similar cognitive language is employed by Brown in the title of his work *The Psychology of Religious Belief* (1987). Belief, of course, is a core cognitive topic within social psychology. Batson,

Schoenrade, and Ventis (1993) confront the issue of a social psychology of religion head-on by asserting that it can simultaneously be both phenomenological and objectively empirical, thus satisfying the criteria for a scientific approach to the field. Thus, their treatment includes prayer, for its essence is fundamentally interpersonal, focusing on relations between people and their God. From a scientific point of view, prayer is also deeply personal (phenomenologically meaningful) and objectively measurable (traditionally empirical).

Social Cognition: Attribution

In contemporary social psychology, emotion is increasingly being linked to cognition through such concepts as schema, attribution, self theory, and social inference in order to understand the nature and meaning of prayer.

The idea of connecting oneself to a deity via prayer is continually stressed in both the inspirational and professional literature on the psychology of religion. The heart of such an association is attribution, that is, how we represent and explain ourselves as well as the God to which our supplications, thanks, and requests are offered. In addition, these understandings are judged in terms of their appropriateness for prayer. Pargament and colleagues' (1988) tripartite framework of deferring, collaborative, and self-directive approaches to God implies attributions to both the Deity and the one who prays.

A background for recognizing the role of attribution within the psychology of religion was provided by general attribution theory (Spilka et al., 1985). The basic assumptions here are threefold: (1) people seek to make sense of their experiences, (2) there is "a need to predict or control events," and (3) a desire exists to "protect, maintain, and enhance one's self concept and self-esteem" (p. 3). In other words, events that challenge or threaten any of these needs are likely to elicit attributions. Many examples of such attribution are presented in Chapter 6 in cases where illness occurs and the patient tries to comprehend why adverse events have occurred. For example, attributions are made to oneself and to God to explain the reasons for the sickness; self-blame, for example, may parallel inferred godly punishment for sin. Such attributions are likely to assume greater prominence whenever, so the theory goes, nonreligious explanations are not sufficiently satisfying. Increased resort to religious possibilities will then probably be sought. Prayer may be a prime solution when other avenues appear closed. Spilka and Schmidt (1983) noted that when vignettes about social, economic, and medical issues were presented to respondents, medical ones were most likely to result in religious attributions and, we infer, prayers. Such attributional thoughts and associated prayer behaviors are first called upon when events (1) occur to the attributor rather than others and (2) are important.

The attributions that are made prior to or during prayer vary with the nature of the prayer. Watts and Williams (1988) detail these various attributions for prayers of thanksgiving, confession, and petition. Still, one can anticipate that the attributions utilized for the self have a higher probability of changing than those that are assigned to the Deity. This is simply because we are likely to attribute greater power, knowledge, and a better sense of what is right and proper to God. These are significant attributional guidelines for understanding the "whys," "whens," and "hows" of prayerful behavior. They, in themselves, are aspects of causal attributions. Unhappily, as productive as attribution theory has been, it has not been directly applied to prayer; so, we have theory but need additional research on this matter.

Social Cognition: Ingratiation

Another social-psychological consideration in prayer is the notion of ingratiation, namely, acting in a manner intended to gain the favor and approval of others. More than a hint of ingratiation may be present in the ways human–God relationships are structured (Jones, 1964). Initiating prayers with effusive praise of God is sometimes motivated by ingratiation. Such behavior works often enough with people, the reasoning goes—so, why not with God? This is not to say that all or most glorification of the Diety is consciously designed to ingratiate onself with God. Formal teaching, personal religiosity, and ingrained habits may, after all, make such eulogizing a largely reflexive response in one's relationship to the Divine.

Cognitive Dissonance

A popular social-psychological theory that is primarily concerned with attitude change has been termed "cognitive dissonance" (Festinger et al., 1956). Fundamentally, it asserts that attitude change follows action, particularly where the latter is at variance with or contradictory to the attitudes held by the individual. Whenever there is obvious dissonance between an action and an attitude, something has to give. The evidence suggests that the resulting change normally occurs in the attitude. We should add that dissonance might occur between two attitudes. The religious injunction to "love thy neighbor," for example, might conflict with one's personal negative feelings toward certain minorities, immigrants, or the like.

Moving into religion and adhering to a biblical explanation of the creation of the universe is difficult for some in the face of scientific theory and data. Such evidence generates cognitive dissonance for certain religious persons, and they may end up revising their interpretation of science, rejecting its assertions while strengthening their religious commitment. Evolving adjustments might translate into an especially strained relationship with creationism but greater harmony with Intelligent Design. Each side might distort challenging conceptions offered by the other, thereby attempting to reduce the perceived dissonance (Ozorak, 2005).

Some empirical research has attempted to use the cognitive dissonance model to test specific relationships between prayer and nonreligious behavior. Adams (2008), conceiving of dissonance relating to workplace inequity in terms of one's job rewards such as money, prestige, and power, hypothesized that resorting to prayer and a perceived sense of inequity should relate positively. In other words, the greater the perceived dissonance attributable to inequity, the more that prayer should help to resolve it. His findings did not support this hypothesis. A second hypothesis proposed that prayer should moderate or lessen discrepancies between supervisory support and workplace inequity, but again the data did not support this expectation.

Using qualitative methodology, Marsden, Karagianni, and Morgan (2007) used prayer in the treatment of 10 Christian women suffering from eating disorders. The 10 women in their sample were interviewed at length. Prayer was conceived as aiding the maturation of religious beliefs to increase appetitive control and thus reduce a sense of sin resulting from dissonance. These researchers concluded that "prayer provided a dialogue and healing relationship with God" (p. 10). As is unfortunately true in some qualitative work, success in controlling the eating disorders was claimed, but the lack of objective results made this claim merely an inference.

Prayer may possess a built-in potential for cognitive dissonance. When one prays, particularly in a petitional manner, the hope is that there will be a positive response to the request made. Obviously, in many if not most circumstances, such a response is not evident. Pray-ers, however, often differ, suggesting that God always answers prayers—albeit not necessarily in ways we recognize. This argument resolves any conflict in line with the expectations of cognitive dissonance theory in that belief is not weakened but confirmed. Here again we need more research to understand what is meant when respondents say that prayers are always answered (whether an answer is always evident or not). Bender (2008) attempted to resolve this matter and found that the nature of the God inferred by the supplicant appeared to be the major factor influencing what constituted an "answer" to prayers.

The General Social Survey (2008) offers an interesting research possibility, given the incidence of prayer in relation to belief in God. Approximately 30% of those who state that they do not believe in God nonetheless admit to praying. Granted that we cannot be totally sure what this apparent discrepancy means, there is the implication of dissonance. A study indicating its resolution might be quite interesting.

Prayer and Gratitude

Moving away from cognition in social psychology to other aspects of this realm, a fair amount of research has related religion to gratitude. Theoretically suggesting that prayer might be an especially fruitful variable to examine in relation to gratitude, Lambert, Fincham, Braithwaite, Graham, and Beach (2009) conducted three studies that supported this hypothesis and further confirmed it as a longitudinal relationship even when controls for initial gratitude, general religiosity, and social desirability were provided. These researchers have conducted several social-psychological studies involving prayer and interpersonal relationships.

This relatively brief excursion into social-psychological ties to the psychology of religion and prayer barely touches on the potential for this branch of the psychological mainstream. The complexity and depth of social psychology are attested to by the multivolume sets of the various editions of the *Handbook of Social Psychology*. All we can do here is illuminate a few of the issues that have been unearthed and suggest that the interested reader delve further into a realm with virtually unlimited research horizons.

SUMMARY

In the foregoing discussion, we have barely dipped into the many possibilities for exploring motivation, cognition, neuropsychology, and social psychology in the study of prayer. Succeeding chapters should further deepen our understanding of these relatively new frontiers for productive social-psychological research.

CHAPTER 3

The Many Faces of Prayer

Multidimensionality

What is prayer? It appears in human experience in an almost
endless variety of forms.
—ELWOOD WORCESTER AND SAMUEL McCOMB (1931, p. 291)

The nature and function of prayer are so complex that we must
view the subject from many sides if we would form
any adequate conception.
—BORDEN P. BOWNE (1910, p. 127)

*E*very scholar, researcher, and layperson who has thought
seriously about prayer recognizes its complexity and
how it can be expressed in so many different ways. To clarify our
understanding somewhat, in this chapter we consider at length the
various dimensions of praying and conclude with an overview of how
a well-structured program of research can best advance this area of
scholarship.

WHY MULTIDIMENSIONALITY?

A large amount of the conceptual and scientific literature mentioning
prayer does just that—simply *mentions* it. There is one exception,
namely, the inclusion of a single item to evaluate the *frequency*
with which a participant engages in praying. On a scale of 1 to whatever (i.e., a Likert scale), respondents are asked to report how often

they pray daily, weekly, monthly, or the like. By quantifying prayer through an interval level of measurement, researchers relate "prayer frequency" to a host of other variables, both religious and nonreligious, to better understand its significance to respondents. Unfortunately, prayer's ultimate role still remains unclear, although a growing number of psychologists of religion sense that it is not only an important component in the daily lives of most people but also represents far more than any single question could ascertain.

Viewed from another perspective, it is hard to know precisely what such data tell us. This dilemma arises because, as with nearly any single piece of data, the vagueness quotient (roughly, the complexity of any phenomenon divided by the number of items measuring it) is necessarily quite high. Consider, for instance, the comparably vague question "How often do you exercise?" The expert mountaineer, casual bocce player, and laid-back health club member might all conceivably report the same subjective score; one who walks a quarter-mile a day and another who runs 6 miles a day might also claim the same overall level of activity. One special difficulty is that single-point measures usually record only gross amounts of activity. Such imprecise information—albeit seemingly precise—can sometimes be worse than none at all because the data point is likely to be ambiguous and not comparable among respondents, especially when employed as an index of individual differences. When faced with including only a single-item measure of prayer, researchers are likely best served by simply asking "Do you pray or not?" because asking an even broader or more open question might result in one's overinterpreting the resulting research data.

Even if one chooses to ignore this psychometric problem, a more pertinent question remains, namely, "To what extent is a person's praying frequency something uniquely psychological?" As an alternative to the foregoing illustration, consider the plight of a cognitive psychologist reduced to asking simply "How often do you think?" Certainly, both praying and thinking involve the brain and are properly within the realm of psychology. The core of psychology, however, is much more than just counting responses, as even the purest behaviorist would prefer data that details respondents' learning history and the experiment's context. In the same sense that a psychologist exploring cognition can do very little with only minimal data, so too the psychologist of religion needs to operationally specify far more than just the frequency of respondents' prayers.

A red herring related to both of these situations encountered from time to time is the argument that one item might account for an amount of variance comparable to (or greater than) combined sets of items specifying different ways of praying. In other words, the argument goes, why not wield Occam's razor to eliminate more complicated explanations when a simpler one might be equally compelling. Based solely on the mathematics, the two sets of very different factors might yield similar numbers, but this feat of calculation, however, is beside the point. That is to say, an isolated question about the frequency of one's prayers, as noted above, provides no additional insight into the prayers' components or context. Psychologists have long agreed that properly understanding the human psyche necessarily involves examining multiple aspects of the phenomenon under study. We advocate the same with respect to exploring prayer: single-item measures appear inadequate, and multidimensional indices are therefore essential.

WHICH MULTIDIMENSIONALITY?

Having settled on the necessity of exploring prayer through a wide variety of means, how should we go about identifying the most relevant ones? Initially, we must make two somewhat independent choices regarding origins and number. By "origins" we mean that there are multiple sources on which one can base a meaningful taxonomy of prayers and their relations. Among the most obvious choices are theological statements, written or unwritten, both academic and popular in form, either within a specific faith tradition or across the religious spectrum. This is a logical place to begin since these provide a record of how practitioners have long viewed prayer in situ. It is through these various formulations that customary ways of praying are transmitted to each new generation. Simultaneously, theologies and particular denominations speak to the expectations and motivations that accompany the act of praying and how prayers can enhance or detract from liturgical practice (Cabrol, 1900).

Some social scientists might view taking this theological route to understanding prayer as, in effect, not only "putting the fox in charge of the hen house" but also "serving the chickens up on a platter." Such notions are unconsciously and subtly introduced into research as "good" versus "bad" religion, which was discussed in Chapter 1

(Kirkpatrick & Hood, 1990). In addition, in Chapter 1 we promised to avoid theology except where it might contribute meaningfully to psychological theory (Spilka, 1976). There is certainly some basis for concern, since theology may have a vested interest in encouraging prayer and possibly prayers of a certain type (e.g., prayers derived from and supportive of predominantly masculine and patriarchal content). Yet, prayers' origins are of fundamental interest to the psychologist of religion because, if we are to fully understand the concept of prayer, specifying its ontological context is critical. Excluding observations arising from religious sources would in this inquiry be tantamount to a chemist's analyzing water by acknowledging the role of hydrogen but not that of oxygen in its chemical composition.

Even allowing for various differences in language and practice across religious traditions, approaches to praying have generally three features, common emphases in the "directionality" of prayer: inward, outward, and upward. The intention implied by these three directions is to encourage via prayer a sense of connecting with, respectively, oneself, others, and that which is supraphysical (God or the Divine) (Foster, 1992; Ladd & Spilka, 2002, 2006). While these prayer directions serve as practical guidelines, it is nearly impossible to avoid their occasionally overlapping. Indeed, prototypical prayers in religious traditions often demonstrate the desirability of integrating these directions rather than exclusively focusing on each separately.

Up to this point we have emphasized the cognitive features of prayer. Multidimensionality, however, may also be understood in terms of how it affects an individual's behavior. We can observe how prayer is physically realized. Are there differences in prayers that are uttered and experienced while one is stationary versus moving? To what extent does posture matter when the pray-er is stationary? What are the implications if one walks, crawls on one's hands and knees, or even dances during prayer? We only touch on a few fascinating possibilities for extensive research when we point out that praying activities may differ dramatically to the extent that they initiate discrete physiological patterns of respiration, tactile sensation, and visual stimulation.

One additional facet of prayer's multidimensionality that we should note is its impact on affective experience. As with any linguistic expression, understanding the emotional tone of one's prayer is central to accurately interpreting its content and meaning. For instance, the single word *help* can carry vastly different meanings, depending on whether it is uttered in anger, surprise, or a fit of joy.

GROUNDING MULTIDIMENSIONALITY

The foregoing observations rest largely on objective data that also take account of theological contexts. We have a glimmer of how prayer works. So, in addition to the theoretical position offered in Chapter 1, we are now in a position to suggest why prayer works in a psychological sense.

Culture and Social Context

Having noted that prayer is multidimensional, we must consider how it is systematically varied and organized across the diverse contexts of actual daily practice. These contexts are like Russian nesting dolls, or matryoshkas, sets of wooden dolls of decreasing size placed one inside the other. The sequence of dolls is analogous to the settings in which we live, with the context of practice, the immediate situation in which prayer occurs, comparable to the innermost doll. Encapsulating it are various constructs (i.e., surrounding contexts and meanings) based on time, place, past determining factors, and future expectations until finally culture and possibly even biology help define the larger picture (i.e., the outermost doll's features).

An important feature of the prayer setting is its social character. Classic experiments in social psychology have demonstrated how behaviors may be altered by the actual or implied presence or absence of other actors. Certainly praying alone or praying with a single other person, versus praying in a small group or even in a large group such as occurs in a church or synagogue, all merit attention. On the surface, this distinction might appear to be a simple experimental manipulation, but there are significant differences involved. Chief among these is that, by common agreement, prayer is never engaged in "alone" in the strictest sense—since prayer assumes the presence of a Being toward Whom the prayer is directed. In some instances, the pray-er may report a feeling of being unsuccessful in connecting with the "Other"; yet, the presumed expectation of at least a dyadic interaction is nonetheless a significant feature. In the group situation, however, the prayer is typically conceived as an occasion when one is connected not only with a singular object (i.e., one's Deity) but also is simultaneously in the presence of other believers. This "wider" presence itself establishes a particular mindset that should be taken into account in the design and execution of studies (Ladd & McIntosh, 2008).

The social context can further expand from the immediate group setting to the level of family and peers, then to denominational influence, locally and in general, and finally to the context of the overall culture. All of these may importantly shape attitudes and values as to what is acceptable and desired in prayer and what is not. These concerns reflect various avenues of exploration in attempting to understand the variety of terminology (with often overlapping meanings) that one encounters in the literature.

One fascinating feature of prayer is that, while it creates a social bond at the group level, it simultaneously produces individualized experiences that can alter physiological responses and influence the interpretation of perceptual stimuli. That is, it has the potential to engage all of one's bodily senses, thereby intensifying the experience for the individual pray-er.

Treating prayer as a multifaceted expression of belief obviously entails concrete measurable action in the midst of embedded and embodied contexts. Theory exists about these important social considerations and their individual correlates, but the relevant research has not yet been undertaken. For instance, multidimensional prayer frameworks have been postulated for a number of years but with only mixed observable effects on these hypothesized forms. Therefore, one is hard-put to know where to start, what framework to select, and when to call research efforts complete. Classic works by Sabatier (1897), Heiler (1932/1958), Eller (1937), and Buttrick (1942) combined traditional faith, philosophy, and the social sciences with psychology. Heiler's nine forms of prayer derived from history, literature, archeology, and all but the physical sciences. Still, the researchers' focus, from a psychological standpoint, was almost exclusively on the pray-er's cognitions and motivations. Many studies have also been undertaken by "religious psychologists" more concerned with faith-oriented phenomena than would be true of specifically scientific undertakings.

THEORETICAL FORMS OF PRAYER

Table 3.1 contains a sampling of prayer forms, or types, that were relevant to psychology during the first half of the 20th century. Some of these forms are still present today. Some overlap among the concepts clearly exists, and various authors have often used the same term and yet described it differently. For example, Stolz (1923) mentions prayer for the cure of disease, but he refers to illness only in oneself. In contrast, Tillett (1926) and others (Puglisi, 1929; Stewart, 1939) specifically refer to efforts to cure sickness in others, and they label these prayers "intercessory." The impression is created that alleviation of the problem in the pray-er might best come under the heading of "petitionary prayer" since it is a request for personal aid, but this label need not be restricted to this usage. Furthermore, prayers of petition are complex. Calkins (1911) considered the desire for forgiveness, the need for moral strength, and

TABLE 3.1. Prayer Forms Found in Early Works Relating to the Psychology of Religion

Adoration	Gratitude
Altruistic	Guidance
Aesthetic	Intercession (intercessory)
Aspiration	Meditational
Communion	Mystical
Confession	Noetic
Consecration	Penitence
Contemplative	Petitional (petition)
Dependence	Praise
Devotional	Problem solving
Egoistic	Ritual
Ethical	Simple regard
Eudaemonistic (emotional)	Submission
(for) cure of disease	Thanksgiving
(for) the dead	
(for) Divine love	
(for) Divine guidance	
(for) ethical betterment	

Note. The following sources were consulted: Buttrick (1942); Calkins (1911); Hallesby (1931/1975); Heiler (1932/1958); Puglisi (1929); Stewart (1939); Stolz (1923); Tillett (1926).

the primitive appeal for material advantage as all falling under the rubric of "petition."

Additional variations on these themes have abounded. References to private and public prayers were common, and they raised the issue of public worship that was mentioned earlier. Hierarchies of prayer were offered. Stolz (1923) placed everything under two headings, petitional and devotional. Puglisi (1929) preferred the key categories of egoistic versus altruistic, which could be viewed as either personal or social. Corporate prayer, which could be tied to specific faiths and their theologies, was most commonly expressed in public church settings, though not exclusively (Buttrick, 1942). One might suggest questions relating to silent, as opposed to vocal or audible, prayer and the likelihood of undertaking such silent prayer in coordinated group settings. Other possibilities were seemingly limited only by the vocabulary and linguistic inclinations of the various authors dealing with the subject. Subtleties in meaning might be lost when attempting to draw easy comparisons; however, we can offer definitions with which most scholars appear to agree.

During the second half of the 20th century, scholars exploring the psychology of prayer often simplified their research offerings, though the basic prayer types they discussed remained unchanged from those of their predecessors. For example, Webb (1962) referred to prayers of adoration, confession, petition, and intercession, while Hinson (1979) invoked the concepts of praise, thanksgiving, confession, intercession, and petition to describe much the same thing. One especially noteworthy detailed formulation was provided by Foster (1992), who grouped 21 prayer forms under three major headings (i.e., inward, outward, and upward prayers). His scheme was quite comprehensive and should be considered further for its valuable instructional potential. At the same time, many of the forms he cited were unique or only rarely found elsewhere in the literature of the day. Table 3.2 presents, in outline form, Foster's framework for types of prayers.

Beyond the surface similarity of providing shared names for different ways of praying or kinds of prayer, these scholars' efforts evidence another important feature. Almost none of them has been systematically evaluated through empirical data. One exception is the framework of Foster (1992), which proved fruitful for research on the cognitive and emotional aspects of prayer (Ladd & Spilka,

TABLE 3.2. Prayer Types According to Foster (1992)

Moving inward: seeking personal transformation

1. Simple prayers
2. Prayers for the forsaken
3. Prayers of personal examination
4. Prayers of a contrite heart
5. Prayers of surrender and relinquishment to God
6. Prayers for self-change, improvement
7. Prayers of decision, commitment, covenant

Moving outward: seeking direction and guidance

8. Praying the ordinary, everyday, and commonplace
9. Petitionary prayers
10. Intercessory prayers
11. Healing prayers
12. Prayers of suffering
13. Authoritative prayers: representing God
14. Radical prayers: appreciation and change

Moving upward: seeking identification with God

15. Adoration prayers
16. Prayers of trust in God's love
17. Sacramental, liturgical, and guidance prayers
18. Consuming and unceasing prayers of God contact
19. Prayers of intimacy: being at one with God
20. Meditational prayers
21. Contemplative prayers

Note. In some instances, we have extended Foster's designation to give readers, hopefully, a fuller appreciation of what he intended.

2002, 2006) and was also successfully applied to psychotherapy (Tan, 1996).

Research directed by theory is relatively rare in this area. The prayer types designated are almost exclusively based on the empirical observation of people when they pray, the settings in which prayers occur, and the content of the prayers. One contemporary exception, however, was some work undertaken by Baesler (2003), whose greatest strength is in communication rather than traditional psychology. Although much of his work is accepted as objective psychological scholarship, many commentators insist that it is heavily tinged with Christian theology. By his own admission, Baesler offers an "interpersonal Christian prayer" framework. In keeping with his communication orientation, there is an emphasis on listening, talking, or dialoguing with God. He elaborates at length on active versus receptive kinds of prayer. Separating theology from a scientific psychological and objective communication approach is difficult to accomplish. Baesler's efforts definitely merit close examination, especially since he presents a lengthy and significant set of questions specifically directed toward furthering new research.

JUNGIAN THEORY AND PRAYER

Most early prayer systems were premised on the religious commitments of their creators. These schemes were primarily constructed *by* the devout *for* the devout. This is not to demean such efforts, since they provide an important avenue into the way prayer is generally viewed and practiced in our society. Psychologists who tackle the problem of differentiating the various types of prayer are often concerned about the classic separation of religion from psychology, a distinction that both historically and contemporaneously psychologists publicly maintain because of fear that scientific rigor might be compromised (Hood et al., 2009; Kirkpatrick & Hood, 1990).

The contemporary empirical approach commonly embraces methods such as factor analysis, often without supportive theory. One exception is the writings of Carl Jung, which have generally been viewed as congenial and useful by religious scholars and some psychologists of religion (Clift, 1982; Michael & Norrisey, 1984). Works such as *Modern Man in Search of a Soul* (Jung, 1933) have been welcomed in religious circles, since Jung has long been regarded as sympathetic toward institutional faith (in stark contrast to Freud). This high regard for Jung seems to be especially evident among Catholic scholars (Clarke, 1983; Michael & Norrisey, 1984).

Clarke (1983) derived his system from "retreat/workshop experiences . . . which have sought to aid Christian growth by correlating Jungian type personality categories with Gospel themes and Christian practices" (p. 661). Even though Clarke employed the Myers–Briggs Type Indicator (MBTI)[1] in his research, no data were provided. Several studies based on Jung's personality system have, however, resulted in a multidimensional scheme for prayer.

According to Jung (1933), the ego in essence possesses two innate attitudes, extraversion and introversion, which express tendencies in which psychic energy turns toward, respectively, either the environment or oneself. Within this construct, there are also four innate functions, two emphasizing perception (sensing and intuiting) and two stressing judgment (thinking and feeling) (Hall & Lindzey, 1978). The combination of these orientations and functions leads to eight possibilities (four for Introversion and four for Extraversion) for defining both individual personalities and forms of prayer. The most full development of the forms of prayer was undertaken by Francis and Robbins (2008), who constructed eight scales to assess prayer preferences, namely, the above four for Introversion (I) and four for Extraversion (E). These are denoted as Sensing (S), Intuition (N), Thinking (T), and Feeling (F). The Jung–MBTI dimensions have also been translated into a multidimensional Catholic framework (Michael & Norissey, 1984). Further validation of this scheme has been undertaken by Ross, Weiss, and Jackson (1996). Various distinctions relating to religious outlook (including prayer) are sometimes evident among the Jungian types, but their significance is not altogether clear.

Catholic theology and Jungian thought have been combined by one scholar into the notion of Centering Prayer (Pennington, 1986). Keating (1999), in turn, attempted to translate the aspirations of Centering Prayer into behavioral guidelines that express, in essence, what contemplation means. In other words, Centering Prayer is considered a form of contemplative prayer. Unfortunately, this concept was characterized by inspirational obscurity, which challenges the empiricist's desire for criteria that can be operationalized. One practitioner, for example, emphasized that "centering prayer is beyond words" (Petrovski, 1996, p. 1G). That this approach was meaningful to the devout is not questioned here. It returns us, however, to William James's (1902/1985) assertion of ineffability as central to mysticism: "It defies expression . . . its quality must be directly experienced; it cannot be imparted or transferred to others" (p. 380). Paul Pruyser's (1968) argument that religious practice is designed to produce religious experience also comes to the fore in trying to understand Centering Prayer. Implying that prayer and religious experience are intimately associated appears to question the possibility of developing objective criteria for Centering Prayer. Still, qualitative clinical indicators may be inferred. Clarke (1983) adopted the idea of Centering Prayer as a subform of Jungian intuition, which is not well distinguished from Jung's thinking and feeling functions.

Fantasy and imagination are key aspects of its focus on fundamental Christian values. Its promise of profundity and its vague definition, however, are antithetical to a strictly scientific approach. One reviewer suggested that it is "like trying to catch a cloud in a net" (Petrovski, 1996, p. 1G). Turning to Jung's feeling function, Clarke (1983) spoke of "prayer characterized by affection, intimacy, and the devout movement of the heart" (p. 669). This last phrase again suggests the difficulty of putting feelings into words that might actually result in potentially definitive research. Feeling Prayer, however, was separately delineated as focusing on the emotion of love as its central component.

Lastly, in Clarke's (1983) scheme, Thinking Prayer introduced the classic battle between Aristotelianism and neo-Platonism, which at its core is the distinction between emotion and cognition in revelation. Clarke notes that rationality and thinking have gotten a bad name in Catholicism as they relate to prayer. Still, he and Michael and Norrisey (1984) emphasized the legitimate role of cognition and other higher mental functions such as memory and self-examination in prayer. For some people, this emphasis on mental activity and intellectualism distinguish Thinking Prayer.

Michael and Norrisey (1984) also employed a Jungian scheme with the Myers–Briggs inventory to clarify the relationships between various prayer types and personality dispositions. Jungian ideas are readily illustrated through expressions of spirituality, not the least of which involve prayer. For example, Sensing is realized by citing mortification of the senses, which is intended to open "souls to the Spirit" (p. 24); thinking is identified with meditation on basic truths; feeling is tied to relationships with the Divine, and intuition is expressed through "contemplative union with God" (p. 24). As with Clarke (1983), such definitions make psychological and theological ideas difficult to differentiate from each other. There is also no simple one-to-one prayer—temperament correspondence. By way of illustration, we read that Jesus prayer and Centering Prayer call upon all four psychological functions as having only one goal, namely, mystical union with God. An ideal form of prayer is offered, Benedictine prayer—again, said to call upon all of the psychological functions. It is regarded as the ideal prayer form appropriate to all four temperaments. Schemes like this are questionable in respect to proper measurement. The criteria suggested by theologically sophisticated scholars may simply be too abstruse for rigorous analysis of their concepts. When situations like this are encountered, a common argument is that a phenomenologically holistic approach is needed, and the reductionism commonly employed by most research psychologists is simply inadequate. A scientific psychology of religion must, however, rely on something more tangible than just inspired aspirations or unanchored spirituality.

THE EMPIRICAL DEMONSTRATION
OF MULTIDIMENSIONALITY

The best way to determine the empirical dimensions of prayer is through factor analysis, and this approach has been used to obtain the information presented in Table 3.3. The question immediately arises why there is not greater agreement among the various factor studies. A number of possibilities need to be considered:

1. Sometimes researchers employ different data categories, and these may vary in their interpretation of the same information.
2. It is common to find like item content with slight changes in the words selected.
3. Studies have examined diverse combinations of old and new items.
4. Linguistic variations and new items may differentially influence response sets (e.g., social desirability and acquiescence). In addition, the same items usually produce dissimilar correlations when the samples are changed (e.g., college students in church- vs. non-church-affiliated schools, adult respondents vs. general populations [e.g., American Protestants vs. Irish Catholics]).
5. Factor analysis is a generic term applied to numerous analytic methods, and not all studies divulge the specifics of the techniques used, such as rotational procedures. Factor solutions need to be cross-validated and the particulars specified regarding what was done.

This latter approach was the goal of Ladd and Spilka (2002), who sought to identify the common factors in several studies. When straightforward initial matchups proved elusive, they turned to the

TABLE 3.3. Types of Prayer Identified in Empirical Studies

	Poloma & Gallup (1991)	David, Ladd, & Spilka (1992)	Hood, Morris, & Harvey (1993)	Laird (1991)	Ladd, Spilka, McIntosh, & Luckow (1996)	Luckow (1997)	Ladd & Spilka (2002, 2006)
Adoration				×			
Good feeling		×				×	
Rituals						×[b]	
Behavioral habits		×					
Colloquial	×[a]						
Thanksgiving		×		×	×	×	
Intercession		×				×	×
Suffering							×
Personal examination							×[c]
Confession		×		×	×	×	
Tears							×[c]
Sacramental	×[b]	×[b]	×[b]		×[b]	×[b]	×
Rest	×	×	×	×	×	×	×
Spiritual petition			×	×		×	
Material petition	×	×	×		×	×	×
Radical							×
Number of types	4	8	4	5	5	9	8

Note. The studies in **bold-faced type** used the same datasets for the primary analysis but different factor-analytic approaches. From Ladd and Spilka (2002). Reprinted with permission from John Wiley & Sons, Inc.

[a]Includes elements of *thanksgiving, confession,* and *spiritual petition.*
[b]The items relate more to physical behavior than to cognitive activity.
[c]Two scales represent discrete aspects of previous confession indices.

work of Foster (1992) and then generated a new set of likely factors based on his overview to give the process a firmer conceptual base. They further detailed their factor-analytic procedure in an appendix so that the method would be transparent and more readily transportable. Foster's categories demonstrated considerable linguistic overlap, and ultimately eight scales emerged that tap into the inward, outward, and upward (I, O, U) "directions" toward which prayers are focused (Table 3.4).

This study further noted that the second-order factors did not follow a pure I, O, U format but, rather, revealed combinations of those dimensions (Table 3.5). The structure of these higher-order factors

TABLE 3.4. Scales with Item Loadings

Inward scales	Upward scales	Outward scales
Personal examination	Sacramental	Radical
.85 examining myself	.91 engaging and exploring	.73 seeking to be revolutionary
.73 evaluating my inner life	.63 connecting with traditions	.63 boldness
.65 devoting myself		.61 radical approaching
.63 committing	Rest	.57 assertiveness
.49 judging myself	.78 quietude	
	.76 silence	Suffering
Tears	.64 stillness	.84 agonizing with others
.77 misery	.56 private experiences	.63 accepting the pain of others
.76 sadness		.62 carrying the distress of people
.56 grieving		
		Intercession
		.82 asking for help for other people
		.74 seeking assistance for others
		.70 searching on behalf of someone else
		Petition
		.84 asking for things I need
		.67 making personal appeals
		.67 asking that physical needs be met
		.53 requesting material things

Note. From Ladd and Spilka (2002). Reprinted with permission from John Wiley & Sons, Inc. Scale concepts from Foster (1992).

TABLE 3.5. Second-Order Factor Loadings and Correlations

Loadings	Scale type
Internal concerns	
.80 Intercession	Outward
.77 Examination	Inward
.76 Suffering	Outward
Embracing paradox	
.85 Tears	Inward
.69 Rest	Upward
.65 Sacramental	Upward
Bold assertion	
.86 Radical	Outward
.72 Petition	Outward

Note. From Ladd and Spilka (2002). Reprinted with permission from John Wiley & Sons, Inc.

suggested certain themes normally associated with praying, namely, internal concerns (IC), embracing paradox (EP), and bold assertion (BA). The IC factor reflects the extent to which self-examination prepares an individual to relate effectively to challenges faced by others. The EP facet captures the experience of people struggling to understand the interface between faith and life-as-lived (see Kierkegaard, 2006). Finally, the BA factor incorporates prayer content emphasizing more explicit requests.

A follow-up study of 570 respondents (Ladd & Spilka, 2006) confirmed both the scales and the higher-order structure in relation to multiple constructs (general religiosity, death attitudes, life satisfaction, coping, etc.). The conceptual model emerging from this work suggests that both the three directions (I, O, U) and themes (IC, EP, BA) appear to be useful. As we noted in Chapter 2, Breslin and colleagues (2010) were not able to confirm the Ladd and Spilka (2002, 2006) analysis. We suggest the need for further work to resolve this matter. Although we present here as instructive the factor-derived scales with which we are most familiar and believe to be most solidly validated, readers should also consider that alternative instruments have been developed by Hood and colleagues (1993) and Poloma and Gallup (1991).

The Acceptance and Utility of Multidimensionality

Although single items to assess the frequency of prayer continue to be used, multidimensional measures predominate in the now numerous empirical efforts undertaken to specify the various forms of prayer (David et al., 1991; Hood et al., 1993; Ladd et al, 1996; Ladd & Spilka, 2002; Laird, 1991; Luckow, 1997; Poloma & Gallup, 1991). The preference for such multiform systems in research also appears to be well established (Janssen et al., 1990; Ladd, Hvidt, & Ladd, 2007; Laird, Snyder, Rapoff, & Green, 2004; Whittington & Scher, 2010). Unfortunately, one major shortcoming pervades this literature, namely, that relatively few efforts have been made to create theoretical schemes that distinguish among and predict the differential effects of the various types of prayers. Laird and colleagues (2004) show that four of their five scales relate moderately to strongly with intrinsic faith but not with measures of extrinsic faith, hope, or agency. These authors offer suggestions for improvement, yet they somewhat optimistically admit that "only a few a priori predictions were made" (p. 254). In essence, the same lack of conclusiveness also applies to the work of Poloma and Pendleton (1989) as well as Whittington and Scher (2010).

Little by little, however, studies explicitly treating prayer content are emerging. Recent work exploring the importance and frequency of prayers in the *St. Joseph Daily Missal* has indicated relationships consistent with expectations about prayer elements, whether the language in the 1,100 prayers was hand- or machine-coded using language recognition software (Language Inquiry and Word Count, or LIWC) (M. L. Ladd, Cook, Becker, & Ladd, 2009). For instance, more common or frequent rituals display less inward and more outward and upward prayer language.

In another example, Ladd and colleagues (in press) explored the idea that prayer to God and conversations with friends display similar patterns in preferred subject matter. In this instance, concurrently the same words and phrases clearly made sense to the participants in the study even though, as hypothesized, the ways in which the linguistic structures were employed might have differed significantly.

Additional experimental work has focused on how the elements of prayer shift, depending on the physical posture of the practitioner (K. L. Ladd, Cook, Foreman, Ritter, & Cora, 2010). Meanings may differ depending on whether the pray-er is seated or walking (K. L.

Ladd et al., 2009) and whether the prayer is taking place in a quiet setting or in a functional magnetic resonance imaging–type context (Cook, Ladd, Ritter, Foreman, & Mertes, 2010).

When one employs factor analysis, the reasons underlying why items load on a factor may be quite unexpected. A common word or terms signifying a similar process can produce a grouping. For example, three of the questions in Poloma and Pendleton's (1989) colloquial type of prayer contain the word *ask*. These are joined with items that include the words *talk, telling,* and *thank*. Calling this factor Colloquial Prayer makes sense as a phrase connoting communication without indicating what the specific item content is. In a later work, this is termed Conversational Prayer (Poloma & Gallup, 1991). Hood and colleagues (1993) replicated Poloma's factors, though they preferred the terms Meditative, Contemplative, Ritualistic, and Liturgical Prayer (among others). The distinction between Petitionary and Material Prayer in Hood and colleagues is unclear and does not appear equivalent to Poloma's Colloquial Prayer (see Table 3.3). Conversational or Colloquial prayer implies style more than a unity premised on components such as in petition. Certainly this last form involves communication. In a similar way, ritualistic and meditational approaches can be viewed as styles where themes such as petition, adoration, confession, thanksgiving, and the like emphasize the substance of communication. As far as we know, these various distinctions have not been analyzed.

Before leaving this topic, we must note a different approach based on linguistic word counts. VandeCreek, Janus, Pennebaker, and Binau (2002) creatively broke with the standard methodology to conduct, as they put it, a "Linguistic Inquiry and Word Count" treatment of prayers solicited from seminarians. The results were categorized into causal expressions as well as expressions of insight and negative and positive emotions. Commenting favorably on the potential presented by this methodology, the authors suggest a variety of future research possibilities.

PRAYER FORMS: THEIR MEANING AND RAMIFICATIONS

We have gained some insight into the complexity and richness of prayer by taking appropriate note of its many forms and expressions.

Even though such scholars as Buttrick (1942) and Foster (1992) identified the primary and mostly spiritual qualities of the prayer forms they undertook to study, we need to place their insights more firmly within the framework of behavioral and social science. As an example, let us look at the psychology of petitionary prayer.

Petitionary Prayer

Capps (1982) pointed up the significance of petitionary prayer by asserting that "the heart of the psychology of religion is the psychology of prayer, especially petitionary prayer" (p. 130). Hendry (1972) similarly believed that "prayer is basically petition—asking, seeking, making requests . . . petition is the heart of prayer" (p. 26). Previously, Heiler (1932/1958) had declared that "the free spontaneous petitionary prayer of the natural man exhibits the prototype of all prayer" (p. 1). The truth of his observation is evidenced in both its character and frequency. In respect to frequency, prayers of petition are said to be "dominant over all other kinds of prayerful expression" (Ellens, 1977). Petitionary prayer's central mission is to obtain something or improve one's personal situation. This description can be interpreted as a desire for simple narcissistic gratification, a rather widely accepted notion. Ellens (1977) refers to this approach as "the pathological paganism of compulsive God manipulators" (p. 48). Recognizing this troubling possibility, Capps notes that theologian Karl Rahner calls such prayers "a testing point for the modern interpretation of prayer (and) a special stumbling block . . . either useless or a fraud" (p. 132). One can argue, however, that petition is elevated whenever one asks for something good or noble, like the enhancement of personal righteousness, spiritual enrichment, or aid for others. Again, this exposition is primarily from a religious point of view. Thus, the various possibilities may range from the egocentric to the allocentric. Representing both motives is a description by Kennedy (1974) of the 1941 sinking of the German battleship *Bismarck* by the naval flotilla commanded by British Admiral J. C. Tovey. The evening prior to the battle, Tovey retired to his cabin and prayed (as Admiral Horatio Nelson had done prior to his victory at Trafalgar). He believed that his ships would ultimately sink the *Bismarck* but was worried that they might sustain serious damage. The prayer calmed him. Feeling that the full weight of responsibility had been lifted from his shoulders (as with Pargament et al.'s [1988] Deferring mode of coping), he resumed command assured of success. Thus, the religious act of praying had, for him, key psychological consequences.

One suspects that many petitionary prayers are not especially enlightened appeals to the Deity. The petitionary pleas of athletes to their God to help them beat the other team or to knock out their opponent in a boxing match may be commonplace phenomena (Hoffman, 1992). Similarly, the heaven-bound entreaties of gamblers for a winning card hand or a successful roll of the dice may not enjoy the outright approval of devout religionists, but these satisfy meaningful psychological needs for those imploring their God for aid. In Chapter 1 we observed this basic function also in control enhancement and stress reduction.

Two studies by Brown (1966, 1968) on adolescents found that the inclination to employ and believe in the efficacy of petitionary prayer generally declines between the ages of 11 and 17. Some variations were observed that were based on respondents' religious affiliation and nationality (i.e., whether they lived in the United States, New Zealand, or Australia). More exacting work, however, needs to be done, as these two early efforts were merely exploratory and suggestive in nature.

Communication: The Essence of Petitionary Prayer

Communication is the most obvious characteristic of prayer in general (Baesler, 2003). It is especially significant in petitionary prayer, as the supplicant wants something—in particular, evidence of a favorable answer. Pray-ers, however, try to communicate not only with the Divine but also to some degree with themselves—as seems evident in the effect that Admiral Tovey's prayer had on his outlook and feelings. Prayer is thus to some extent reflexive, telling seekers that they have done something that is potentially effective. In other words, petitionary praying is an indication that the person expects to benefit—at least, by feeling more capable of accomplishing a goal. One is therefore less helpless or impotent or certainly feels different. Anything may be requested via prayer, but we must ask how effective such prayers are objectively and subjectively. Since communication has many facets, it is reasonable to analyze the intentional basis of prayers. Are they designed to persuade, inform, beguile, suggest, inveigle, ingratiate, encourage compliance with our wishes, or merely reflexively benefit us psychologically and physiologically (Ellens, 1977)?

Another important consideration that pertains to petitionary as well as other forms of prayer is that those of many practitioners include the caveat "if it be Thy will," whether spoken or unspoken. This caveat establishes a context that simultaneously encourages a freedom to express deeply one's own needs and yet emphasizes the atypical character of the human–supranatural exchange. Even the well-trained observer might overlook this subtext when dealing with prayers that seem crass or purely materialistic (e.g., "Please give me a new car!").

Other Prayer Forms

Petitionary prayer, including "intercessory" variations (see Chapter 7 for details about these), has often been studied and thus (we might hypothesize) is also the easiest for which to develop a theoretical perspective. One may rightfully ask, "What about all the other forms?" Responding to this query poses something of a dilemma. For all practical purposes, other prayer forms have been little used and then not very successfully. This is a poorly explored realm. Multidimensionality obviously negates exclusive reliance on debatable single items such as prayer frequency. In other words, currently variations on multidimensionality are mainly little more than fragmentary descriptions. As an initial step, Ladd (unpublished data, 2010) conducted a pilot study that focused on several factor-derived kinds of prayer previously discussed by Foster (1992). Prior to a hierarchical analysis in which these types roughly fell into the inward, outward, upward scheme, the primary factors were labeled as follows:

1. "Examine"—with self-examination and confession.
2. "Tears"—elements of "misery," sadness, and grief.
3. "Petition"—"petitions for material and physical needs.
4. "Radical"—prayer as argument, aggression, self-assertion.
5. "Rest"—quiet, the quality of being subdued in the presence of the Divine.
6. "Suffering"—identifying with the distress of others, "agonizing with others."
7. "Intercession"—praying to help others.
8. "Sacramental"—valuation and utilization of rituals.

To better understand how these forms of prayer illuminated perspectives on personal faith, they were related and compared to various measures of intrinsic, extrinsic (personal and social), and quest faith. The results were not heartening. Statistical significance was detected in only three instances for quest, four for personal–extrinsic, none for social–extrinsic, and five for intrinsic faith. The coefficients were generally low, attaining only the .05 level or less owing to the small sample size ($N = 215, 217$). Again, the statistical relationships were not strong. Where significant, a Quest orientation related negatively to the prayer forms, whereas all other variables correlated positively. As could be expected, prayers for petition associated with a personal–extrinsic outlook and an intrinsic perspective were most consonant with the other prayer types. Although work along these lines needs to be expanded and extended, one can see its hypothetical potential in the findings thus far reported.

We would be remiss if we did not take note of the fine work of Janssen and his coworkers (Bänziger, Janssen, & Scheepers, 2008; Janssen, Prins, Van Der Lans, & Baerveldt, 2000). Although they initially constructed measures for four types of prayer, they were able to confirm only three in their later studies. The initial four were defined as follows:

1. "Religious"—traditionally Christian, reinforcing faith in God.
2. "Meditative"—passive, self-oriented immersion in thought; heightened self-awareness.
3. "Psychological"—directed toward self-change, increasing the sense of control and self-direction.
4. "Petitionary"—meant to affect external and possibly internal factors; objective and problem-oriented.

The petitionary and religious focus coincided, leaving the other three viable. Even though these researchers sought to draw out possible similarities with a few other systems, the need to further assess psychometric and experimental correspondence within their own systems is abundantly evident.

SUMMARY

Very little argument opposes the view that prayer consists of a variety of dimensions, although much debate is devoted to how best to identify and describe these dimensions. With variations in the style, content, and intensity of one's practices and beliefs, we propose a three-dimensional scheme. In the final analysis, our primary concern is how researchers explore the different meanings of praying in relation to the psychology of those who engage in these practices. We might, for example, ask whether some employ prayers of adoration in an ingratiating manner and how this possibility affects other religious expressions, personality, and social behavior. Single-item measures of prayer frequency obviously have a place in the research toolkit, but such rudimentary instruments provide only limited understanding of one's inner life. While there has been some modest progress in clarifying prayer's cognitive aspects, its affective, social, and behavioral components have yet to receive comparable systematic attention. These are wide-open areas where researchers could easily spend an entire career.

We are invariably drawn back to the realm that is clearly the weakest, namely, theory construction. Simply put, the concept of multidimensionality has opened an inviting door to the really creative psychologist of religion. Hood and colleagues (2009) put it best in observing that "measurement-based research has clearly established the multidimensionality of prayer, and future research will undoubtedly contribute to a deeper understanding of the subjective experience of prayer" (p. 308).

NOTE

1. The Myers–Briggs Type Indicator is probably the most well-known and popular objective questionnaire designed to measure Jungian personality tendencies.

CHAPTER 4

The Individual's
Development of Prayer

The lowest and crudest notion concerning prayer is that it
consists in asking God for things. . . . This is the notion
with which childhood always begins, and the only one
which childhood can entertain.
—BORDEN P. BOWNE (1910, p. 130)

And beads and prayer books are the toys of age.
—ALEXANDER POPE, "Epistle on Man," II, l. 280 (1948)

*I*n this chapter, each individual's development of prayer is
conceived as a lifespan development process and is thus not
restricted to the preadult period. In addition, human growth is conceptualized in "evo-devo" fashion, focusing on the numerous interactions among evolution, genetics, and postnatal growth and development (Carroll, 2005).

Kelemen (2004) has carefully reviewed the literature on how
even young children conceive a potential role for Divine intention and
purpose in explaining natural phenomena. With considerable caution
she suggests that, by the age of 5, children's ideas about agency, invisible companions, and artifacts imply that the very young may well be
"intuitive theists." In other words, nonhuman factors—even supernatural agents—readily appear in children's understanding of natural processes. Such cognitions may also make children more receptive to adults' religious ideas. Other research work on the hidden

causes perceived by 10- and 12-month-old infants show them capable of inferring a "hidden causal agent" without any explicit evidence that it really exists (Saxe, Tenenbaum, & Carey, 2005). A case can be made, though far from proven, that this view implies an innate (i.e., "genetic") component of religion—or at least a predisposition toward ideas and beliefs favorable to religion's emergence. This natural inclination has repeatedly been demonstrated (D'Onofrio, Eaves, Murrelle, Maes, & Spilka, 1999). Bouchard (2004) estimates that the innate proclivity toward religiousness affects some 11–22% of 16-year-olds and 30–45% of adults. We may well ask: Where does prayer fit into this overall scheme?

In certain quarters, then, the psychology of religion has adopted an evolutionary–genetic framework in relation to religions' origins and development (Atran, 2002; Atran & Norenzayan, 2004; Boyer, 2001, 2003; Feierman, 2009; Hood et al., 2009; Kirkpatrick, 2005). As might be expected, this framework fully takes into account the importance of prayer (Atran, 2002; Feierman, 2009). One of the most graphic evolutionary possibilities for a rudimentary form of prayer was embodied in the ritualistic animistic action of chimpanzees described by Jane Goodall (1988; Guthrie, 1993). Animism per se (i.e., animated action) is premised on the view that inanimate objects or occurrences possess human-like qualities or are the result of the behavior of unknown beings. This is usually regarded as the initial stage in the development of religion (Gould & Kolb, 1964). Though a highly speculative notion, it would be quite significant to know if the chimpanzees' animated actions assumed some external intentionality, meaning that the chimps attributed agency to some force beyond themselves. If so, religion might be in the offing!

Suggestions that evolutionary elements influence the psychological development of religion and prayer are strongly implied by Lawson and McCauley's (1990) conception of the evolutionary basis of ritual. However, there is far more to prayer than just its ritualistic aspect. Psychological development during one's early life has been extensively studied, and the type that particularly concerns us emphasizes cognition and emotion. This is also a time when social and moral sensitivities, sex roles, ego, and personality development become part of the overall picture. Unfortunately, as the *Handbook of Spiritual Development in Childhood and Adolescence* (Roehlkepartain, King, Wagener, & Benson, 2006) attests, research on prayer as it relates to any of these aspects of growth is virtually absent.

The fact that cognitive processes and contents are active and changing throughout life means we need a theoretical framework that can encompass one's entire lifespan. The ideas of Piaget point toward such a system, although Piaget's formulations are most relevant to the time period prior to adulthood. We will shortly see how this theory has been applied to prayer. The theoretical scheme for religious judgment devised by Oser and Gmunder (1991) looks promising for the task we are undertaking, but it has yet to be employed to the development of prayer. Another life-spanning scheme for development has been proposed by James Fowler. His *Stages of Faith* (1981) is in part subtitled "the quest for meaning," and cognition via a Piagetian conceptualization of it is central to Fowler's formulation. This effort goes well beyond traditional cognitive elements to include morality, social awareness, and motivational considerations that one would expect to encounter in a much wider perspective on personality. Fowler appropriately cites the views of Erik Erikson (1959, 1963) as embraced in his lifespan developmental theory. There is, however, no explicit recognition or treatment of prayer. While Erikson's various posited stages are successively identified with one's advancing years, these stages are increasingly complex, cognitively and psychosocially. We might therefore hypothesize a growing multidimensionality across and within the identified forms of prayer associated with such stages.

Alternatively, increasing complexity may not actually be a virtue in the practice and understanding of prayer. Various traditions, in fact, speak explicitly of the goal of reducing complexity in order to move toward more profound experiences. This point of view suggests a divide between theories emphasizing a growing complexity and those aiming toward simplicity. One may be able to resolve this issue by citing the insights of Wolfram (2002) as they relate to "new science" or through the more easily accessible notion of "simplexity" (Kluger, 2008). The dynamic interplay between simplicity and complexity must necessarily be explored (Fuller, 1975). Hofstadter (1979) raises interesting questions concerning the development of systems over time without settling on definitive answers. These writings admittedly cross the boundaries of traditional psychology, but, as with any evolutionary approach, they provide broad intellectual maps that suggest new directions in our understanding of prayer's development. In other words, let us not perceive everything as solely simple to complex growth.

PRAYER IN CHILDHOOD

Support for the Lawson–McCauley (2002) framework for ritual may be inferred from Childs's (1983) theorized connection between prayer and "private speech" in the young child. Placed in the context of communication, children's self-regulatory functions are considered "adaptive for survival" (p. 30). Childs further conceives of prayer as possibly "far more social than just a conversation between the person who prays and the deity" (p. 32). Additional support appears in the work of Ulanov and Ulanov (1982), by whom prayer is regarded not only as private communication but also fundamentally a deep form of speech that voices concerns that are difficult for the person to meaningfully articulate.

These observations concerning private or inner speech may reflect evolutionary–genetic roles for language and prayer, as contrasted with what is learned. These evolutionary–genetic emphases also better enable us to understand both the form of prayer and its content at different ages. Unfortunately, research and writing on the early development of prayer to date is highly speculative and often theologically premised (Hoffman, 1992; Koppe, 1973; Lee, 1963). Tatala (2009) asserts that religiousness is first manifested at ages 2 or 3. A period of "magical" religion is said to follow from years 3.5 to 6.5. Six additional stages are offered to cover the entire lifespan. Neither the source of these hypothesized intervals nor research affirming them is given. Such thinking, however, might contribute to eventual theory construction if it were systematically developed (Godin, 1958; Meissner, 1961).

Piagetian and Associated Cognitive Possibilities

Although a few attempts have been made to study children younger than 5, most early developmental work deals with later childhood (7–12 years). This history may primarily reflect the fact that prayer is typically operationalized in terms of language and the ability to engage in dyadic interchanges. To the extent that scholars are able to develop other views, explorations of prayer at earlier ages should become increasingly feasible. As for the current state of affairs, Rosenberg (1990) notes that the dominant theoretical framework and methodology used can be termed "Orthodox Piagetian" (p. 50). This fixation on Piaget emphasizes the current state of the study of childhood cognition and the assumed ways it is understood to unfold (Hood et al., 2009).

Reflections on how children younger than 5 are viewed were pressented by Andre Godin (1958), who offered a combination of psychoanalytic inferences and common adult views on the way children think, act, and feel. Typically, close identification with one's parents sets the stage for a child's initial religious understanding of prayer, first in general attitudes and emotions (which Godin believes are derived primarily from the mother). Concepts of deity are added later, along with prayerful practices learned from parents. The two become connected in a utilitarian, self-protective petitionary sense. Godin (1971) emphasized that this early orientation possesses a magical and superstitious quality that, though slowly accepting traditional religious forms, may be present even into adolescence.

Woolley and Phelps (2001) made a serious effort to evaluate prayer practices among 3- and 4-year-olds by studying the thinking of children up to the age of 8. Responses were elicited through interviews, assigned tasks, stories, pictures, and parental questionnaires. The influence of high and low religious parents was especially evident in the responses of the 3- and 4-year-olds. Respondents who came from religious homes had a definite concept of prayer and an understanding of what was desirable when praying. The researchers described the 3-year-olds as possessing "a very vague and inconsistent awareness of prayer" (p. 156). By the age of 4, however, prayer involved the concept of God and religion in the home and was definitely an influential shaper of behavior. Physical postures during prayer were more important for the two youngest age groups than for the older respondents, who more typically emphasized their mental outlook. One can see in this study the expected growth in thinking about causality and acceptability on the part of the children. This observation further suggests the desirability of explicitly studying longitudinal changes in the formation of prayer concepts as they relate to nonreligious ideas.

Utilizing a Piagetian approach with children ages 5 to almost 13, Long, Elkind, and Spilka (1967) identified three developmental stages that implied a specific biological basis for concern with differentiation and abstraction. Stage 1 was observed in 5- to 7-year-olds and revealed a global, undifferentiated, vague, and fragmentary understanding of what prayer is. Stage 2 appeared in 7- to 9-year-olds and evidenced the growth of a distinctly concrete and differentiated idea of prayer in which volition and affect were more prominently featured. Stage 3 (observable in children 9–12 years of age) demonstrated more advanced mental development with abstract, differentiated, and self-reflective notions that encompassed both the cognitive and emotional components of belief. Signs of a systematic organization premised on learned ideologies from religious groups were also now present. Psychological parallels may be drawn between the Piagetian ontogenetic orientation and the broader historical–cultural evolutionary views of Heiler (1932/1958) and Hodge (1931). When we focus on the specific linguistic content employed by children, the growth in verbal organization and vocabulary attributable to one's advancing age and educational experience is evident. The character of ritual prayer stages most likely reflects evolutionary and genetic effects, while the linguistic elements probably emanate from culture and learning. Woolley and Phelps (2001) believed that a child's understanding of prayer began earlier than suggested by Long and colleagues, although the level of the child's comprehension was quite rudimentary.

In an attempt to confirm and extend the Long and colleagues work, Worten and Dollinger (1986) studied 90 students from the first, fourth, and seventh grades, but unfortunately they did not specify the respondents' ages. Other work shared similar shortcomings (see Rosenberg, 1990), making direct comparisons problematic. In addition, in many studies the children came from religiously affiliated schools, making comparisons with public school students questionable. In general, the basic findings of Long and colleagues (1967) were verified by these studies, while other hypotheses concerning maternal influence were not supported.

Ronald Goldman's (1964) extensive work on prayer took a somewhat different path than the foregoing work, as his attention was directed toward the actual content of prayer and its forms over the 6–16 age range. Thus, preadolescence and adolescence now entered the developmental picture. A lack of rigorous data analysis coupled with limited age samples posed interpretive challenges to all these scholars. The average number of prayers increased slightly with age, but the researchers really did not know what this meant because there was little replication of methods and interpretation in most cases. Several types of altruistic prayers—namely, those for others—became more numerous over time, and a similar pattern prevailed praying for oneself. One possibility is that both egotism and altruism were positively correlated with age in this sample. No pattern was detected for petitionary prayers for protection and recovery (what Goldman terms "Set Prayers," which are standardized, repetitive ritualistic offerings).

An especially interesting observation touching on cognitive development and the Piagetian approach is Goldman's (1964) characterization of the stages of prayer as generally moving from the magical (up to 9 years of age), to the semimagical (9–12), and finally to the nonmagical (from 12 onward). Godin (1971) likens this scheme to that of Long and associates (1967).

We cannot overlook the exhaustive study of Francis and Brown (1991), in which nearly 5,000 11-year-olds participated. One noteworthy observation of the analysis was that 37% of the boys and 19% of the girls claimed that they never prayed. In an effort to determine factors that affect attitudes toward praying, an extensive path analysis was undertaken. Not surprisingly, researchers found that the parents' relative religiosity and church attendance closely paralleled their child's attitude toward prayer and its practice.

May (1977) conducted another large-scale study of about 5,000 English schoolchildren ages 10–18. Responses were given to four questions by respondents divided into three age groups: 10–11, 14–15, and 16–18. (Responses for the 12–13 age group were not presented.) Other than frequencies and the corresponding percentages, no additional statistical analysis was reported. Given the large sample sizes, small variations would undoubtedly be significant, if statistically treated. The data presented regarding how people pray, the possible results of prayer, and the reasons for praying are interesting but offer little developmental information.

An extremely important set of studies, one of which dealt with prayer, was undertaken by Kalevi Tamminen on Finnish children from 1974 to 1986 (Tamminen, 1991). Displaying sensitivity to both the theoretical and methodological issues involved, Tamminen selected students ranging in age from 7 to 20 for four separate investigations. To understand the sources of influence on the children and adolescents, their teachers and parents also completed questionnaires. Some 1,000 children and adolescents were assessed.

One may view the pattern of answers over the 12 years sampled, but statistical tests were not usually employed. Selecting a few of the many observations reported, we find that the incidence of regular prayer seemed to decline over time and correspondingly a strong trend toward never praying increased. No consistent tendencies were evident regarding physical practices, mental characteristics, or denoting what was considered important in prayer. Unfortunately, the various tests did not always yield comparable findings. Reliability issues common to single-item measures might have been a factor here. A general pattern of positive correlations between God belief and actions in prayer were obtained over all the age/grade levels. Most significant was the finding that the perceived reality and nearness of God generally correlates with a belief that prayer has a demonstrable effect. Whether or not this perception was in line with the desires of the pray-ers was not ascertained. Tamminen, however, provided a great deal of information that invited subsequent follow-up and theoretical speculation.

Something Different: Softening the Hard Science Stance

Even though we are inclined to hold tightly to research approaches that extol theory, measurement, and statistics in the "hard" sense, some promising variations should be noted. In this regard, at least two thinkers merit special mention and attention, namely, psychiatrist Robert Coles and teacher Vivienne Mountain.

Robert Coles, a physician and child psychiatrist affiliated with Harvard University, has written extensively on the spirituality, religion, morality, and other aspects of the lives of children. The author of over 50 books and 500 articles and the winner of a Pulitzer Prize, he offers insights into the personal faith of children and youth from a wide variety of viewpoints. The informality of his writing provides a refreshing look at how his young respondents cope with life. His book *The Spiritual Life of Children* (Coles, 1990) and five-volume series *Children of Crisis*, among others, depict prayer from unique personal perspectives. Their insights provide opportunities for psychologists of religion to create and test theories that can enrich our knowledge of the place of prayer in the lives of the young.

Vivienne Mountain, an Australian school teacher, employed Glaser and Strauss's (1967) concept of grounded theory in her study (2005) undertaken to understand children's prayers. While possibly unfamiliar to most scholars, the systematic qualitative approach embodied in grounded theory is helpful in understanding the process and experience of prayer from the individual child's perspective.

Summary

We have just briefly reviewed some 40 years of research on children and prayer. During this period, the theory and applied research on cognition and emotion during childhood advanced considerably. The various studies demonstrate much variety in the methodologies and mental and physical phenomena associated with prayer. Some of this work extended into the adolescent years, so its range is greater than would be optimal for generating focused results.

Despite some serious efforts to deal with developmental issues, most scholarly attention has been directed at defining the diverse types of prayer rather than placing this information within the psychology of childhood cognition and emotion. Although Piagetian influences are much in evidence, contemporary research on cognition often resorts to a more demanding information processing alternative (Bukato & Daehler, 1992) that merits further examination.

The study of prayer in childhood needs to be better defined and its various elements integrated with one another. Some initial efforts in this direction may be observed in the work of Long and colleagues (1967), Goldman (1964), Tamminen (1991), and more recently Woolley and Phelps (2001). However, still needed are theory-guided efforts that apply contemporary and cross-disciplinary developmental concepts to the perceived roles, components, and effects of prayer. It is often difficult if not impossible to compare the results from the various studies. When the bedrock work in the field is examined objectively, a major problem is the lack of correspondence between the various investigative methods utilized—whether interviews, stories, pictures, questionnaires, or the like. Also, findings have too often been expressed in simple frequencies or percentages that leave further interpretation to readers when something more definitive is needed. Finally, the language used needs to be better defined and the main concepts coordinated across the various studies. Incidentally, where the research is conducted also has ramifications for its correct interpretation and the wider applicability of findings. While thus far research work in the United States, England, and Finland predominates, the various cultural and national differences in religion and in the specific contexts for prayer have yet to be controlled and more widely assessed.

PRAYER IN ADOLESCENCE

Age is a continuous variable without neat dividing lines designating childhood, adolescence, young adulthood, and the like. Researchers studying children and prayer have generally included respondents from ages 5 to 16. The common upper limit given for adolescence is usually 18, but again this is a convenient convention that may be employed or ignored at will.

Using data from almost 3,300 13- to 17-year-olds who participated in the National Study on Youth and Religion, Smith and Denton (2005) reported that 40% of the respondents attended worship services once a week or more, while some 65% reportedly prayed alone during the same period. The corresponding figure for personal prayer once or more daily was 38%.

This last finding was closely mirrored in the 1995 National Longitudinal Study of Adolescent Health (AddHealth; Smith, Faris, Denton, & Regnerus, 2003), whose sample of 13- to 18-year-olds showed 40% praying daily. As might be expected, considerable variation characterized the different religious denominations, with the frequency of prayer lowest among Jewish teens (the latter group's families were also least likely to engage in prayer at mealtimes or in joint religious practices involving parents and children). Although the massive AddHealth study was not theory-oriented, its authors proposed a general thesis they termed "moralistic therapeutic deism." According to this thesis, both prayer and worship are integral to this system, thereby fostering an altruistic morality code and emotional support network to rely on when personal problems arise. The survey data focused on the frequency of prayer, while in-depth interviews revealed the significance of prayer to the teens.

Taking the field as a whole, we might consider reported research first from an atheoretic standpoint. Janssen, De Hart, and Den Draak (1989, 1990), for example, discussed one particular Dutch study in two separate articles. Employing the general rubric "praying practices," they asked specifically what Dutch adolescents do when they pray. Noting that the 5,000 Dutch youth averaging 16.8 years of age responded in 1983 to a national survey of political and religious issues, the researchers gave no additional information on the findings of this initial work. In 1985, however, they conducted a follow-up study of 192 of the respondents (who by then would have averaged 18 to 19 years old). The authors, however, were unclear as to whether they were dealing with 192 individuals from the same 1983 study since in one place they refer to "Dutch youth averaging 17 years old" (p. 104). Elsewhere in the latter (1990) article they indicate a return to "the original answers" from the sample. Since no basic data were provided in the 1989 article, readers cannot meaningfully compare the two samples. So, for all practical purposes, the research in the 1990 article claims to cover the what, how, and why of prayer and praying in the second group. Even though the authors listed only percentages, this latter article could serve as a very useful introduction to the whole area. The authors' analysis of the structure of prayer and its content is creative and original.

The tasks of adolescence are basically the gaining of cognitive and social-emotional maturity. These may mean, among other things, logically analyzing problems, controlling egocentrism, appreciating others, and finding purpose in life, including pointing toward future commitments in relationships and work (Berk, 1993; Goldhaber, 1985).

Prayer and Formal Operational Logic in Adolescence

The Piagetian framework for adolescence stresses placing the concrete in abstract perspective. The issue is to understand what is done in terms of deductions from inductive generalizations. Starting at about age 12, as the young person leaves childhood and enters adolescence, there is an increased tendency to think logically (Piaget, 1958). Generally, the examples provided to illustrate formal operational logic tend to be mechanical intellectual exercises seemingly independent of personal and social behavior (Goldhaber, 1985). Furthermore, although this rather popular cognitive process has been seriously challenged, it continues to be widely applied (Keating, 1980). For example, Marcia (1980) asserts that the achievement of personal identity requires formal operations. Studying the role of prayer in late-age adolescents, McKinney and McKinney (1999) investigated the "prayer lives" of 77 religious college undergraduates ranging in age from 18 to 23. In addition to keeping a prayer diary for 7 days, respondents answered questionnaires concerned with prayer and their ego identity. No meaningful statistical relationships were found between these measures, and there was little more than a brief selective presentation of a few relationships in this article. Researchers also subjected the content of the prayer journals to dramaturgical and semiotic analyses, but no specific data for interscorer agreement or objective criteria were included, thereby undermining any substantive conclusions. The authors postulate the existence of six types of prayer: adoration, petition, thanksgiving, reparation, communication, and relaxation. While petitionary prayers predominate and are briefly described, none of the other types is specifically defined. The potentially helpful organizing themes of identity and its formation unfortunately are not pursued through the entire work. One suspects that these might have been more active matters of greater concern with younger adolescents, especially where formal operations could have been developing and involved. Although some provocative methodology is suggested, this work leaves many gaps to be filled.

In Marcia's (1980) discussion of formal operational logic and identity formation, an aspect of the latter, purpose-in-life (PIL), invites further scrutiny. Francis and Burton (1994) shed additional light on this topic. Studying some 647 12- to 16-year-old Catholic adolescents, significant positive associations between PIL and both participation in private and church prayer are reported. Francis and Burton further claim that this cross-validates an earlier study of theirs that produced similar results. The early- to midadolescent age range of the respondents was again probably best for observing the development of formal operations.

Given the controversial nature of formal operational logic and the possibility that it relates to prayer development, further research is needed to understand what is happening here. Mere correlation is not enough, as the process remains obscure. One must keep in mind that the broader involvement of religion per se lies in the background of the prayer findings.

There is a major potential confound in all of the work on adolescent correlates of prayer, namely, the relatively common pattern of experiences of youth in regard to home life and education. One can hardly partial out these influences in any depth and, even worse, we cannot accurately define them. Despite this difficulty, Francis and Brown (1991) looked at parental behavior and attendance among students at church-affiliated schools. No inclusion or discussion of Piagetian views was presented, the entire emphasis being on the home–school–worship–private prayer complex. A pattern of weak to moderately significant correlation coefficients characterized these relationships. In addition, the sex of the adolescent was also a factor, undoubtedly a product of parent–child relationships. Mothers and daughters showed more joint involvement than fathers and sons. Parent attendance at church linked strongly to their child's attitude and practice of prayer. The causal nature of these findings, however, remains elusive, providing fertile ground for further examination.

The Question of Adolescent Egocentrism and Altruism

Adolescence is usually pictured as a time for developing mature ego identity (Marcia, 1980). This means, among other things, establishing a sense of self selectively separate from childhood attachments and external controls. It is also a time for consolidating one's sexual orientation and social and moral relationships more or less independently of the expectations of past authority. With a growing tendency toward abstraction, self and superego processes increasingly imply personal choice. Churches and synagogues are often significant resources for new judgments and understandings. With regard to faith, we see changes in the nature and content of the prayers adolescents employ. Theoretically, childish egocentricity should be supplanted by growing social and altruistic inclinations. Some hints were offered by Goldman (1964), who instead of providing definitive analyses supplied simple data counts to be further interpreted by his readers.

May's (1977) work is also pertinent in this regard, for although he did not undertake exacting analyses, his large research samples and the evident trends in the data implied that altruistic and empathic prayers decline during adolescence based on responses from his 10- to 11-year-olds versus those from the 16- to 18-year-olds. This finding is opposite to what other studies' data suggest.

Brown (1966, 1968) carried out a number of studies that in some ways overlap with those of May's later work. These could imply a growing intellectual maturity. Studying over 1,000 youth ages 12–17 from the United States, New Zealand, and Australia, Brown observed a "consistent" reduction in belief in the "causal efficacy of petitionary prayer" (1966, p. 208). Apparently adult moral approval and personal threat can influence this judgment. Brown suggested a growing tendency on the part of adolescents to evaluate when prayer might or might not be effective. When "personal danger" was a factor, petitionary prayer was regarded as most effective.

In a subsequent research effort, Brown (1968) found that the perceived appropriateness of prayer was influenced by the respondents' religious affiliation, whether Catholic, Anglican, or Protestant (mostly Methodist or Presbyterian). In general, Catholics showed the strongest belief in the efficacy of prayer, though still with qualifications. Further data breakdowns suggested that the age effect might really be a function of ability. If anything, this work suggested that respondents' understanding of prayer was mostly dependent on a number of other psychosocial factors.

The Structure and Content of Adolescent Prayer

In 1990, Janssen and colleagues (1990) tackled the problem of identifying the structure of adolescent prayer in general, defining it in terms of seven factors: (1) the motivating need, (2) the action (specifically, how it is expressed), (3) the direction (i.e., at whom it is directed, (4) the time (when practiced), (5) the method (the procedure employed), (6) the effects, and (7) the outcomes. The researchers then examined the content of the prayers in their sample and came up with answers that made sense not only for late adolescents but for a broad range of ages. Praying was stimulated by problems of all kinds, constituting some 81% of the needs listed by the respondents. Considering respondents' great concern with needs, surprisingly only one-third of the prayers featured a petitionary quality. Praying overwhelmingly took place in the evening or at night, with church cited as the location only 11% of the time. The methods of praying were rather prosaic, as were also the desired effects that related to the problems brought up. Pray-ers naturally desired to have their difficulties resolved. The researchers also attempted to compare respondents from three religious groups as a whole with those characterized as unaffiliated and nonpraying youth. Since these were highly variable in composition and of relatively small size, it was difficult to generalize beyond this particular content. The structure–content approach employed here, however, does offer a potentially constructive way of understanding prayer in relation to a wide variety of such independent variables as gender, age, education, and religious affiliation.

The great potential rewards for work among young people can be readily appreciated based on the impressive collective efforts of the Search Institute, whose report *With Their Own Voices* (Roehlkepartain, Benson, Scales, Kimball, & King, 2008) explored what youth and young adults think about spiritual development. This organization is known for its extrordinary work, this effort being perhaps the prime example. Drawing on data from 6,853 participants representing eight nations and ranging in age from 12 to 25, the report offers readers the minimum necessary to deal with the basic intentions cited above. Private prayer, meditation, and religious worship revealed a consistent pattern, with the highest percentage of participation shown for Cameroon (53–71%) and the lowest for the United Kingdom and the Ukraine (10–32%). Unfortunately, but in keeping with the descriptive nature of the data, the reasons for these variations were not discussed.

When we look at daily private prayer participation among respondents in the age groups 12–14 and 22–25 over all the nations sampled, there is an orderly decline from 31% to 17%. This downward progression is also evident for respondents' participation in public worship or prayer services. The implication is that there is more or less an orderly reduction of their participation in prayer and worship as respondents age from early adolescence to early adulthood.

Summary

Summing up a variety of prayer studies, one is likely to perceive more contradiction than an orderly and gradual growth in egocentric and altruistic inclinations in prayer from childhood through adolescence (Goldman, 1964; May, 1977). Good beginnings such as the work by Tamminen (1991) need to be extended, repeated, and coordinated with what has been done in order to comprehend prayer in the perspective of adolescent needs and religious/spiritual orientations. Some scholars attempt to resolve the complexity of the area, but each research and theoretical venture is largely isolated from the others (Janssen et al., 1990; Oser & Gmunder, 1991; Rosenberg, 1990; Tamminen, 1991). As a result, the broad developmental trends in adolescent religion are difficult to perceive and communicate to others.

A few studies have looked at the subjective correlates of faith (including prayer) during these years. Smith and colleagues (2003) attempted to determine the feelings of youth toward their faith and concluded that about two-thirds of those participating in very large surveys are not alienated or hostile toward organized religion, while about 15% are. One gets the feeling that we need a focused conference among researchers to delineate clearly the dimensions of what constitutes prayer, how and why it is practiced, its perceived and actual effects, plus designation of the subtle expressions the resulting factors imply. In other words, a strong need exists for coordinating and integrating the research and determining what deserves to be further replicated and extended longitudinally. As already noted, one obvious failing in the field is the insufficient attention paid to multi-dimensionality. Multiple confounds abound—ranging from efforts to compare dissimiliar nations to a failure to define and assess appropriate age ranges. One gets the impression that the controversial Piagetian insights are probably inapplicable by the age of 15 or 16, and by then also one's practice of prayer is likely evolving both in content and complexity into adult forms and expressions.

PRAYER IN ADULTHOOD

The General Case

Once we leave adolescence, the stage-like Piagetian designations slowly fade away. There is a well-developed psychological inclination in all of us to hone in on clear-cut structural guidelines. The more popular ones are presented below, but the validity of their implied limits and divisions can easily be questioned. Although Stevens-Long (1990), an acknowledged specialist in this area, commonly employs such compartmentalizing terminology, she also states clearly that there is "little reason to think of stages" (p. 153). Certain ages have customarily been designated as transition periods when in reality the processes discussed are more fluid and often possess a uniquely individualistic quality. Too readily a resort to the language of categories is an intellectual convenience that bears watching closely and warily. Still, it has its uses, as in the next paragraph.

Even though some of the studies cited under adolescence extend into early adulthood, we now enter the period labeled by Stevens-Long (1990) as "post formal operations" (p. 134). She provided a fine analysis of theoretical thinking about young, middle, and late adulthood along with a number of suggestive possibilities that structure adult life as it relates to cognition and personality. Unfortunately, none of these appears to have been applied to prayer. While Piaget's theories and formulations facilitated our better understanding of prayer in childhood and early adolescence, contemporary views of aging preclude notions of psychosocial uniformity in adulthood (Spacapan & Oskamp, 1989). As a rule, informed discussions of religion and prayer are noticeably absent from works dealing with adult life, aging, and gerontology (Cunningham & Brookband, 1988; Eisdorfer & Lawton, 1973; Stevens-Long, 1984).

In Chapter 2 we noted that the standard basic measure used in this area is a single item assessing the frequency of prayer. This is commonly supplemented by another question on attendance at religious services. Prayer is treated as private practice, and worship is its public counterpart. A recent national study utilizing these items was reported by the Pew Forum (2010). In this study, over 35,000 participants ranging in age from 18 to 65 and older were sampled, with the age breakdown as follows: 18–29 (Millennials), 30–49 (Generation X), 50–64 (Baby Boomers), and 65+ (the Greatest). Clearly, the current Millennial group of young adults engages less in prayer, meditation, and worship than their older cohorts. In all of these behaviors, the percentages increase with age. (See Table 4.1.)

The main contribution of such descriptive data as these is their recency. The surprising amount of variability that attends these figures is likely a function of who is sampled, the data collection procedures, and other methodological matters. For example, Benson and his associates from the Search Institute (Search Institute, 1990) gathered information on 5,000 Christian church–affiliated respondents over a 4-year period ending in 1990. In this instance, we would normally

TABLE 4.1. Pew Forum (2010) Survey Data on Prayer, Meditation, and Worship by Age

Age	Pray daily	Meditate weekly	Attend services weekly
18–29 (Millennials)	48%	26%	33%
30–49 (Generation X)	56%	35%	36%
50–64 (Baby Boomers)	61%	46%	40%
65+ (the Greatest)	68%	56%	53%

Note. N = 35,556.

have expected higher rates of prayer frequency than with the more generalized Pew sample cited above. However, while Pew indicated daily prayer for 56% of its Generation X group (ages 30–49), Benson and his associates (2006) observed that only 33% of their sample of 30- to 49-year-olds prayed daily. Their finding of 43% for those ages 50–69 contrasts with Pew's 61% for a slightly younger cohort. If we used the Pew Forum's trends, the 5 additional years in Benson's comparable cohort data should have yielded percentages quite a bit higher, and yet, instead, they were lower.

Rodney Stark's (1968) earlier data on over 1,400 church members further illustrated this problem. With respect to prayer, his 30- to 49-year-olds yielded a 50% estimate, and for his 60+-year-olds the finding was 70%. Change over time may provide a partial explanation, but other factors must be considered.

Another problem is the age breakdown utilized. Sometimes there is a year or two variation among studies, whereas other instances reveal 5 to 10 years' difference. Levin and Taylor's (1997) study indicated prayer at least once a day for 27.6% of its 18- to 30-year-olds. If we include more than once a day, the number jumps to 40%. The midlife years' definition in this study was not comparable to the Pew Forum or Search Institute categories. If we look at the category of 61+ years in the Levin and Taylor data, 72.9% stated that they pray daily one or more times. Comparability of data across studies is obviously a common problem in this type of research work.

In sum, when we conduct an overview of studies, we see a 10–20% variation across the age groups even with very large numbers of participants. Fundamentally we are dealing with the most elemental consideration for prayer, namely, its frequency.

Early Adulthood: The Millennials

When comparisons are made over decades from the 1970s to the present, one conclusion stands out—namely, that twice as many of the Millennials are currently unaffiliated with religious institutions than was true of their peers in the 1970s. Only 4–5% fewer 18- to 29-year-olds prayed daily in the 1980s and 1990s than appears to be true today. More Millennials may be currently choosing everyday prayer on the basis of personal needs than was the practice 20 and 30 years ago. During the earlier times, affiliation with religious bodies conducting standard rituals was higher than it is currently.

The richness of research on contemporary young adults is well illustrated by Christian Smith's (Smith & Snell, 2009) more recent follow-up to his landmark work on adolescents in the 2005 volume titled *Soul Searching* (Smith & Denton, 2005). Referring to his earlier 13- to 17-year-old sample (now 18–23 years old), he analogized this cohort to 18- to 29-year-old Millennials, terming this period "emerging adulthood" (p. 4). He further placed his sample deeper into the context of adulthood, noting that this young group engaged in less daily prayer and public worship attendance than their elders. Some inconsistencies with the Pew Forum data should also be noted. This much can be said with relative certainty: considering adulthood in toto, people's weekly attendance at worship services steadily increases from 15 to 40% as adulthood progresses, and a similar pattern is observable for daily prayer, with participation growing from about 40% to some 80%. Given the various generations from the Baby Boomers on, we are always ready to anticipate some substantive basic changes, but Smith informs us that his emerging adults are ultimately similar in prayer frequency to those younger respondents that preceded them. Among Smith's Catholics, however, weekly church attendance has generally declined 10% over the past 30 years.

Fortunately, Smith has recognized the importance of placing prayer in parental and peer contexts, enabling its meaning to become clearer. Moderate-sized correlations with other variables speak to the complexity of prayer's usage and the often forgotten fact that it is a significant part of both current and past religious life patterns (e.g., parental religiosity = .36). The frequency of prayer in adulthood is thus discussed as a function of earlier familial and adolescent experiences. It may be our cultural emphasis on individualism that causes us to look at concurrent rather than consecutive influences. Smith terms his inclusive approach "qualitative comparative analysis," in which attention is afforded both individual and sociocultural levels in order to reveal causative interdependencies.

Smith adds another very important consideration, namely, the affirming and reinforcing character of prayer, its allied devotional practices, and the attendant supportive beliefs. This consideration is further broadened to include such psychological referents as personal identity and interpersonal relationships. Since there appears to be a reduction in institutional involvement, prayer *could* speak to the growth of an individual's personal framework with its own unique values. Another insight comes to mind in the perception that college spans the closing years of adolescence and the beginning of adulthood. While college does not necessarily lessen the religiosity of committed students, it may affect those who were little attached to religion at the outset.

Smith's analysis—probably more than any other research treatment—offers a path to understanding prayer in adulthood. We wish, however, that he had gone beyond merely citing prayer frequency to dealing more substantively with multidimensionality.

Looking beyond our own country, research in the United Kingdom with 18- to 29-year-olds has been undertaken by Maltby and Lewis (1999). They placed prayer and worship in a religious context like that described by Ladd and Ladd (2010), which we discussed briefly in Chapter 2. Focusing only on frequency of prayer and church attendance, the researchers found that both measures related positively and significantly to an intrinsic religious orientation for men and women. An extrinsic–social perspective linked up significantly to church attendance but not to private prayer. Interestingly, the latter variable was negatively associated with personal extrinsity. One can argue that these relationships are compatible with Ladd and Ladd's findings on multidimensionality as it relates to intrinsic commitment and extrinsic utilitarianism, with the former's positive connection to private prayer and the latter's possible rejection of it.

Benson and the Search Institute's (Roehlkepartain et al., 2008) multinational study of 22- to 25-year-olds generally revealed a lessening of prayer and worship inclinations from adolescence onward. Unfortunately, for most of the work covering the millennial years, a need clearly exists for understanding the feelings and motives of these young people regarding prayer. We have accumulating data but few hints regarding its foundations.

Moving into Midlife

The relative freedom of early adulthood generally gives way to a period of consolidation. These years, usually 30–60, involve the establishment of personal/social stability plus integration into various organizations and communities through marriage and family, work, friendships, and institutional religion. Erikson (1959, 1963) calls it the stage of maturity. All of these may be motivational sources for prayer that relates to one's satisfaction with life.

Very little of the research on prayer distinguishes middle adulthood as a definable period of change. Levin and Taylor (1997) break their sample into four age groups and provide specific data on their frequency of prayer. In their sample some 45% of 31- to 40-year-olds indicated they pray one or more times each day, increasing to 58% for 41- to 60-year-olds. These authors attempt to associate prayer with age and other demographic variables, but in the few instances where statistical significance was achieved, the relationships were weak and few of their explanations provided any grist for future research. One can perceive alternative ways of analyzing these data, but there is little reason to believe that different analytical schemes would alter the fundamental conclusions.

Expanding their concerns to gender and race, Levin and Taylor (1997) examined prayer frequency for whites and blacks by age and sex. At all age levels from 18 to over 60, more women than men and more blacks than whites prayed. In either gender or race, prayer frequency consistently increased with age (which was attributable in part to the likelihood that the older respondents were exposed during their early years to greater religious training than their younger counterparts). Levin and Taylor assessed a variety of demographic factors, most of which correlated poorly, or at nonsignificant levels, with prayer frequency. The main influencing variables appeared to be the degree of organizational religiosity and one's relative personal feeling of closeness to God. Extending this work to deal with prayer's multidimensional aspects is recommended by these researchers. Of course, this avenue had already been opened by Poloma and Pendleton (1989) and Poloma and Gallup (1991). Poloma and her colleagues performed a great service by developing scale-based measures of what they termed Meditative, Petitionary, Colloquial, and Ritualistic prayer. The first three scales proved to be instructive indicators, but the last produced relatively low values, possibly because of small variations among the respondents. Unfortunately, these instruments yielded low regression coefficients with indices of well-being and satisfaction with one's life as well as religious satisfaction (Poloma & Pendleton, 1989). Further work (Poloma & Gallup, 1991) also failed to provide the expected results. Continuing this effort with other religious measures remained essentially unproductive in the mid-adulthood age range. In general, some constructive possibilities were observed when the prayer variables were placed in a broader personal religious context with such indices as closeness to God and prayer experience (Peacock & Poloma, 1999).

Correlates of Prayer in Adulthood

Much if not most of the research on prayer in adulthood concerns its use with stress and health. This relationship is discussed in much greater detail in Chapter 6. Similarly, adjustment issues are treated in Chapter 5. This leaves very little research on prayer with adults that is not directed toward either health or well-being applications or coping with life's problems.

Prayer in Old Age

The concluding years of life present numerous problems that people usually do not wish to recognize and accept. Retirement is common, and what it portends for most of us is either unclear or negative. The undesirable dangers posed by financial, social, personal, and medical stresses are abundantly clear. Cognitive change in old age is complex and not just a tale of simple decline, although one reluctantly becomes increasingly aware of such shortcomings as difficulties with memory (Park & Schwarz, 2000). Finally, there is the inevitability of death.

The fact that older adults are the fastest-growing segment of our population has spawned innumerable senior centers and stimulated every kind of organization to develop ways of working with this group. Religious institutions are often in the forefront of such efforts, and those over age 65 tend to be quite active in such programs.

The relative scant theoretical research available on religious and spiritual behavior during middle life contrasts with that available on older adults. With respect to prayer frequency, a sampling of various studies undertaken is presented in Table 4.2. Although there is a fair amount of variation, the differences in when and how the data were gathered and who constituted the samples probably accounts for the bulk of these variations.

Without question, Table 4.2 tells us that prayer is important to older adults. In a series of studies, Krause, Chatters, Meltzer, and Morgan (2000) attempted various assessments of the effects of prayer and its relationship to selected personal characteristics. Working with whites

TABLE 4.2. Prayer Frequency Given as Daily or More

Source	Age	Percentage
Pew Forum (2010)	65+	68%
Levin & Taylor (1997)	61+	72.9%
Koenig, George, Blazer, Pritchett, & Meador (1993)	75+	55.9%
Stark (1968) (all church members)	60+	71.2%
General Social Survey (2008) (2000+ data)	55+	69.1%

and blacks ages 65 and older in focus groups, Krause and colleagues observed variations among the participants in beliefs about the timing of prayer and the Deity's response. Some expected the response to come immediately, others when God deemed it appropriate. The answer, both in the speed of the response and its content, was assumed to be in the best interests of the pray-er. Underlying these views was the premise that one can always trust God. Krause (2004) hypothesized that such "trust-based expectancies" would support psychological well-being. National samples of some 750 older adult (66+ years old) whites and the same number of blacks were interviewed face-to-face regarding trust-based prayer expectancies and both the frequency of prayer and church attendance (worship). The expected ties with self-esteem were found and were stronger for blacks than for whites (Krause, 2004).

We should also note that Krause and Tran (1989) earlier studied worship and prayer with respondents 55 years and older. Utilizing the terminology of organizational and nonorganizational religiosity, these researchers demonstrated that these forms are at heart, respectively, worship and prayer. Although statistically significant results were reported for the association of organizational religiosity with esteem and nonorganizational religiosity with an enhanced sense of control, the relationships tended to be weak.

When the issue was coping with stress among 60- to 89-year-olds who responded to 66 possible ways of dealing with distressing events, prayer placed first in their rankings. The gap between prayer and the next closest alternative means of coping was larger by far than that between any other of the possibilities provided (Manfredi & Pickett, 1987).

Prayer and Death

Death, as the inevitable termination of life, is naturally very much the subject of prayer and supplications. For obvious reasons, it is of special interest to older adults but owing to various illnesses and the demise of friends and relatives, among other possibilities, many young people also express intense death anxiety or death depression. As might be expected, religious promises of life after death tend to alleviate these worries somewhat (Alvarado, Templer, Bresler, & Thomas-Dobbins, 1995).

A fairly large number of studies have been conducted in this area, more dealing with church attendance and worship than specifically with individual prayer. Happily, much of this work is methodologically sophisticated and summative in nature. A large meta-analytic review by McCullough, Hoyt, Larson, Koenig, and Thoresen (2000) focused on 20 major studies involving a total of almost 126,000 respondents. Religious involvement, mainly consisting of worship but also including private or nonorganizational activity that implied prayer, was associated with lower mortality rates. The main moderator variables appear to have been social ties and healthy living styles, which in our own chapters on health and prayer (see Chapters 6 and 7) have been shown to be physically and mentally beneficial (Strawbridge, Shema, Cohen, & Kaplan, 2001).

Also representative of this work was research by Strawbridge, Cohen, Shema, and Kaplan (1997) on over 5,000 people who attended worship services for an average of 28 years. In this study, greater church attendance was positively correlated with reduced death rates. A possible confounding factor in such research is that focusing on public worship often ignores those too sick to attend church; that is, homebound persons might not live sufficiently long or be sampled. The work of Fry (1990), which specifically addressed this problem, concluded that prayer was a major coping mechanism for dealing with one's fears about pain, personal safety, and the uncertainty of life after death.

Summary

Our intention in this section was to zone in on the three major periods in adulthood: young adults, comprising persons 18–29 years old; midlife adults, those 30 to 49 years old; and older adults, persons 60 and older. We concluded by noting how the reality of death was dealt with, most notably by older adults. Try as we might to find continuities from one time period to another, we may have to recognize that such may not exist. Peacock and Poloma (1999) suggested that very different early-life experiences by the various age cohorts makes the notion of a general smooth course for life relative to religion unlikely. These authors, however, acknowledge that normative attachments lessen as one's age advances. Krause (2000) believed that "there may be multiple patterns of religiousness over time" (p. 142). In other words, as people age, they individualize. Even so, they are apt to undergo numerous like experiences: such things as marriage and family involvements, work, retirement, and physical and mental decline and illness. The role of age per se is often minimized in this research work and possibly rightfully so, as the common events encountered constitute the real concerns of those involved.

Peacock and Poloma (1999) cite a review of 556 studies on life quality—of which only 28 dealt with religion and even fewer, 18, emphasized older adults. These, however, could perhaps provide guidelines for examining prayer during the earlier periods of adult life.

Similar difficulties plague all three of the adult age ranges because of reliance on frequency of prayer or worship as opposed to employing multidimensional frameworks. Still, the evidence suggests that people generally increase in their overall religiosity as they age (Krause, 2000). There is also evidence that people increasingly resort to prayer as they grow older (Pew Forum, 2010). One hypothesis remains untested, namely, whether the older a person is, the more likely that person was exposed to religious education when young. At most, this influence appears to be only a moderate one, particularly since the tendency to pray is strong throughout adulthood. We need to know much more about the form and content of these prayers. Does prayer multidimensionality take on different meanings in the age groups over time? Given normative changes, is there a growing differentiation within and across the various multidimensional expressions in prayer? Such possibilities should be identified and their religious and spiritual significance spelled out. Let us also be aware that the variables to which types of prayer may be related can also be multiform in nature. An excellent example is the work of Dunn and Horgas (2000), in which prayer is correlated with eight coping styles. Two of these, optimistic and supportive coping, correlated significantly with prayer frequency. Does this simply mean that these forms are the ones most often used? If so, why? Finally, we must consider developing theories and dimensions that aid us in comprehending the complexity that undoubtedly underlies this entire domain.

SUMMARY

Change over time does not necessarily mean that some orderly development is taking place owing to patterned modifications in cognition, personality, or other psychological processes. A number of theoretical works by Piaget (1958), Oser and Gmunder (1991), and Fowler (1981) have been offered to explain alterations in the understanding and expression of prayer in childhood and adolescence. The Piagetian framework and language has greatly appealed to researchers in this area, and although different research approaches have been applied to children and youth, a case can be made for the validity of Piaget's enumerated stages of development. These apparently weaken in adolescence or simply get less attention. Nothing comparable has been found for adults.

Beyond classic Piagetian models, such researchers as Woolley and Phelps (2001) and Barrett (2004) are bringing to bear "theory of mind" constructions, especially in reference to the earliest ages. These approaches contend that children automatically attribute intentionality to both humans and nonhuman referents, predisposing them to engage in prayer-like behaviors. In addition, young children also readily accept "superhuman" powers; so, the possibility of miracles or otherwise perceiving prayers as answered is rarely questioned. Such approaches rely far more on the early intuitive abilities of children than do the Piagetian formulations based on exposure and learning. This movement toward alternative conceptualizations means that the challenge to meta-analyses can only increase.

In general, adulthood has defied cognitive or psychosocial developmental structuring, despite researchers' best efforts at conceptualization, such as those of Erikson. As noted above, a number of scholars are convinced that there is no standard developmental pattern for adults, since individual experience and contexts may differ radically. One might argue that the possibility for generalizing about life diminishes as one's life progresses through the years. The conceptions of prayer held, the experiences encountered, and the practices in which people engage inevitably would broaden, meaning that the multidimensional aspects increase for prayer styles and contents, just as a like diversification occurs in other aspects of one's life.

CHAPTER 5

Prayer in Coping and Adjustment

Prayer has functional value for the individual.
—HORATIO W. DRESSER (1929, p. 54)

I try to get myself together. And that for me is prayer.
—JAMES B. PRATT (1927, p. 330)

*P*rayer is a central expression of faith. In prayer's full setting, all references to the supernatural are basic to the
ways in which humans have interacted with the world since their
earliest appearance in the evolutionary record. In essence, all living
entails coping, and prayer is coping behavior. At every moment, physically and mentally, a person acts to survive and achieve gratification.
For most people, religion, spirituality, and prayer are integral parts of
this universal process. Pargament (1997) points out that prayer serves
multiple functions, not only in coping with the sorrows and distresses
of life but also in better dealing with all the good things that happen.
For some, it provides a sense of a secure closeness to God and related
enriching experiences. In other words, prayer offers the individual
a means of dealing with both negative and positive experiences in
the present and the projected future. Pargament's fine volume, *The
Psychology of Religion and Coping*, elaborates on this fundamental
theme.

Coping is obviously complex; hence, we need to keep in mind
that prayer as coping behavior is concerned with perceived images

and intentions of the Deity, one's personal feelings of deservedness, expectations of a positive result, and other possibilities. In deliberately focusing on coping per se, Pargament and colleagues (2000) elucidated its many facets by developing a scale that they termed Religious Coping Questionnaire (RCOPE). Jalowiec (2003) also constructed a coping instrument based on his own theory that encompassed eight specific coping styles. The latter were applied to prayer by Dunn and Horgas (2000) in work that is discussed later in this chapter. Unfortunately, although these styles were studied in their original incarnations, a more useful approach would be to make them directly relevant to prayer, perhaps enabling us to better understand the roles played by prayer as a coping mechanism.

Prayer in general is too frequently equated with petitionary prayer because its many subforms (discussed in Chapter 3) imply some element of desire. Admittedly, in the broadest sense, this predisposition denotes a general petitionary quality.

PRAYER, COPING, AND CONTROL

Beginning in Chapter 1, we noted the close relationship between effective coping and a sense of control. Even though reference to this theoretical association has appeared elsewhere in this volume, it is much easier to discuss than to demonstrate. First, it is surprising that so little research has examined the relationship of prayer to control. Second, most of this research concerns health and, third, a substantial proportion of the studies failed to find any definitive associations between the two, prayer and control (Saudia, Kinney, Brown, & Young-Ward, 1991; Williams, 2009). The Pargament and colleagues (1988) coping scheme of deferring, collaborative, and self-directive modes of relating to the Deity is basically concerned with matters of personal control. Specifically, these coping schemes refer to both external and internal expressions of control. This work might be extended to deal with primary (actual) and secondary (imagined) forms of control (Weisz, Rothbaum, & Blackburn, 1984).

Researchers studying control have developed a number of measurement scales to cover a variety of pertinent ideas, such as internal versus external control, control by chance (or its absence), control by God, and a framework embracing interpretive, predictive, and vicarious types of control (Hood et al., 2009; Wallston, 2005).

PRAYER, LIFE SATISFACTION, AND WELL-BEING

Probably the most elemental indication of personal success or failure
is how one perceives her life situation. To feel good, to have a positive
sense of well-being, and to believe that one's life has real purpose (or
purpose-in-life, PIL) plus high self-esteem all communicate personal
effectiveness, self-satisfaction, and happiness. Actively manifesting
these qualities translates into successful coping.

Many scholars in the psychology of religion wax enthusias-
tic about the close association between prayer and self-satisfaction
(and its various expressions). Poloma and Gallup (1991) perceive the
importance of prayer to be a function of its "improving a sense of
well-being" (p. 5). McCullough and Larson (1999) attest to positive correlations between prayer and various characteristics of such
a state. These findings open related research doors. Diener and Chan
(2011) reviewed 160 studies and found that happiness correlates positively with better health and longevity. Could prayer be part of such
a complex? In a like manner, Meraviglia (1999) cites research theory
that includes constructive associations with prayer relative to meaning and purpose in life. Starting simply by measuring frequency of
prayer and church attendance, Maltby and Lewis (1999) show that
for both sexes private prayer is moderately and positively associated
with self-esteem and to a similar degree negatively related to trait
anxiety. This last construct has been extensively conceptualized
and measured by Spielberger (1985). Matby and Lewis showed that
church attendance—meaning public worship—is independent of trait
anxiety and negatively correlates with esteem among women. This
last association makes little sense unless we hypothesize that, the
lower that female respondents' self-esteem is, the more these women
engage in worship. Lim and Putnam (2010), however, contradict this
last observation by noting cross-gender social networks that become
part of church attendance. They conclude, "for life satisfaction, praying together seems to be better than either bowling together or praying alone" (p. 927). Nicholson (2010) quotes a neurologist, Sapolsky,
who asserts that the "single best predictor of an ability to deal well
with stress is how socially connected you are" (p. 1). Prayer is indeed
a social connector, and so is collective worship.

Ellison and Taylor (1996) studied a large national sample of
blacks, attempting to ascertain the respondents' relative recourse,
in solving their major personal problems, to what the researchers

termed "organizational and subjective religiosity" (i.e., respectively, public worship and private prayer). They ultimately concluded that worship and prayer are both beneficial.

More recent research by Sharp (2010) has been concerned with how prayer can help one to manage one's emotions. Sharp views prayer as "an imaginary social support interaction" that facilitates the expression of "individual emotion management strategies" (p. 417). One is thus able to vent negative emotions by obtaining positive assessments of such actions, and thereby reduce situational threats. These constructive evaluations are a function of the nature of one's perceived interactions with God. In a series of creative experiments, Bremner, Koole, and Bushman (2011) recently confirmed Sharp's hypotheses. They were able to show that prayer helped people cope with anger that was aroused by frustrations and incitements that were independent of what was prayed for. This latest study opens up a potentially productive new avenue for prayer research.

LIFE SATISFACTION AND THE
MULTIFORM NATURE OF PRAYER

We have shown that prayer is clearly multidimensional. For well over a century, theologians and psychologists of religion have theorized about various types of prayer. Their operationalization and application is evident in the available research on life satisfaction, as demonstrated in studies in which up to 19 kinds of prayer were evaluated. A pervasive difficulty afflicting this research area is the tendency to assign the same name to different scales (e.g., measures of petitionary prayer), even when they vary from one scale to the next. Since such instruments are found in studies by different authors, one is rarely able to determine the degree to which such indices are really measuring the same variables.

As we previously noted, prayer is widely regarded as a coping mechanism, an assumption that is also supported by Pargament and his associates (1988). Bänziger, Van Uden, and Janssen (2008) took the next step and related their three forms of prayer (petitionary, meditative, and religious) to Pargament's three coping styles (deferring, collaborative, and self-directive). Of the nine possible resulting dyadic relationships, statistical significance was observed in four, with three showing moderate to reasonably strong correlations. The self-directing style negatively linked to what the authors term "religious" prayer, and yet it affiliated positively with the deferring and collaborative orientations.

Credit must again be given to Janssen and his coworkers (2000) for the thoughtful manner in which they treated prayer's multidimensionality. As discussed in Chapter 3, their initial four types of prayer (petitionary, religious, meditative, and psychological) offered a creative framework premised on the need for prayer, its action, direction, effect and method, time and place. These forms were also analogized to those developed by Poloma and Gallup (1991) and Hood and colleagues (1993).

Margaret Poloma of the University of Akron is the premier early researcher in the area of life satisfaction. Recognizing the complexity of prayer, she employed both general and specific measures. In her initial research with Pendleton (Poloma & Pendleton, 1989, 1991a), data were collected by telephone in the Akron Area Survey, and the relationships adduced between prayer frequency and various indicators of satisfaction, though often statistically significant, tended to be low but positive. The same was true for the colloquial, meditative, ritualistic, and petitional prayer forms that were developed for this study. These forms were correlated with four indices of well-being.[1] In a variant of this study, Poloma and Pendleton (1991b) reported the same variable relationships, again with only small changes in coefficients from the previous effort. This work essentially set the stage for the many studies of a similar nature that followed. Virtually all illustrate a common problem, relatively low correlations, possibly indicating both prayer's complexity and the fact that it is embedded in a broad matrix of other religious concepts.[2]

In most of this research, the prayer type names are usually inferred from factor analyses. Frequently, these evidence an intellectual stretching to make a best fit. Although the instruments display reasonably good reliability, conceptually their implications are unclear and lead to theoretical weaknesses when related to such variables as the life satisfaction indices studied here. In a parallel research study on forgiveness, similar shortcomings were evident between the prayer scales, forgiveness, and life satisfaction (Poloma & Gallup, 1990).

Having opened this door to prayer research, Poloma joined with George Gallup, Jr. (1991), extending her work to almost 2,000 participants in a national sample. Despite the team's efforts to evaluate the effectiveness of prayer, their results were more descriptive than truly analytical. Even though the authors concluded that "the effects are profound" (p. 128) relative to life satisfaction, purpose-in-life, forgiveness, and similar variables, their interpretive enthusiasm seems excessive. Given the sample size, any significant correlations are quite weak and the percentages cited can only be viewed as suggestive. In a similar but considerably smaller-scale study, five forms of prayer were factorially developed (Carlson, Friedman, & Spilka, 1991). Denoted as Habitual, Ritualistic, Petitionary, Meditative, and Self-Improvement, they were related to the Hassles and Uplift Scales of Lazarus (1981). As expected, "Uplifts" were positively associated with self-improvement prayer, and "Hassles" were negatively affiliated with petitionary prayer. This finding was opposite in direction to the prediction. The remaining eight correlations were nonsignificant.

A similar investigation was undertaken by Williamson, Morris, and Hood (1995). Their four prayer scales fared no better when correlated with measures of Existential Well-Being and Happiness, and no significant associations were found.

The concept of happiness has been studied in relation to church attendance, hence worship, by Childs (2010), but her single-item measure "First, taking things all together, how would you say things are these days?" raises validity questions. Although the response choices used the word *happy,* the imputed meaning appeared indistinguishable from life satisfaction or well-being. Using a sophisticated analysis for the two times she sought answers, she inferred that for the first assessment church attendance boosted "happiness." A causative effect, however, was questionable and was not supported, as well, in the second administration. She also believed her data suggested that one's perceived relationship with God was a factor in the results. Clearly, additional work would be needed to validate either the findings or the judgments made.

This last point should not be taken lightly. We know that self-esteem is dependent on how others perceive us—so, why not take our view of how God judges us? In a recent effort, Schieman, Bierman, and Ellison (2010) creatively introduced a new way of conceptualizing this question. They employed the concept of "mattering" as the degree to which people feel their well-being "matters" to God—in other words, how much they feel God values them. "Mattering" also brings in the issues of divine control and interest, important concerns to the older adults participating in this research. Utilizing this notion in a sophisticated manner by measuring prayer and church attendance, researchers inferred that both of these variables indirectly affect the sense of mattering through the idea of Godly control. Variations in these relationships were assessed with regard to such demographic factors as group affiliation, gender, and education. Scholars working in this area should consider possible perceived roles for the Deity's views in regard to mattering and self-regard.

The popularity of this kind of research is apparent in other studies. Whittington and Scher (2010) sampled some 430 respondents recruited from computer online religious listservs and e-mail lists. With this fairly large sample, they related six forms of prayer to four nonreligious indices of satisfaction. Fifteen of 24 possible associations were statistically significant, but only produced three correlations above .30, while seven were below .20. Two of six correlations with self-esteem and three of six with life satisfaction attained the .05 level. In other words, the large sample permitted some degree of "statistical significance" but featured mainly low and weak relationships. The lack of any substantive results in this effort was regrettable.

The multidimensional approach continued with Bade and Cook (2008), who used sophisticated methodology to assess from one to 11 possible forms of prayer before finally settling on four. The authors argued that, since their work was exploratory, no theory was necessary, a questionable stance. They discussed coping behavior and the effectiveness of prayer for "personal difficulties," but only three of their scales associated moderately to what they vaguely called "self-spirituality."

Also lacking theory and selectively offering data, a study with potential by Richards (1991) employed 19 measures of prayer and three that could be viewed as more or less positive personality inclinations. The chief one of these is PIL (purpose-in-life). The researchers declined to offer the specific data, proffering instead only highly selective and rather obscure findings. Described as an exploratory study, it was never followed up subsequent to its 1991 publication.

One standout research effort in developing theory on the forms of prayer was undertaken by Carlson, Bacaseta, and Simanton (1988). Focusing on what they labeled "devotional meditation," the researchers likened it to progressive relaxation and transcendental meditation. In a study comparing the three group regimens—devotional meditation (prayer), progressive relaxation, and a control—the researchers found that the devotional meditation group scored lowest on anxiety and anger and manifested a significant lessening of muscle tension. Replication of this work with larger samples and more rigorous experimental controls would be a desirable goal to pursue.

AGE, PRAYER, AND WELL-BEING

Chapter 4 revealed sensitivity on the part of researchers to issues of individuals' religious change over time. Much of the early-life developmental work was premised on the widely recognized ideas of Jean Piaget. Rew, Wong, and Sternglanz (2004) took a different approach by considering the possibility of "protective resources" in elementary school children. While emphasizing health behaviors, these authors also treated religious activity as adaptively protective. Prayer was regarded as a way of helping the child ward off distressing situations. In essence, they postulated that prayer could support personal resilience in important ways. Their review of the pertinent literature stressed social connections and humor as further buffering aids. The social aspect emphasized good relationships with one's parents, while humor was considered an element of spirituality that allowed for the positive reframing of difficult circumstances. These researchers used objective measures of these variables in studying some 271 fourth through sixth graders. Both social connectedness and humor were found to be related positively to prayer frequency and more effective coping behaviors.

Continuing this work on well-being and prayer with school children, Leslie Francis and Darryl Gibbs (1996) focused on self-esteem among 8- to 11-year-olds. No meaningful relationships were observed. Another effort was more successful with respect to PIL among churchgoing 12- to 15-year-old youth (Francis & Evans, 1995). The fact that rather large samples, totaling more than 2,300 respondents, were employed made a .31 coefficient for churchgoers quite impressive. Nothing comparable was demonstrated for non-churchgoers. Francis and Burton (1994) also investigated PIL with Catholic adolescents and again found support for a positive association with prayer and church attendance, albeit a weak one.[3]

Most of our opening references to prayer and well-being dealt with young and middle-aged adults; hence, we need to examine the more stressful period of old age. The massive amount of evidence showing the widespread use of prayer in the general population has been confirmed for specific age ranges. Stark's (1968) early work showed that, over all age ranges, older Protestants participated most in what he termed "public ritual involvement" and "private devotionalism." These terms translate into, respectively, public worship and private prayer, which Stark did not relate to well-being. Still, there are other data confirming that increasing age correlates with a growing inclination to cope with life's problems through prayer (Gurin, Veroff, & Feld, 1960). Koenig, Kvale, and Ferrel (1988) also confirm this for the combination of prayer and Bible reading.

Prayer is considered by Dunn and Horgas (2000) to be a form of "spiritual self-care." These researchers reported that 96% of their sample of 50 individuals 65 years of age or older utilized prayer to cope with life's difficulties. No other adaptive response was as frequently employed. This confirmed the earlier work of Manfredi and Pickett (1987), whose research found that "prayer was . . . the most frequently used coping strategy among the elderly" (p. 106). Parallel concurrent research in which 100 persons, ages 55 and older, were interviewed reported 556 coping strategies for dealing with stress. Prayer came in second behind "trust and faith in God" (which may mean the same thing as prayer), but no relationship between the two items was given (Koenig, George, & Siegler, 1988).

Criticizing the literature on aging and research for its cross-sectional nature, Markides (1983) studied more than 500 respondents, 60 and older, over a 4-year period. He was also able to compare whites and Mexican Americans. Neither group showed a significant association between life satisfaction and church attendance (worship or private prayer) in either the first or second testing. Issues such as confinement to the home owing to poor health may have confounded the relationship with church attendance. Since well-being correlates strongly with physical health (Levin & Markides, 1986), positive ties to well-being might simply result from healthy older individuals being in church more.

Krause (2004), using a national sample of persons ages 66 years and older, offered a different perspective. Finding no relationship between prayer frequency and self-esteem, he simply suggested that the latter was expected from prayer. This explanation seems rather forced, given that Krause offers no specific rationale to support it.

In general and specifically for the young and old, private prayer and public worship are positively but not strongly related. These findings suggest greater complexity in this realm than initially thought. It may also speak to a weakness in theory as well as shortcomings in scale construction and data analyses. Too often attempts to assess prayer do not consider its integration with other aspects of personal faith. Poloma and Gallup (1991) recognized this problem when they included a number of additional religious indices relating to forgiveness.

A radical possibility is implied by McKay and Dennett (2009) regarding the potential benefits of particular misbeliefs. We may ask whether positive illusions about oneself result from religious attachments and actions such as prayer and worship. The religious or spiritually committed person may feel especially blessed, favored, and benefited by the presence of the Divine. If so, his self-perceived well-being could be enhanced. The question is whether prayer and worship are uplifting experiences that enhance the supplicant's self-image.

In sum, the results of most of this work are positive. Although the associations detected are generally weak, they do provide noteworthy insight into the richness of the religious or spiritual domain underlying participation in prayer.

COPING WITH STRESS: PRAYER, PERSONALITY, AND MENTAL HEALTH

Personality Characteristics and Prayer

The term "personality" seems to be falling out of favor as researchers increasingly focus on specific mental and behavioral processes. The time for grand theories of personality also seems to have passed, and concepts now must be anchored in measurement. A popular translation of Jungian ideas into a more contemporary scheme may be found in the Myers–Briggs Type Indicator (Coan, 1978; Mendelsohn & Sundberg, 1965), which was previously cited in Chapter 3. Not to be dissuaded by earlier disappointing results noted in Chapter 3, Leslie Francis and his associates undertook the same basic study with at least five different groups: undergraduate students, an older adult group, another one composed of general churchgoers, one featuring churchgoing Methodists, and lastly 16- to 18-year-old Catholic and Protestant high school students (Francis, 1996, 1997; Francis & Bolger, 1997; Francis & Daniel, 1997; Robbins, Francis, & Edwards, 2008). In all of this work, personality was operationally defined by the tripartite scheme of Eysenck, which was developed by the late 1970s (Eysenck & Eysenck, 1976).[4] Francis and his colleagues correlated respondents' frequency of prayer with the three scales of the abbreviated Revised Eysenck Personality Questionnaire plus a lie scale. These measures assess Psychoticism, Neuroticism, and Extraversion. Neither of the last two traits significantly correlated with prayer in three of the studies. Psychoticism related negatively to prayer frequency and church attendance in three studies. This work confirmed that of Maltby (1995) and can be viewed as corroborating the often asserted claim that churchgoers tend to be well-socialized normal people.

In the most recent work by Francis and Robbins (2008), some 2,306 16- to 18-year-olds participated. Using the three Eysenck scales, a lie scale, and frequency of praying, researchers found that only three of eight correlation coefficients from the two studied groups were significant, ranging from .11 to .22. Given the large samples used, extraneous variables might have affected the data to produce such questionable findings. In addition, these coefficients could be regarded as trivial. Still, if any relationship makes sense, it is the prayer–psychoticism link that was noted in three of the studies.

Prayer and Psychological Disorders

The generic phrase "psychological disorders" can mask an immense variety of mental states, ranging from simple distress to extreme disturbances. Without considering the seriousness of conditions, we enter the domain of the American Psychiatric Association's *Diagnostic and Statistical Manual of Mental Disorders* (DSM). This volume is now being published in its fifth edition, and the following citations range over a number of the editions. For example, a noteworthy effort in this area by Koenig and colleagues (1993) utilized the third edition. These researchers emphasized the category of anxiety disorders and covered seven different diagnoses. An accurate and well-agreed-upon identification of each of these conditions leaves much to be desired. Studying 1,300 respondents over the age of 60, Koenig and his colleagues examined both prayer and church attendance in relation to respondents' expression of anxiety. Again, the relatively low correlation coefficients were statistically significant (e.g., .08, .10). When possible confounding variables were removed, significant associations with church attendance disappeared. Still, those who prayed and read the Bible manifested higher levels of anxiety—and then prayed more. The same was true of church attendance in uncontrolled analyses. The authors struggled to find some positive indications that prayer and church attendance had beneficial effects, but these were not readily evident.

A similar problem confronted Ellison, Boardman, Williams, and Jackson (2001), who obtained respondents' church attendance and prayer frequency data from the 1995 Detroit Area Study. The 1,300-plus participants provided little support for additional praying as their stress increased, most of it attributable to health problems. Signs of stress buffering for their long-term difficulties would imply that respondents' mental health benefited from their faith. In specific terms, six models were tested, and the researchers found that church attendance correlated negatively with psychological distress in all six instances. In other words, as attendance increased, distress decreased. Prayer displayed the opposite tendency; that is, the more distress that was encountered, the more that respondents prayed. In one instance, the amount of prayer was independent of the amount of distress. With respect to psychological well-being, more inconsistency was evident. Well-being and prayer related negatively or were independent of each other. Church attendance and well-being were positively associated in all models. Questions of consistency in the findings may be raised with regard to the issue of a large sample yielding extremely low coefficients that nonethless result in statistical significance. The likelihood that extraneous influences affected the results cannot be ruled out, although the authors were quite aware of these problems and exercised caution in interpreting the data.

Another study with a much smaller sample ($N = 85$) resulted in slightly more robust findings (Harris, Schoneman, & Carrera, 2005). In this study the researchers employed the multidimensional Prayer Functions Scale of Bade and Cook (1997) along with solid indices that measured anxiety control and trait anxiety. Prayer acceptance of the source of stress related positively to trait anxiety, whereas prayer seeking God's assistance negatively linked to trait anxiety. The former implies that the origin of stress may be reasonably acknowledged along with recognition that appealing to the Deity could be the only way of resolving the difficulty. In other words, perceptions of God's potential help is consistent with one's greater control of anxiety. As expected, a stress-deferring or avoidance prayer style correlated with less anxiety control, possibly leading to poorer mental health outcomes.

As we continue to see, the findings relating to mental health measures and individual prayer and church attendance are not all clear and definitive. Employing a sophisticated analysis with some 1,500 survey respondents in Texas, Acevedo (2010) found public worship and church involvement to be correlated positively with mental health but individual prayer inversely related to mental well-being. The latter was also true for evangelical identification. Acevedo suggests the operative favorable mechanism was likely social support, which would accord with findings on the alleviation of stress presented earlier (Nicholson, 2010).

One is hard pressed not to conclude that the ways in which data are sometimes presented serve to obfuscate rather than clarify the roles of faith and prayer in coping with stress. Lindenthal, Myers, Pepper, and Stern (1970) interviewed some 900 respondents regarding psychopathology, church attendance, and prayer. The percentage of individuals falling into categories labeled as "unimpaired," "moderately impaired," and "very impaired" were determined from scores on a previously validated index of mental status. No criteria were provided justifying the cutoff points that defined the three groups. This practice of arbitrarily setting limits and ranges is potentially opportunistic in that one can conveniently select boundaries that confirm the researcher's position. One may also argue that pathology is less a discrete than a continuous phenomenon. In any case, the percentages that were offered confirmed the authors' thesis, namely, that church attendance and prayer appeared to effectively counter mental disturbance. Of course, more exacting and informative findings would have resulted from the use of correlation and regression techniques. On balance, the analysis provides little meaningful information.

Another study deals creatively with God imagery in relation to prayer and psychopathology (Bradshaw, Ellison, & Flannelly, 2008). Given that prayer obviously is directed toward the Divine, it is surprising that researchers had not previously linked the two in the quest to understand what prayer means when employed. Work on the multidimensionality of God images harkens back almost a half-century, summoning up a number of conceptually rich and complex schemes (Gorsuch, 1968; Spilka et al., 1964). In addition to the frequency of praying, Bradshaw and his coworkers (2008) employed the simple dichotomy of a Remote God and a Loving God. These appear similar to the close and distant deities invoked earlier by Spilka and Reynolds (1965). In this latter work, a distant God was related positively to holding prejudiced attitudes, whereas closeness was associated with an antiprejudiced viewpoint. Nothing comparable exists in the present research. Again, owing to the large sample, in this study low correlations can be claimed as statistically significant; however, very few attained this status. Prayer related negatively to depression with a −.05 coefficient that was almost identical in size to the coefficient indicating the .05 probability level for statistical significance. In terms of practical meaning, one can barely put their faith in such results. Church attendance correlated −.10 with both depression and a paranoid outlook, both favorable outcomes but again quite weak. The situation was slightly better with the God indices. Coefficients for a Loving God were similar to those with prayer, being very weak and close to the significance level. Perceptions of a Remote God were slightly better, suggesting a positive association with depression and hostility, the last possibly indicating a result akin to that noted above with prejudice. Much stronger was the connection between church attendance and a Loving God as well as antipathy toward a remote one. Unfortunately, for the most part, sound theoretical thinking and methodology failed to be realized in this study.

Another study that looked at 103 nonpsychotic depressive patients included prayer in a short scale labeled "problem solving." Prayer was related to behavioral changes assessed as effective or ineffective. Some 56% of the participants considered prayer effective and 1% as ineffective. The total problem-solving measure was also significantly correlated with effectiveness (Parker & Brown, 1986).

Clearly, a variety of troubling conditions have been evaluated relating to prayer. J. I. Harris and colleagues (2010) studied churchgoing Christians immediately after they attended services. The respondents who were selected had recently suffered traumatic experiences. The object was to determine whether prayer had any effect on posttraumatic growth (PTG). Normally, those subjected to trauma develop negative outlooks toward themselves and the world. An inventory to assess PTG was employed to determine whether negativism was successfully countered. A Prayer Function instrument provided information on four specific types, or roles, of prayer: acceptance, assistance, calming and focusing, and deferring and avoiding. When noninterpersonal trauma survivors were compared with interpersonal trauma survivors, the latter group showed significant improvement as compared to the former ones on the acceptance and assistance types of prayer. Total PTG related solidly and significantly to all types of prayer. Interestingly, there was no noteworthy correlation with a simple frequency of prayer. The authors postulated that the calming and focusing function might be worthy of special attention in counseling circumstances.

A number of studies focus on the relationship between faith and drug and alcohol use, some worthy of special attention in counseling situations. The Alcoholics Anonymous creed and practice can be viewed as relevant to this category of research. An interesting project directly related to prayer and intoxication was undertaken by Lambert, Fincham, Marks, and Stillman (2010). Using a large sample of college students and employing prayer along with solid theory and good controls, prayer frequency was distinguished from other religious factors, thereby revealing "a unique effect on alcohol consumption" (p. 9). In all four of the studies conducted in this project, alcohol usage and prayer were negatively associated. This work ought be expanded to other forms of addiction with noncollege respondents.

We have sampled the research on coping not only as it relates to everyday matters but also to certain mental health concerns. Happily, there have been two relatively recent meta-analyses of research in these areas, one focusing on adolescents and the other on adults (Hackney & Sanders, 2003; Wong, Rew, & Slaikeu, 2006). Unfortunately, church attendance and prayer are sometimes joined with other variables and respectively coded as institutional and personal devotion. In addition, the combinations of variables treated in the two studies overlap but are not identical.

Some Conclusions

In general, research on the foregoing personality problems suggests that prayer plays a favorable role, although many of those who have conducted this research discuss that role in more supportive terms than the findings merit. Again, quite often large samples result in very weak though statistically significant findings. In most instances, controls are lacking for other religious factors and associated sociocultural influences that should, at least, be statistically removed. In more than a few of these efforts, a heavy burden was placed on the simple self-denoted index of prayer frequency. Research of this nature might be especially fruitful in assessing theory-based multidimensional prayer forms. Another consideration concerns the various measures of well-being and pathology. Although they are grouped together here, these are complex concepts, and we do not know if the same variables are being evaluated. Certainly, life satisfaction per se may be quite different from purpose-in-life or self-esteem.

In many of the studies discussed, God images and relationships that entered the picture were only obliquely discussed. The notion of the Divine "mattering," cited above, suggests a need for more research on the perceptions of God-like images and perspectives held by pray-ers and church attenders.

PRAYER AS THERAPEUTIC

Although prayer has many functions, we have repeatedly demonstrated that it is used, first and foremost, in attempting to cope with one's problems. For example, Carson and Huss (1979) explicitly termed prayer "a viable therapeutic and teaching tool" (p. 37). To prove their point, they carried out a small sample study ($N = 20$) on hospitalized schizophrenics. Treatment and control groups were formed, each composed of 10 student nurses who were individually paired up with a specific patient. The first group had regular prayer and scriptural reading sessions with one of the researchers. Although the emphasis was on the student nurses, the expectation was that they would carry the effects of their experience to the patients with whom they worked. Testing confirmed constructive change in the nurses. Even though the respondents did not perceive response modifications in the patients with whom they worked, the overall effects were inferred from postassessment test results. Unfortunately, no objective data were provided, and although subjective judgments colored this experiment, potentially instructive research extensions were evident.

Prayer is widely employed in pastoral care settings and also by parish clergy during hospital visits (Hulme, 1990; Vandecreek & Cooke, 1996). Although Hulme (1990) restricted his discussion of pastoral care solely to Christians, the practice is also widespread among other faiths (Kirkwood, 2002; Lartey, 2003; Last, 2009). A survey of Christian psychologists who belonged to the Christian

Association for Psychological Studies (CAPS) revealed strong support for the use of prayer in clinical/counseling situations (Lange, 1983). Some 90% of Lange's sample viewed prayer as "an important agent in therapy," while 79% agreed that "therapists should pray regularly for clients" (p. 39). Magaletta and Brawer (1996), however, pointed out that there are ethical factors to be considered if such activity is to take place.

Despite some good theoretical thinking about the utilization of prayer, there appears to be relatively little research on such possibilities. For example, utilizing Foster's (1992) theologically oriented multidimensional scheme for prayer (discussed earlier in Chapter 3) Siang-Yang Tan (1996) convincingly showed how it could be applied to psychotherapy. In a like manner, Finney and Malony (1985a) offered a theoretical framework for the similar use of contemplative prayer in therapy. In a suggestive small-sample study, they emphasized the usefulness of contemplative prayer as "an adjunct to psychotherapy" (Finney & Malony, 1985c, p. 284). Unfortunately, other researchers have not built upon this instructive work.

The foregoing research efforts mostly discussed what was rather informally done; however, they also showed the potential for what might occur. Such possibilities are inherent in the excellent qualitative investigation of what Griffith, English, and Mayfield (1980) termed the "therapeutic aspects" of a regular Wednesday meeting at a black congregants' church. This study focused on the dehumanizing features of certain urban environments and the "community support mechanisms" (p. 128) provided by churchgoers. Griffith and colleagues concluded that group prayer was mainly directed at bolstering the individual. Abramowitz's (1993) presentation of how prayer was therapeutically employed with elderly Jews demonstrated the constructive use of institutionally based formal ritual prayer. He apparently reasoned that studying how institutional ritual was integrated and coordinated with private prayer might well reveal indicators of coping and self-therapeutic efforts. In this light, Jewish liturgy might be viewed as not leaving room for individual private prayerful innovation.

Some scholars have proposed that prayer be used therapeutically, both within standard clinical practice and as an adjunct (Sullivan & Karney, 2008). Doubts and continuing contention over these possibilities are, however, abundantly evident (Marks, 2008; Worthington, 2008).

THE ROLE OF PRAYER IN ROMANTIC
RELATIONSHIPS, MARRIAGE, AND FAMILY

The popular aphorism "The family that prays together stays together" may contain more than a grain of truth. Research on prayer and family relationships, while not prolific, is quite sophisticated in theory, research design, and analysis (Beach, Fincham, Hurt, McNair, & Stanley, 2008a, 2008b; Butler, Stout, & Gardner, 2002; Fincham, Beach, Lambert, Stillman, & Braithwaite, 2008).

The earliest work involving prayer and marital adjustment was reported by Gruner (1985), who was concerned with a variety of devotional practices among members of several denominations. The study found that, among all the respondents (N = 416), a moderate correlation coefficient of .33 was obtained with prayer and marital adjustment. Similar statistical significance was observed within all of the religious groups. Possibly the most recent research effort in this area was a nationwide survey of some 1,400 people (Ellison, Burdette, & Wilcox, 2010). Ethnicity was one concern of the researchers; hence, data were gathered on black, Hispanic, and non-Hispanic white couples. Attention was focused on both organizational (church) worship and nonorganizational (home) devotion. The researchers provided some fine conceptual thinking in directing the analyses and interpreting their findings. Six models were employed in assessing combinations of the variables. Given the large subsamples, low coefficients attained statistical significance and yet were meaningfully consistent. Although the models were necessarily complex, the attendance of both marital partners at church services and their joint participation in in-home practices (e.g., prayer) related positively to satisfaction in their relationship.

Sometimes an important element may appear so obvious that it tends to be ignored. Prayer, by definition, involves attempted contact and involvement with a deity; yet, most often this consideration remains in the background as researchers concentrate on prayer frequency, church attendance, or various multidimensional prayer practices. Butler and his associates postulated that truly religious couples thought of God as being present in their relationship. Butler and Harper (1994) term this arrangement "the divine triangle." Undertaking a qualitative analysis of prayer as it relates to conflict situations, Butler, Gardner, and Bird (1998) asserted that prayer brings God directly into the conflicted setting. This, they theorized, should reduce negative emotional reactions, aid in reconciliation, facilitate self-change, and support problem solving. Delving more deeply into the roles played by prayer when couples interact negatively, Butler and colleagues (2002) came up with 10 functions from which reliable subscales were constructed as components of a 102-item Prayer Conflict Scale. These were administered to religious couples who had been married for at least 7 years. Based on the results, the researchers' hypotheses were confirmed, further buttressing the utility of prayer in resolving marital conflict. These findings had useful implications for both self-therapy and marital therapy.

A general observation is that work in this area is better organized theoretically and methodologically than in virtually any other research realm concerned with prayer. For example, Beach and his colleagues developed a comprehensive theoretical framework that both informed and organized their research efforts (Beach et al., 2008a). They then sought informed commentaries to help evaluate and further develop their approach (Beach et al., 2008b). Next, they undertook three research studies that sought to estimate the relative significance of prayer for one's partner versus prayer in general, as well as assessing factors that might mediate prayer's effects on relationship satisfaction (Fincham et al., 2008). In a much more sophisticated manner, these efforts drew heavily on earlier research that produced similar results, such as that by Dudley and Kosinski (1990).

Continuing in this line of research, Fincham, Lambert, and Beach (2010) sought to show that prayer might help to counter infidelity. Studying romantically involved undergraduates, they theorized that prayer could both activate positive and supportive emotions and further enhance a current loving involvement. Three studies were conducted. The first hypothesized that praying for one's partner should strengthen an existing attachment. The second study postulated that required praying for the partner for 4 weeks would result in less extradyadic romantic behavior. The third study had independent observers rate the commitment levels of the pray-ers. In the first study, with a sample of 375 participants, prayer at two different times correlated negatively with infidelity. The correlation coefficients were low though statistically significant. In the second study, again prayer related negatively to infidelity when additional measurement controls were used. Further support for the prayer effect was found in the third study, although the results could be viewed as quite tentative in this instance.

These infidelity studies raise the question of whether the motivation to avoid infidelity was positively or negatively (e.g., guilt) motivated. In addition, we wonder whether there might be an influence from social desirability influencing the results. Fincham and his coworkers certainly, however, deserve credit for creative and methodical research.

We cannot overlook writings that, though more general and not focusing on prayer, largely set the stage for thinking and research in this area. We are referring specifically to the comprehensive meta-analytic review and directive conceptualizations of Mahoney and associates (Mahoney, 2005; Mahoney, Pargament, Murray-Swank, & Murray-Swank, 2003; Mahoney, Pargament, Tarakeshwar, & Swank, 2001; Mahoney & Tarakeshwar, 2005).

SUMMARY

In this chapter, we have tried to establish the significance of prayer for coping behavior in a number of areas central to the psychology of religion. The literature overwhelmingly endorses a positive role for prayer, but its conclusions should be regarded cautiously because of the concern we often express in this volume regarding how large samples tend to result in weak (albeit statistically significant) findings. The theoretical foundations for much of this research, however, are usually clear and instructive. The orderliness and meticulous thinking that has gone into studies of prayer in relation to romantic, marital, and family relationships should serve as an instructive model for research in the field as a whole.

NOTES

1. Identifying four domains as aspects of satisfaction, Poloma and Pendleton (1989) developed four semantic differential measures: Existential Well-Being, Religious Satisfaction, Negative Affect, and Happiness. These were also combined into a total Life Satisfaction Index.
2. In Poloma and Pendleton (1991b), of the 16 correlations computed, 14 were below .20, hardly justifying the pair's optimism. Furthermore, if one applied the Bonferroni adjustment to the entire table, the .05 level of significance accepted by the authors became .003, reducing the originally claimed 14 significant coefficients to just 8.

3. The correlation coefficient for prayer rounded out to .20 and for church attendance .17. The authors' suggestion that prayer proved to be a "stronger predictor" of PIL is perhaps overstated since prayer had only a 1% advantage over church attendance. Such a small difference could have arisen from other factors, including chance and unreliability.

4. Eysenck's three scales are based on his personality theory, which overlaps with the common understanding of these concepts in personality in general. Extraversion describes an outgoing person high in positive qualities and expressions. This is opposed to introversion, in which opposing traits are dominant. Neuroticism emphasizes negative affect, especially stress. Depression and anxiety plus poor emotional control are dominant expressions. Psychoticism implies poor contact with reality, inappropriate aggression, and impulsiveness (Eysenck & Eysenck, 1975).

CHAPTER 6

Prayer and Health

Prayer can be of great assistance in the healing of disease . . .
very largely through its power of suggestion.
—JAMES B. PRATT (1927, p. 331)

Prayer offered by the sick person or by his friends tends to
soothe the mind, dispel fears, encourage confidence and hope,
and lifts the soul into a higher region than the earthly.
—JOHN H. RANDALL (1911, p. 63)

One reason for praying stands out above all others, namely, seeking out God's help in maintaining one's health (Bell et al., 2005). Survey estimates of the proportion of people resorting to such prayers range all the way from 25 to 75% (Bader et al., 2006; Eisenberg et al., 1993; Jantos & Kiat, 2007; McCaffrey, Eisenberg, Legedza, Davis, & Phillips, 2004; O'Connor, Pronk, Tan, & Whitebird, 2005; Straus & Stoney, 2005). While it is not always clear what respondents' physical condition was, most researchers imply that the great majority were currently healthy. Similar work with the ill, as might be expected, reveals an even higher incidence of health-related prayers. Whenever the chief concern was with pregnancy, 95.5% of the mothers-to-be prayed for their babies (Levin, Lyons, & Larson, 1993). Two studies of cancer survivors yielded prayer percentages of 61.4 and 68.5% (Gansler, Kaw, Crammer, & Smith, 2008; Ross, Hall, Fairley, Yhenneko, & Howard, 2008). Using a sample of more than 4,400 people over the age of 40, O'Connor and colleagues (2005) observed that 47.2% reported they prayed for health. Some 90% of this sample believed that such prayers actually helped improve their health.

Two kinds of health prayers are observed, namely, those for one-self and intercessory prayers for others. We look at the former in this chapter and deal with the latter in the next one. Another concern in this complex realm is the important distinction between physical health and mental health, but both types are treated.

The prayer–health relationship has many facets. The key over-arching assertion is that prayer benefits one's health. One study of 1,200 baby-boomers and older cold-war cohorts (Sutherland, Paloma, & Pendleton, 2003) found no relationship between health and prayer for the boomers but a significant negative association for the cold-war cohorts, who by virtue of age alone might have suffered from more illnesses. This latter correlation may simply mean that sicker respondents pray more frequently for their health, as the discrepancy between the two groups was not explained.

Another investigation of over 1,000 Presbyterian church members noted that the frequency of prayer was negatively associated with physical health and positively with mental health (Meisenhelder & Chandler, 2000b). The first finding may be telling us that the sicker that people are, the more they pray. Both of these observations were confirmed in a study of church lay leaders (Meisenhelder & Chandler, 2000a).

PRAYER AND HEALTH: A CONFLICTED AREA

Possible health–religion–prayer connections have fascinated profes-sionals and laypeople for many years. The literature on such asso-ciations has also stimulated reviews that illustrate both the best and worst of scholarship in this complex area (Powell, Shahabi, & Thoresen, 2003). Researchers fit into one of two camps, those claiming beneficial effects for faith and prayer and their critics, who argue that much if not most of the publications are based on poorly designed and analyzed studies. This bifurcated view leaves the issues largely unresolved. Currently, from the viewpoint of science, the crit-ics hold the more defensible position (Sloan, 2006). In one survey of 266 research works considered relevant to religion's impact on health concerns, only 45 supported the optimistic stance (Sloan & Bagiella, 2002). Sloan (2006) is devastating in his critique of the favorable studies, emphasizing how methodologically and analytically defective they are. Other commentators have recognized similar shortcomings (Howard et al., 2009; McCullough, 1995).

Of course, attempts have long been made to assess the scientific credibility of research on faith as it relates to health (Powell et al., 2003; Seeman, Dubin, & Seeman, 2003). Only a small portion of this work is regarded as acceptable for scholarly citation, however. Hill and Pargament (2003) have tried to place the literature in proper perspective by analyzing the concepts of both religion and spirituality in relation to the measures employed in this research area.

Orderly contrary arguments that meet scientific criteria have also not been readily available, although some (possibly many) may disagree with this assessment (Dossey, 1993, 1996). Our task is to offer what we believe to be a balanced and cautious view of the area.

HOW MIGHT PRAYER INFLUENCE HEALTH?

When a religious person prays in order to solve a personal health problem, whether or not his physical health changes in any way subsequently, the proffered explanation is usually in terms of the prayer being answered. As a purely theological question, this set of circumstances is outside of the realm of science and thus the empirical orientation of this volume. One alternative possibility is to assume parapsychological or paranormal influences might account for favorable consequences. This matter is discussed at greater length in Chapter 7 on intercessory prayer.

Fortunately, Breslin and Lewis (2008) suggest some potential factors that enable us to understand scientifically the impact of prayer on our physical or mental well-being. In their analysis we have (1) prayer responding as a placebo effect; (2) pray-ers who live more healthful lifestyles than those who either don't pray or pray little; (3) prayer serving as a diversion from illness; (4) prayer acting as a psychological support that aids the body's immune function; and (5) prayer stimulating social support that helps patients cope better with their health problems. McCullough's (1995) review of research adds evidence of a relaxation response, a heightened sense of security and well-being, and positive expectations, all of which appear to benefit the immune system. A number of authors include in their theories both religious and spiritual forces as well as parapsychological "latent energies" (Breslin & Lewis, 2008, p. 17). These arguments are surprisingly common in the writing on health and religion (Levin, 1996). While such positions may be heartily embraced and vehemently defended by their proponents, their lack of specific causative mechanisms may well be beyond scientific interpretations and methods. In most instances, we exclude these efforts. The crucial question is whether scientific research can be conducted that would properly evaluate these alternatives.

ORIENTATIONS TO PRAYING FOR HEALTH

The use of prayer by individuals for their own health maintenance has been approached from at least three vantage points: (1) versions that claim to be premised on traditional medicine; (2) religious invocations or faith healing largely based on Judeo-Christian doctrines and scriptural interpretations; and (3) healing practices that utilize psychological ideas and language that have "one foot in religion and the other in medicine" (Fuller, 1989). Since our concern is solely with empirical testable theory, neither theological nor traditional religious or spiritual approaches (as in choice 2, above) are discussed.

Variations in Traditional Medicine

A number of medical professionals have begun using the phrase "complementary and alternative medicine" (CAM) and have created a journal bearing the same name. This publication offers commentary and research covering a broad range of nonmedical or borderline procedures, including acupuncture, yoga, meditation, touch healing and prayer, among others. Much of this writing focuses on practical applications and employs a nonscientific language that makes the research or findings difficult to evaluate. One reads of miraculous cures, the power of the mind, psychic healing, and similar possibilities that often are not readily amenable to exacting scientific analysis. This nascent movement began on the fringe of mainstream medicine but is now well represented by a full-fledged professional organization, the National Center for Complementary and Alternative Medicine, which operates under the auspices of the National Institutes of Health. During fiscal years 2009 and 2010, they have overseen the distribution of some $31 million in grants, using a rigorous set of criteria. CAM's

gradual movement toward more widespread acceptance is also suggested by the $121.9 million in grant research funds dispersed in fiscal
year 2007 by the Office of Cancer Complementary and Alternative
Medicine under the direction of the National Cancer Institute. Very
little of this funding has thus far supported research on prayer.

Despite questions regarding the validity of what Eisenberg and
his associates (1993) have termed "unconventional medicine," their
national study reported that one of every three persons resorted to
at least one such unconventional procedure during the year prior to
data collection. In 2008, some 40% of patients used CAM methods and CAM workshops and clinics. A surprising number of these
gatherings are sponsored by major medical organizations such as the
Mayo Clinic (Deardorff, 2009). Approximately three-quarters of
the patients in the Eisenberg and colleagues study kept their resort
to unconventional approaches secret from their physicians. Such
unorthodox alternatives have been reported for cancer, arthritis, and
chronic back pain. The 2002 National Health Interview Study found
that 43% of their more than 31,000 participants utilized prayer
for their own health purposes in the year prior to data collection
(Barnes, Powell-Griner, McFann, & Nahin, 2004). One study of over
1,000 people who have used CAM indicated that most respondents
did so *not* because of their dissatisfaction with traditional medicine.
Rather, they were motivated more by the feeling of having greater
control over the health-seeking process and the fact that these methods were compatible with their personal value systems and beliefs
about the meaning of illness (Astin, 1998). Note that these actions fit
well within the theoretical framework for petitionary prayer that we
discussed earlier.

Smith and colleagues (2008), in a study of 276 undergraduates,
asserted that those willing to use prayer as a CAM method are especially open to new experiences and sensitive to internal emotional
states and also appear to be both spiritual and religious. In a somewhat
similar and traditional manner it has long been known that minorities
that possess their own folk medicine practitioners are also inclined to
use both prayer and CAM-like procedures (Arredondo, 1978).

Spiritual Healing

The CAM approach is becoming culturally legitimized as medicine.
Spiritual healers explicitly mix religion with medicine through the use

of such methods. Stein (2006) states that "healing rooms" in which prayers are offered for health are popular in religious institutions. CAM's advances are not without strong critics from both medicine and religion. Medical critics regard such efforts as wasting research money and time, while religious ones believe that they trivialize faith (Stein, 2006). Regardless of the professional debate over CAM's status, over half of those surveyed believed that intervention by God can occur and might save family members or themselves even after physicians have indicated that nothing more could be done medically.

Certain variants of spiritual healing strive to identify themselves with the prestige and terminology of science and medicine, although they remain firmly rooted in notions that are clearly alien to both realms. For example, frequent references may be made to electromagnetic energy, seven layers of the body's human energy field, "prayer consciousness," and other unconfirmed notions. These purported treatments are then held out as the solution to one's physical illness and defects (Johnston, n.d.). Such ideas are alien to the mainstream of science and medical knowledge precisely because they are not amenable to testing within the parameters of the scientific method. One avenue of research that has received considerable attention involves bringing religion into the relationship between patients and medical personnel (Maugans & Wadland, 1991). In this study, 64% of the physicians sampled were religious; 89% believed they had the right to discuss religion, and 88% had done so with patients. These interactions mostly related to terminal illness (69%) and near-death situations (68%). In other related research, patients who initiated prayers were both more satisfied with and involved in their health care decisions than were patients who did not pray (O'Connor et al., 2005).

Psychological Methods

Approaches that stress faith usually also emphasize the role of ritual and imagery as aiding in the healing process. A concern with cognition through symbolism and meaning is normally central to these methods (Achterberg, Dossey, & Kolkmeier, 1994; McGuire, 1988). McGuire (1988) conducted extensive research on prayer-for-healing groups in suburban Christian churches. These groups are usually successful in creating a sense of power and mastery in their members, the overall effect of which reduces members' anxiety and bolsters their hopes.

WHY SHOULD PRAYER
BE BENEFICIAL FOR HEALTH?

Theoretical Considerations

We have already shown that people turn to prayer for their health concerns, and the more impaired they are, generally the more they pray (Lindenthal et al., 1970). In a similar vein, Pargament (1997) declared that "people have looked as much to religion in their search for health as they have to medicine" (p. 54). One representative group of interest might be renal transplant patients. They confront a broad spectrum of stressors such as fear of kidney rejection, high costs, undesirable physical symptoms, and anxiety about social acceptance. A common coping mechanism employed is prayer (Sutton & Murphy 1989). The predominant view that prayer also has discernible beneficial effects is likewise evident though controversial (Hollywell & Walker, 2008).

We have suggested that prayer is often employed when one's sense of control is in question. Sick people are frequently frustrated and subject to a variety of psychological pressures. In Chapter 1, we offered a stress–coping–control perspective that is pertinent to the physical effects of stress and ill health. At that time, we cited the work of Ballantyne (2009), DeNoon (2009), and Mozes (2009) regarding the deleterious effects on one's heart of driving in heavy traffic. Other research has suggested that stress may speed aging, shorten one's lifespan, and actually nourish cancer (Epel et al., 2004; Sood et al., 2010). Because of the biological complexity involved, some of the possible effects of prayer and worship on the physical expressions of stress will now be presented in a rather simplified way. The interested reader can find more technical treatments of this subject matter in the presentations of Charney (2004), Cox (1988), Koenig, McCullough, and Larson (2001), Rabin (1999), and Sterling and Eyer (1988).

The Biology of Stress, Simplified

Poor health and illness are stressful and may in part or whole even *result from* stress. Essentially all bodily systems and functions may be affected. One possible entrée to this subject is provided by what is commonly termed the HPA (hypothalamus–pituitary–adrenal) axis, which encapsulates how the endocrine and central nervous systems are involved in this process.

The limbic system in the brain is primarily concerned with emotional control and expression. Working in conjunction with the limbic system is the hypothalamus, a structure central to the maintenance of a wide range of physiological functions. It is basically concerned with homeostasis, that is, the process of regulating and preserving optimal body performance. Activation of the limbic system by stress causes the hypothalamus to secrete corticotropin-releasing hormone (CRH), which stimulates the pituitary gland to secrete, in turn, adrenocorticotropic hormone (ACTH). Utilizing various neural pathways, ACTH causes the cortex of the adrenal glands (which are located directly above the kidneys) to produce cortisol. Known as the stress hormone, cortisol plays a key role in the complex pattern of stress responses, helping to prepare the individual for what has been termed the "fight-or-flight response." This encompasses a broad spectrum of physical "emergency" reactions such as increasing blood pressure and heart rate plus releasing sugar from the liver. In addition, the body's immune system is partially suppressed in order to prepare for action in critical situations, with some functions enhanced and others constrained. These reactions, however, are not designed for extreme arousal for any extended period of time. Acute and prolonged operation of the HPA axis may have such deleterious consequences as a heightened potential for infection, tumor development, and cardiovascular problems, among other difficulties. But brief arousal normally results in positive changes that help one to better deal with stress.

RESEARCH ON PRAYER AND HEALTH

The significance of religion and prayer for both research and life applications is well documented in the *Handbook of Religion and Health* (Koenig et al., 2001). This encyclopedic overview of a massive body of literature has been the object of critical evaluation by Sloan and Bagiella (2002) and Sloan (2006). These authors correctly point out that the enthusiasm demonstrated for religious or spiritual-religious explanations by so many researchers has largely overwhelmed the emphasis on objectivity and rigor in the scientific evaluation and design of many studies and data analyses in this field. We concur with that observation, reiterating our position that there is nothing inherently wrong with such belief systems or explanations. They simply must be subject to ultimate evaluation by scientific methods and criteria.

The Immune System

The body's first line of defense is the immune system. If a problem originates externally and is physiologically caused by such foreign agents as viruses, bacteria, or other biological phenomena, an immune response results. Internally developing physiological maladies such as tumors also activate immune reactions.

A few recent studies have examined religious practices and prayer as they relate to heightened cortisol levels that are a function of stress (Dedert et al., 2004; Tartaro, Luecken, & Gunn, 2005). Since these normally vary during the day, Dedert and his associates (2004), assessing nonorganizational religiosity (NOR), combined "prayer, meditation, or Bible Study" into a single item. The validity of this approach is questionable. No significant relationships were found with mean cortisol levels, and those endorsing this NOR item maintained a normal daily cortisol pattern. Participants who scored low evidenced a flattened daily pattern. The meaning of this observation is unclear and may reflect an effort by the researchers to find something that appears statistically significant even if its meaning is obscure. Better-designed theory-guided work is needed in this area.

Using a very small sample ($N = 4$), Katz, Weiner, Gallagher, and Hellman (1970) reported that hospital patients who pray secrete less cortisol than those who use other psychological defenses. Considering the tiny sample size, we only offer this observation as suggesting the need for replication of the experiment and further study.

Tartaro and colleagues (2005) reported that "significant repeated measure effects on cortisol were found for frequency of prayer" (p. 760). Those scoring highest in prayer frequency revealed lower cortisol reactivity on a "very frustrating" (p. 757) computer task than those who prayed little or not at all.

In Chapter 2, we discussed the issue of meditation as operating both independently of prayer and tightly tied to it. Regardless of the presence of religion, in practice there appears to be one basic meditative process. But this interpretation may not tell the entire story. Helminiak (1982) asserts that "the very activity of meditative practice is prayer" (p. 774). Others have postulated similar associations with prayer in general and Christian prayer in particular (Gross, 2002;

Maloney, 1976). Urubshurow (1992) further developed this theme by analyzing Catholic and Tibetan Buddhist practices. Canter's (2003) brief summary of the physiological effects of *nonreligious* meditation, however, showed this to be a troubled area with mixed results. Design flaws and shortcomings in analysis pervade this entire literature. Clearly, we need more exacting work that distinguishes between religious and nonreligious meditation's effects.

In his research overview of this area, Shapiro (1982) pointed out the close association between meditation and both relaxation and self-regulation. Left unclear was whether something else might enter the picture when the person brings his religious ideas into the act of meditation. Conceiving self-regulation as control, we can understand how stress and cortisol might be constructively affected by prayer. This is illustrated by Sudsuang, Chentanez, and Veluvan (1991), who asserted that Buddhist meditation evidenced a lowering of cortisol levels along with a variety of other desirable modifications in such stress-related variables as heart rate and blood pressure. Unhappily, an exacting review of this work by Seeman and colleagues (2003) considered it to have a number of methodological weaknesses, though they concluded it still possessed some validity. Cross-validation of this research is needed, plus a better appreciation of the possible confounding differences in those constituting the experimental and control groups. In other work, Carlson and colleagues (1988) compared groups identified with devotional meditation, progressive relaxation, and a control. Favorable changes were implied relative to muscle tension and activity, but again these observations require further confirmation. Unfortunately, few serious studies attempting to relate HPA axis measures to religion and prayer have been reported.

Cognitive-Behavioral Stress Management

An indirect way to better understand prayer and coping with stress may be provided by studying the strategies employed to combat stress. Conceptually, these strategies overlap with spiritual techniques (including prayer) to the extent that the associated beliefs, experiences, and behaviors are aspects of what is formally designated as cognitive-behavioral stress management (CBSM) (Antoni, Ironson, & Schneiderman, 2007), or more broadly cognitive-behavioral therapy (CBT) (Kendall & Bemis, 1983). Said to reduce cortisol levels in stressed healthy persons (Hammerfald et al., 2005), HIV-infected gay men (Antoni et al., 2000), and women under treatment for breast cancer (Cruess et al., 2000), CBSM has also been successfully used to treat HPA effects other than those resulting from heightened cortisol secretion (Antoni et al., 2007; Lutgendorf et al., 1997; McGregor et al., 2004). Although none of these approaches explicitly identifies prayer or religion in dealing with stress, there are still some interesting parallels between prayer and CBSM. Holahan and Moos (1987) discussed praying "for guidance and/or strength" (p. 949) as an active cognitive strategy. Dealing with older adults, Koenig and colleagues (1988) noted that prayer was primarily employed to regulate and control emotion. Both of these orientations are part of CBSM. Formalized Christian CBSM methods have been developed, and these use prayer and other religious aids such as Scripture and imagery (Pargament, Ano, & Wachholtz, 2005). Only occasionally, however, do authors of these cited studies not discuss at length specifically what they did that was therapeutic or stress-managing. *Mosby's Dictionary of Complementary and Alternative Medicine* (Jonas, 2005) defines CBSM as combining meditation with cognitive-behavioral strategies. As already noted, meditation appears to be integral to prayer, but this process is not spelled out as it relates to CBSM. However, Antoni and colleagues (2007) do clearly ally CBSM with instruction in relaxation, imagery, and meditation.

Our suggestion that relaxation training parallels prayer was examined in a study of muscle tension reduction through electromyogram recording (Elkins, Anchor, & Sandler, 1979). The researchers compared various groups of conservative church members. One group underwent relaxation training, while the other took part in a 10-day focus on prayer. No evidence of stress or need for relaxation or prayer was indicated. Unfortunately—as is so common in this literature—it is not difficult to critique this effort in relation to theory, methodology, and analysis. Where statistical significance was obtained, its meaning was unclear.

We have only skimmed the surface of immune system function, but may indirectly touch on more of its operations in succeeding sections. One can follow probable immune system breakdowns attributable to acute and chronic stress through their effects on cardiovascular operation, the malfunctioning of white blood cells, the development of endocrine and neural deficits, cancer, and the depression of cellular immunity as well as sugar and protein metabolism, among other problems. Unfortunately, research involving how prayer relates to these possibilities is scarce, but where it exists more often than not it appears to possess beneficial potential, largely through its enhancement of relaxation and of internal controls. Unfortunately, the paucity of direct prayer research is compounded by specific problems with the criterion "medical variables." These difficulties will be more evident in the next section.

Cardiovascular Problems

Cardiovascular data have long been popular among researchers seeking to understand the potential influence of prayer on illness. One reason for such attention is that cardiovascular conditions are the primary cause of death in our nation (U.S. Bureau of the Census, 2008). An early step in dealing with these issues is determining a patient's blood pressure (BP). A frequently cited study asserts that "blood pressure is the most important predictor of life expectancy" (Markandu, Whitcher, Arnold, & Carney, 2000, p. 31). The specific indices of greatest concern are the systolic and diastolic blood pressure levels, the former denoting when the medical examiner first detects the heart's "beats." Systolic blood pressure (SBP) reflects contraction of the heart, while diastolic blood pressure (DBP) measures its relaxation phase.

Claims that religion and prayer improve one's cardiovascular prognosis, however, are often questionable methodologically, as this is an area with many measurement problems. Rather than detailing these here, as they divert us from our chief concern with prayer, we take them up at the end of this chapter.

Religion, Prayer, and BP[1]

There is a complex literature in this area, in part because researchers often provide little or no information on the procedures employed. For example, regarding BP assessment in their study on BP and prayer, Koenig and colleagues (1998, p. 193) wrote that the "usual manner" of collecting the data was employed, citing another source for the details of the procedures used. A brief review of the literature would suggest that "usual" might be difficult to define, and readers should not have to search the literature to obtain the necessary information. Still, Koenig and colleagues describe a BP methodology that seems medically quite acceptable. Timio and colleagues (1988) standardized their work by using one observer and one mercury sphygmomanometer. Levin and Vanderpool (1989) reviewed 13 studies in which BP was measured, but they provided no details on how it was computed. None of the researchers dealt directly with prayer—even though religious attendance, as already noted, connotes public worship, and much evidence suggests strong relationships among most religious variables (Hettler & Cohen, 1998). Still, many other factors temper the attendance–worship association such as family teachings and habits as well as social needs, a variety of personal motives, and even economics. Most likely, many of these variables are mutually supportive (Roberts & Davidson, 1984).

In their work, Larson and his associates (1989) took three BP readings over a period ranging from 45 to 80 minutes using a seated patient's left arm. Mean readings constituted the final data. Although prayer was not directly assessed, almost 500 white men were categorized as either high or low in church attendance. A few differences favorable to religion were observed, particularly when smokers and nonsmokers were compared. BP differences were in the 5- to 7-point range, hardly making for confidence since questions regarding the measurement method were unresolved. All of these studies seem problematic.

We cannot overlook the difficulties encountered in the impressive effort of Koenig and colleagues (1998), who studied almost 4,000 older persons. Although the blood pressure findings favored religious attenders, including Bible readers and frequent pray-ers, the differences were trivial and within the normal range of expected error. Statistically significant differences with large samples are not very informative, and effect size analyses might be undertaken. Beyond the methodological points already made here, readers are referred to Sloan (2006) and Sloan and Bagiella (2002) for further treatment of the weaknesses in much of the reported research.

Alexander and his associates (1996) return us to the linkage between prayer and relaxation. Their study compared hypertensive older blacks who were divided among three groups: ones utilizing transcendental meditation, progressive relaxation, or a lifestyle/education regimen (the control group). In most instances, the SDP and DBP readings appear to have been favorably influenced by meditation and relaxation. It is unfortunate that relaxation via prayer and religion in general were not included as potential factors in this fairly sophisticated study.

Studying over 3,000 adults, Buck, Williams, Musick, and Sternthal (2009) observed outcomes opposite to what has traditionally been expected. In their data, prayer was positively associated with heightened DBP.

A general weakness in the study of prayer is the fact that most research has dealt solely with the Judeo-Christian tradition. However, at least two studies have looked at Muslims in relation to blood pressure. Again, we must confront problems with the findings and their interpretation. Al-Kandari (2003) focused on normal nonhypertensive Kuwaitis and reported that religiosity "is intensively associated with both systolic and diastolic blood pressure" (p. 471). In the article, religiosity is defined in terms of commitment and activities, the latter being explicitly prayer. Nowhere in the article do we see the BP averages. In addition, the basis for the conclusiveness expressed in the "intensively associated" sentiment is never expressed. The significance of adjusted regression coefficients is given, but the data on which they are based are not provided. We are further told that "many religious activities . . . are highly related to physiological matters" (p. 471), but the evidence is not supplied. One gets the impression that a scientific undertaking is being placed in the service of institutional faith.

A second study of Iranian Muslim women also claimed that prayer lowered blood pressure (Safavi, Sabuhl, & Mahmoudi, 2007). An experimental group of 30 women listened to tapes of prayers at least three times during a 10-day period. Blood pressure was taken on the fourth, seventh, and 10th days. A control group had individual participants' BP registered at the beginning and end of the experiment. All participants had pressures within the normal (120–140 millimeters of mercury [mm Hg]/80–90 mm Hg) range. The intervention group evidenced a trivial shift in both SDP and DBP relative to the controls. The data analysis was presented in a somewhat obscure manner, with probabilities less than .05. Our recomputation of the significance between the groups at the end of the study shows only negligible postintervention group average differences of 1.17 mm Hg for SBP and 0.04 mm Hg for DBP, neither of which is statistically significant.

Where correlation differences favor prayer and faith, these may be influenced by prayer countering stress, enhancing security, and promoting relaxation. However, we must again recognize that prayer is part of a larger complex that reflects the likelihood that pray-ers generally have more social support from co-religionists and usually come from more traditional homes that reinforce desirable health habits in terms of food, sleep, exercise, and a low probability of smoking or using drugs and alcohol. Nowhere is this more evident than among Mormons as it relates to cancer and mortality (Enstrom, 1989). Given all of these possible confounds, greater caution is required in study design, analysis, and data interpretation.

Stress and Cardiovascular Disease

When we go beyond the study of blood pressure to more severe cardiovascular problems, we again encounter sources of error that generally appear to go unreported. The electrocardiogram (ECG) is a major, if not the most important, initial source of information about the condition of one's heart. Unfortunately, research indicates that ECG intrareader reliability and interreader agreement are low (Weston, Bett, & Over, 1976).

Negative stress effects may be a more serious contributor to poor health than elevated blood pressure. Identified coronary risks account for some 50–60% of the possible causes of cardiac illness, according to O'Keefe, Poston, Haddock, and Hartis (2004). These researchers next turn to what they call the "mind–heart connection" (which we earlier alluded to in Chapter 1). While earlier in this volume we discussed the psychology of stress, our focus now is on its physiological underpinnings and associated health problems. This process begins with cortisol and the function of emotion as well as the activation of the sympathetic branch of the autonomic nervous system (Curtis & O'Keefe, 2002). In other words, we are back to discussing the HPA axis and the immune system. This context better enables us to understand how heart attacks and other cardiac conditions relate to such matters as occupational stress (House, 1974), marital difficulties (De Vogli, Tarani, & Marmot, 2007), bad weather and the winter holiday season (Spencer, Goldberg, Becker, & Gore, 1998), and social isolation (among other possible stressors). The real-life effects of these factors are demonstrated in a 2004 study of job layoffs among older workers (Gallo et al., 2004). The risk of heart attacks and strokes among this sample were more than double that of the general population. Other similar research revealed an 83% greater probability of developing a stress-related disease among sample respondents versus a control group (Luo, 2010). The specific physiological mechanisms that transform stress into hypertension and coronary disease have been well explained and supported by Katkin, Dermit, and Wine (1993).

The physical aspects of coronary disease are generally only peripherally touched upon as they relate to religion and prayer (Kaplan, 1976). One may be initially impressed by the large sample sizes of thousands of participants, but this aspect can obscure many sources of error. Wherever positive findings have been reported, the role of a healthy lifestyle on the part of religiously active persons and a higher likelihood of social isolation among the less religious cannot be ignored (Brummett et al., 2001; Ellison & George, 1994; Kaplan, 1976; Uchino, 2004). Many researchers covary sex, age, status, race, education, and other factors, but they often fail to do that with indices of lifestyle, a practice that is advantageous to religious samples. This inclination plus other design problems are well illustrated by a few scholarly attempts to evaluate research on religion, spirituality, prayer, and cardiovascular health (Powell et al., 2003; Sloan, 2006). Although these efforts question the often highly sanguine judgments of religionists and parapsychologists, they do not always agree on the possible health benefits of religion and prayer. These research reviews reveal how a few knowledgeable professionals can uncritically put aside the necessity for rigorous scientific assessment. Many people succumb too easily to the temptation to believe and ignore without objective proof counterarguments. In one study, 96% of patients awaiting cardiac surgery used prayer to cope with this stressful situation, and some 70% ended up considering it their most helpful behavior (Saudia et al., 1991). In this study, scores on a Helpfulness of Prayer Scale (HOPS) were positively related to those on a Multidimensional Health Locus of Control scale administered to the cardiac surgery patients, but, surprisingly, no significant correlations were found between these two instruments. The authors point to a lack of variation and questionable reliability for the HOPS as the reason for the negative results. Unfortunately, the essential details for the HOPS measure and the appropriate correlational data were not presented. Other criticisms of the analyses are possible, making this entire effort problematic. A potentially useful theory came to naught most likely because of the researchers' dubious operationalizing of the concepts and questionable data analysis.

Examining the research on prayer and its potential physical effects on coronary disease, we find little room for optimism. Both

Sloan (2006) and Sloan and Bagiella (2002) analyzed Luskin's (2000) review of 12 studies in this area and concluded that none met the criteria for acceptable empirical research. Similarly, of the 39 studies examined in Koenig and colleagues' (2001) volume, only four were deemed to have passed muster.

Efforts to associate prayer with the physical aspects of cardio-vascular illness are few and usually woefully inadequate in design and analysis. Findings are commonly negative but sometimes imply other research possibilities. The bulk of the work that appears to be productive deals chiefly with psychological variables among those who are ill.

One issue discussed in Chapter 1 that is particularly central to much of this work is that of meditation as prayer versus nonreligious forms of meditation. The dividing line between these two forms of meditation is not always clear. Most of the cited research literature treats prayer as a theistically focused practice and meditation as com-paratively nontheistic in orientation.

Liu, Wei, and Lo (2009) conducted an interesting study that, much to its detriment, employed relatively small samples. The researchers, focusing on the efficiency of the cardiac system, com-pared an experimental group of 20 experienced Zen Buddhist par-ticipants to a control group of 20 normal, healthy subjects. Although four measures of coronary efficiency were evaluated and statistical significance was reported in favor of the meditators on all variables, a Bonferroni adjustment indicated significance only for an ejection fraction index (which was, by all accounts, an important factor). Sloan (2006) has also criticized various design aspects of this type of research.

More pertinent is the work of Ikedo, Gangahar, Quader, and Smith (2007), who attempted aural stimulation of cardiac surgical patients while under general anesthesia. They conducted a random-ized, controlled, double-blind study with prayer, relaxation, and pla-cebo groups. However, no meaningful statistically significant find-ings emerged.

Blumenthal and colleagues (2007), in a study that examined death rates and repeat coronaries among 501 patients, calculated hazard ratios based on respondents' attendance at worship services as well as their prayer frequencies. All results, however, were negative.

In sum, while many passionate and fervent statements found in this literature assert that religion and prayer are proven aids to general health and cardiac improvement (Dossey, 1993), our brief review of the more solid work in this area simply does not support that assessment.

Prayer and Psychological Responses to Cardiac Problems

Fortunately, when we turn from considering physical phenomena to psychological matters, the picture improves. Much of this research is concerned with cardiac patients' mental coping efforts prior to and immediately following surgery. Naturally, depression is a fairly common response to this situation and is regarded as the best predictor overall of future heart attacks and death (Carney et al., 1988). In one study, 27% of 151 patients who had coronary artery bypass graft (CABG) surgery indicated they suffered from depression during the year following the surgery (Ai, Peterson, Saunders, Bolling, & Dunkle, 1996). Prayer was the most common therapeutic activity, employed by 67.5% of the patients. Describing private prayer as the "patient's last spiritual coping tool for pursuing control over their health," Ai, Dunkle, Peterson, and Bolling (1998, p. 597) in a separate study viewed prayer as a suppressor variable rather than a moderator variable. Continuing this work, Ai and her associates (2010) more recently found that intention to pray correlated positively with more effective coping, optimism, hope, and lower levels of depression. Most likely, one's intention to engage in prayer is part of a more general religious coping response.

In a number of recent studies of CABG patients, probably because of the impact of their depression on outcomes, greater attention has increasingly been directed toward patients' relative optimism versus pessimism, and the results have been mixed. Prior to surgery, Ai and colleagues (2007) found a low but significant positive correlation between prayer and optimism. In part, this finding was a confirmation of previous work that showed that preoperative positive coping was associated with better postoperative coping. Unexpectedly, in this work, the utilization of prayer postoperatively was associated with poorer functioning. One inference might be that if things don't work out as anticipated or hoped, one prays more (Ai, Peterson, Bolling, & Rodgers, 2006).

This finding contradicts earlier research by Ai, Dunkle, Peterson, and Bolling (2000) that concluded postoperative prayer reduced depression immediately following surgery, producing a sense of greater psychological well-being a year later.

These are some of the potentially important research studies by Ai and her colleagues that suggest prayer can be helpful both before and possibly after CABG. Much of this work was undertaken with the same participants and is not always in agreement, suggesting the need for further validation of the reported findings. Finally, we must note that Ai and her associates (2006) made a serious effort to place their work within certain theoretical contexts. Ai's work is consistent with a recent study of 2,800 patients that suggests that subsequent coronary health correlates positively with patients' relative optimism. For that reason alone, we see further potential for prayer in this area of study (see Barefoot et al., 2011).

Especially relevant to the view supported here is a discussion of prayer that relates specifically to locus of control (LoC) and coping style like that offered by Pargament and colleagues (1988). The control issue (which we alluded to briefly in Chapter 1) has not been resolved, and when applied to physiological responses to stress it may need further specification. As pointed out by Houston (1972), we would expect one's internal locus of control to correlate positively with less arousal. However, Houston's research found this association to be truer of *external* control. We theorized that external LoC might also be favorably associated with prayer and if so have a calming influence. As noted above, Saudia and colleagues (1991) postulated that prayer as a coping mechanism prior to CABG was unrelated to LoC. Since 96% of the participants in Saudia and colleagues' study used prayer to deal with their upcoming CABG, lack of variance in the data plus a questionable analysis might account for the failure to find statistically meaningful results. Ai, Bolling, and Peterson (2000) reported that 68% of their sample also prayed but after their surgery. Pargament (1997) wanted to show how religion relates to one's internal LoC and coping behavior; however, since religion uses a possibly *external* referent—God—this alternative cannot be eliminated from further consideration. Despite the constructive development of God–person control offered by Pargament and colleagues, the coping–control–religion triad may be much more complicated than is currently realized.

Oxman, Freeman, and Manheimer (1995) also studied cardiac patients who underwent CABG surgery. Prayer was not directly assessed in this study, but religious attendance was measured. Although the authors report a p value of .06 for this measure, the Bonferroni adjustment for all 18 variables assessed suggests .003 would be meaningful if an initial .05 level were selected. The authors were more lax than this in their interpretation of the findings.

Burazeri, Goda, and Kark (2008) undertook a fairly large sample study of Muslims and Christians in Albania who suffered from "acute coronary syndrome." Experimental and control groups were delineated for purposes of the experiment. The utilization of prayer tended to be low and highly varied, as might be expected, given the differences in distinguishing these two religious groups. A number of cardiac precursor and disposing physical factors were covaried in order to focus on religion and prayer. Statistical significance in favor of these variables using odds–ratio analyses (a means of comparing two groups relative to the probability of an event) was reported. Burazeri and colleagues concluded that a variety of possible mechanisms, such as social support and personality factors, could result in "protective associations with the religious observance variables" (p. 941).

In an interesting if rather informal qualitative study of eight patients recovering from strokes, prayer was treated as a coping strategy to regain control and increase their self-efficacy (Robinson-Smith, 2002). The results suggested that vesting power and control in God increased their sense of self-control. The rather detailed understanding that the interviews yielded might usefully be employed as hypotheses to guide further research along these lines.

Summary

Our overview of the research and thought on prayer and cardiovascular problems raises more questions than it answers. Inconsistency and research inadequacies unfortunately dominate this literature. At the very start, one encounters disagreements regarding definitions of and proper assessment tools for the physiological measures. The avenue leading from stress influences ultimately to control mechanisms is still viable but requires much more research support. There are indications that prayer may well enhance control, reduce stress, and aid cardiac well-being. Schnall (2008) asserted in his study that some "facet of religion or spirituality may protect against cardiovascular disorder" (p. 2). He failed, however, to define such mechanisms—even as he noted that deaths significantly declined as attendance at religious services increased (perhaps implying the indirect involvement of worship and its social aspects). Being conservative methodologically and not wishing to overinterpret his results, Schnall cautiously implied that protection against death from cardiovascular disease might involve social support and healthy lifestyle factors. The door, however, was partially left open, as he put it, to "other important mechanisms" (p. 14).

The need for well-designed follow-up studies is evident. Moreover, the association of religious expressions such as prayers with more general health lifestyles deserves further examination (Strawbridge et al., 2001).

Cancer

The extensive literature on prayer and cardiovascular problems has little in common with that for the relationship between prayer and cancer, since cancer's awesomeness minimizes notions that stress might be one possible cause of it. Furthermore, the likelihood of restoring health via prayer seems like such a long shot that it does not enter the scientific approach to this disease. There are, however, instances of religious denominations with low cancer rates, specifically, the Mormons and Seventh Day Adventists (Levin, 2001). Andreas Hoff and his associates (Hoff, Johannessen-Henry, Ross, Hvidt, & Johansen, 2008) conducted an extensive review of the research on the incidence of cancer among practitioners of various religions. They confirmed the previous findings cited for Mormons and Seventh Day Adventists, but with some qualifications. As has already been noted, the basic cause underlying a low cancer risk (as for illness in general) is a healthy lifestyle, featuring low usage of tobacco or alcohol, high-fat foods, and the like.

Submitting "prayer and cancer" to a Google search yields pages in the millions, the overwhelming majority of which offer hopeful prayers. The research literature, however, is not so sanguine and mainly concerns coping with psychosocial responses to cancer. Prayer, religion, and spirituality are recognized as important resources. For example, in one study, prayer was first among 19 possible "complementary methods" utilized by over 4,000 cancer survivors. Some 61% of respondents in this study employed it (Gansler et al., 2008). In a review of 11 coping strategies, prayer ranked 9th among early-stage cancer patients, with only 9.4% resorting to prayer. The situation was very different among advanced-stage patients, where it ranked first, with 35.3% of respondents indicating they prayed (Gotay, 1984). Other research studies alluded to religious activity as being closely associated with happiness, life satisfaction, and less perceived pain (Yates, Chalmer, Follansbee, & McKegney, 1981).

One study of cancer patients undergoing chemotherapy in Iran also revealed the need to consider psychological response differences that were attributable to sex, age, educational level, and marital status (Mahboubeh Rezael, Adib-Hajbaghery, & Fatemeh, 2008). These and other associated variables were commonly controlled via covariance in most research.

After a rigorous analysis of appropriate databases, Thune-Boyle, Stygall, Keshtgar, and Newman (2006) selected 17 studies dealing with spiritual coping strategies, which included "attendance at a place of worship or frequency of prayer" (p. 159). The researchers found that seven factors posted positive results, while three were nonsignificant, and seven were negative. Four of the last group were actually regarded as harmful to the patients. Methodological shortcomings in this research, as with the studies in the cardiovascular domain, are frequently present. Prayer was particularly resorted to when hope was low and the expected outcome of the illness was poor.

Thus far, we have referred to cancer generically, although the specific form of the disease may be significant, both physically and psychologically. Consider the possible different meanings of breast cancer to young, as contrasted with older, women. What about male views of prostate cancer? Cancers that portend short life expectancies such as pancreatic and liver cancer and certain brain tumors and sarcomas must convey different ideas to those affected than skin and other conditions that are often readily curable. Research that appreciates the significance of such variations is rare. Pretty much across the board, social support through worship and prayer may be a relatively silent factor in purported effects on cancer statistics. Sprehn, Chambers, Saykin, Konski, and Johnstone (2009) demonstrate in their study that mortality is associated with some fundamental social connections. Five- and 10-year cancer survival rates generally favor married persons over widowed, divorced, and never-married peers, totally independent of the spiritual realm. We have discussed prayer's important social aspects and thus must ask whether religion, spirituality, and prayer might also affect survival rates. In other words, what are the rates among those with religious attachments who pray versus those without such bonds? Theoretical and programmatic directions congruent with this view have been suggested by Cole and Pargament (1999) for a spiritual or psychotherapeutic intervention for people with cancer. They emphasize the necessity of confronting issues of meaning and control as well as the attendant social ramifications. Feher and Maly (1999) offer evidence for this position, noting that 70% of their breast cancer sample believed that their faith offered them social support, much of it through their own and others' prayers. Prayer is therefore far from being an individual or separatist phenomenon, its effects seeming to thrive on group participation.

Summary

Considerable research and theory has been directed at attempting to understand how religion and spirituality relate to cancer. The emphasis is almost exclusively on the patient's psychological state and his or her adjustment to others. Comparatively little research has been directed at prayer and none at prayer forms. Some research efforts focus on meaning, control, and the social significance of praying, but these generally require further evaluation. The usual issues of design and analysis defects can also be readily detected.

HIV/AIDS

Mention of HIV/AIDS in the religious community elicits feelings ranging from ambivalence to extreme forms of hostility toward those so affected. Historically and contemporaneously, the Judeo-Christian and Islamic traditions' rejection of homosexuality has embraced every possible negative reaction. Pronouncements such as those of Jerry Falwell that AIDS is God's punishment for both sinners and the society that tolerates them abound in the conservative religious literature, though opposing positions within Christian circles appear to be growing. One representative indication of the latter is the "annual Black Church week of prayer for the healing of AIDS" ("Seventh annual black church," 2006).

As with cancer, religion or spirituality was not expected to alter the actual disease process but rather affect the psychological state of the patient. Ironson, Stuetzle, and Fletcher (2006) have asserted that the course of the disease may be a function of religion or spirituality, a claim that we believe requires further confirmation. We would hope to see a more direct test of the role of prayer in future work.

We may first ask the question "What happens to the religious/ spiritual character of individuals who contract HIV/AIDS?" As so often occurs when a threat or danger is present, we find in one study that 52% of African Americans and 37% of whites asserted that their religious/spiritual feelings became more significant, with about 20% reporting a lessening of these feelings and the remainder saying they were unchanged (Cotton et al., 2006). Although these findings opened the door to additional praying, this variable was not assessed.

Coping with HIV/AIDS means dealing with a wide variety of symptoms and correlates: nausea, fatigue, anxiety, anger, depression, repeated hospitalizations, medications' side effects, the development of a variety of associated conditions attributable to immune system damage, and, of course, the possibility of death. The likelihood of this last alternative has been steadily declining since the mid-1990s as new drugs and procedures have steadily lengthened patients' life expectancy and lessened their discomfort. It is interesting to see that prayer was regarded as the second most important resource after physicians in making decisions about medication among African Americans (Meredith, Jeffe, Mundy, & Fraser, 2001). While 93% of this group viewed prayer as very or somewhat important in making their decisions, only 59% of whites felt similarly. This disparity was also true for women versus men and for those with less than a high school education as compared to their more educated counterparts. In part, we may be observing the influence of relative degrees of religiosity on all of these variables.

In another sample of African Americans, attention was directed to prayer as a "self-care strategy" (Coleman et al., 2006, p. 16). Men and women were compared, and over 50% of both genders claimed that prayer was highly effective. No significant gender difference was observed for anxiety, but males did employ prayer more frequently than females to deal with nausea and depression. Women found prayer to be more helpful in combatting fatigue than men.

A broader possibility is suggested by Carson and Green (1992). They administered the Spiritual Well-Being (SWB) scale (Ellison & Smith, 1991) to 100 HIV/AIDS patients along with other questionnaires, their object being to determine whether psychological hardiness could be predicted in this sample. Hardiness was based on the theory of Victor Frankl (1963, 1969), which stressed meaning and purpose in one's life. Prayer may tentatively be seen in as many as seven of the 20 items in the SWB instrument. Granted that this is a weak but suggestive theoretical argument, it may be more directly assessed in future studies. Of possible spiritual/religious actions, prayer was rated highest, and the SWB scale correlated .42 with hardiness. This study confirmed earlier work by Carson (1993), hence the Carson–Green collaboration can be viewed as cross-validation of his previous research. Again, prayer was associated with significant beneficial effects in HIV/AIDS patients.

Summary

Pargament and his associates (2004), on reviewing the literature on religion or spirituality and HIV/AIDS, concluded that relatively few (mostly qualitative) studies constitute this realm. Our survey confirms their judgment. Bosworth (2006) suggested that medical developments and capabilities within the prior 15 years had reduced the level of threat and the likelihood of death—and hence that HIV/AIDS was now to be commonly viewed as a chronic illness. Prior to this time, religious commitments, prayer, and worship assuaged one's fear of death (Kaldjian, Jekel, & Friedland, 1998). Currently, there might be a reduction of religious/spiritual concerns and the incidence of prayer, but this speculation requires additional research to properly confirm it.

OTHER RESEARCH ON PRAYER AND HEALTH

Illness per se is stressful. Even with medication, discomfort is most likely to be an unwanted companion. As we have seen, turning to prayer in such circumstances is customary, if only to feel that one is doing something that might help to remedy the situation. When the surprisingly extensive literature on health and religion/spirituality is surveyed, the impression is created that researchers are attempting to assess virtually every kind of ill health. The parameters of research have already been identified: Is the condition the result of stress and lack of personal control? Can prayer counter these problems and affect physiology in a constructive way? If the disease process cannot be influenced by prayer, can its negative psychological correlates be neutralized?

Arthritis

Although arthritic conditions can affect people of any age, they are overwhelmingly associated with the elderly. Technically termed "rheumatoid illnesses," there are a number of such chronic diseases, the chief ones being rheumatoid arthritis and osteoarthritis. The primary problems to which therapy is directed are pain and physical limitation. Medical and pharmaceutical research is regularly developing medications that counteract rheumatoid arthritis, but the same is not true for osteoarthritis, for which drugs to control and suppress pain are available but whose side effects can be very serious. Shortcomings in treatment have apparently caused an estimated 90% of arthritics to employ unconventional remedies including prayer to aid them in coping with their discomfort (Cronan, Kaplan, Posner, Blumberg, & Kozin, 1989). In a community sample of over 300 arthritics, more turned to prayer (44%) than to any of the other 18 alternatives provided. Some 54% considered it very helpful.

One study of low-income African American and Hispanic patients revealed that 29% of the former and 35% of the latter prayed weekly for help with their arthritis (Bill-Harvey, Rippey, Abeles, & Pfeiffer, 1989). Some 92% of the African Americans thought their prayers helped greatly, while only 25% of the Hispanics felt similarly. These numbers were potentially unstable, as there were only 33 respondents in each group.

VandeCreek and associates (2004) found religious and nonreligious coping methods to be positively related among rheumatoid arthritis patients. In other words, any possibility for help was explored. Worship attendance and prayer inferred from private religious practices were consistently used as positive coping methods. The authors suggested that these were probably directed more at resolving emotional concerns than problem solving. The authors of this work are to be commended for their sensitivity to possible shortcomings in this research.

Laird (1991) attempted to develop multidimensional measures of both prayer and the impact of arthritis. Prayer use was associated with favorable emotional adjustment and less concern with health, although the opposite was true for confessional prayer. Better social adjustment was also observed for a receptive form of prayer in which one is open to "wisdom, understanding and guidance" (p. 6) from the Divine.

Lastly, evaluating what might be called the psychology of arthritis suggests a need to unite prayer with a sense of personal control to better understand how people cope with these illnesses (Tennen, Affleck, Urrows, Higgins, & Mendola, 1992; Younger, Finan, Zautra, Reich, & Davis, 2008).

Other Possibilities

A number of studies have looked at the use of CAM for multiple sclerosis (MS). A nationwide study found 65% of patients with MS had employed at least one such procedure. Of 13 such approaches, prayer came in second in both frequency of use (27.3%) and judged effectiveness (Nayak, Matheis, Schoenberger, & Shiflett, 2003). In a Canadian survey, prayer placed sixth, with 36% employing it (Page, Verhoef, Stebbins, Metz, & Levy, 2003).

The little research that has directly attempted to assess prayer and MS is at best mixed in its findings. One study failed to show any effects for either prayer or worship in terms of influencing anxiety, depression, the quality of health and life, or the psychological well-being of patients with MS (Makros & McCabe, 2003).

Indirect possibilities for positive results are, however, suggested by research on spiritual well-being (SWB) and MS. McNulty, Livneh, and Wilson (2004) claim that SWB counters the effect of uncertainty and mediates adaptation to MS. More sophisticated work along these lines involving multiple forms of prayer, frequency of usage, and issues of control needs to be undertaken.

Despite the fact that we have sampled the literature in each of the foregoing areas, the reader might correctly infer that we could keep going for some time explicating the research on other medical conditions that investigates the prayer/spirituality variable complex. We will simply mention that similar research exists on childhood cystic fibrosis (Pendleton, Cavalli, Pargament, & Nasr, 2002), kidney transplantation and renal disease (Martin & Sachse, 2002; Sutton & Murphy, 1989), pain (Andersson, 2008; Ashby & Lenhart, 1994; Turner & Clancy, 1986; Tuttle, Shutty, & DeGood, 1991; Wachholtz & Pargament, 2005), and pregnancy (Levin et al., 1993). A parallel area that also merits inclusion concerns caregivers—especially family members who deal with ill children—disabled relatives, and elderly parents (Chang, Noonan, & Tennstedt, 1998; Pearce, 2005; Richards, Wrubel, Grant, & Folkman, 2003). These research studies report both positive and negative findings, necessitating a review of the design, methodology, and analysis of how these studies were conducted.

A POSSIBLE NEGATIVE INFLUENCE OF PRAYER

Thus far in this chapter we have focused only on the potential positive effects of prayer. At least one study, however, has pointed to the likelihood of some adverse occurrences (Rehman & Asfour, 2010). Observed among devout Buddhists and Muslims, these consist of what are termed "prayer nodules" that are well-localized, painless, discolored callous-like lesions on the knees, ankles, and lower legs. They apparently can result from frequent lengthy periods of meditation by Buddhists or from regularly repeated participation in prayers by Muslims. Some 75% of Muslim men and 25% of Muslim women reportedly possess such conditions. Although they may become infected, their primary undesirable quality appears to be cosmetic.

SUMMARY

At this point, we must say that the potential is present for the constructive utilization of prayer primarily in relation to the psychological aspects of the medical conditions that have been discussed. Still, caution rather than enthusiasm is warranted at this time. The work cited in this chapter almost uniformly avoids the evaluation of prayer as a multidimensional construct. When more than a single item is used, the constellation is heavily focused on issues of practice as opposed to content. This makes us wonder about the extent to which prayer is actually being measured or whether the word itself is a proxy for religious activity in general. The effects witnessed may well have more to do with an abstraction than with either the reasons underlying the spiritual discipline or the precise nature of the practice. That being the case, if a theoretical avenue is to be pursued, we recommend that proposed by Pargament (1988), that is, an emphasis on coping and control. It is entirely feasible that praying is an important signifier of the potential for success in the face of physical adversity. Improvement is seen as a physical blessing; poorer health can be buffered with perceived spiritual blessings. We further hope that researchers would seriously consider confirmation of their findings via cross-validation. Given the importance of research on health, replication should be the sine qua non of such efforts. This area is too sensitive not to undertake such replication. Regardless of what is found, one thing is abundantly evident, namely, that people will inevitably turn to prayer whenever one's health is threatened.

NOTE

1. There are three sources of error encountered when one's BP is measured: (1) the individual evaluating the BP, (2) the instrumentation employed, and (3) the person whose BP is assessed.

   The person evaluating BP. One study of a relatively small sample of nurses in a British hospital revealed error rates of up to 35% in their knowledge and use of BP equipment (Carney et al., 2002). Without assessing statistical significance, Neufeld (1986) compared physicians and nurses and found that, even though the former showed less variation in their BP measures than the nurses, the groups did not appear to differ in the mean systolic and diastolic indices obtained.

   Blood pressure instrumentation. Three types of monitors are employed to determine the BP. A stethoscope may also be required to obtain arterial pressure readings. The first device is a mercury sphygmomanometer. An observer records the height of a column of mercury in millimeters (mm). Second, an aneroid sphygmomanometer utilizes a meter without fluids that responds to pressure. The third instrument is electronic or digital. Although agreement among these monitors tends to be high, comparisons indicate that all can be sources of measurement error. Furthermore, the three types employ a cuff that is usually but not always placed around the upper arm. The cuff size, air leakage, and the rate of deflation may all contribute to measurement problems. For example, Pickering (1994) found that 96% of physicians use too small a cuff, which is likely to produce readings that are inappropriately high. Moreover, only about 25% possess a large enough cuff.

   The term "gold standard" is popular in this literature, but it may refer to different procedures and equipment. Perloff and colleagues (1993), in the sixth edition of the American Heart Association's (AHA) guidelines for BP measurement, suggests that this standard is direct assessment with a catheter inserted in an artery. Other methods have been called "imprecise" (Kirkendall, Burton, Epstein, & Fries, 1967). Many professionals consider the mercury sphygmomanometer to be the "gold standard" (Jones, Appel, Sheps, Rocella, & Lenfant, 2003; Pickering, 1994; Tholl, Forstner, & Anlauf, 2004); however, research suggests that it too may have problems.

The AHA has provided recommendations for BP measurement with sphygmomanometers (Kirkendall et al., 1967; Perloff et al., 1993). Different sources indicate the acceptability of the 2- to 4-mm Hg range of variation. The Association for the Advancement of Medical Instrumentation recommends the 4-mm range (Canzanello, Jensen, & Schwartz, 2001). Adherence to these directions may be problematic, as one study of 114 physicians in clinics in Newfoundland revealed that none completely followed these guidelines correctly. In addition, 8% of the mercury sphygmomanometers used were out of calibration by 4 to 6 mm Hg, while 40% of the aneroid devices were similarly defective, 30% of the latter having errors in excess of 10 mm (McKay, Campbell, Parab, Chockalingam, & Fodor, 1990).

Although official doctrine accepts 2- to 4-mm Hg variation across instruments, 5 mm and in one instance up to 10 mm variations were considered accurate (Ali & Rouse, 2002; Burke, Towers, O'Malley, Fitzgerald, & O'Brien, 1982; James et al., 1988). More than a bit of sarcasm is evident in one article's title, "The Mercury Sphygmomanometer Should Be Abandoned before It Is Proscribed" (Markandu et al., 2000). These researchers claimed that over 50% of the 500 mercury sphygmomanometers they evaluated were seriously defective. Other workers suggested that the range of 30–50% faulty instruments was common (Bailey, Knaus, & Bauer, 1991; Burke et al., 1982; McKay et al., 1990; Mion & Pierin, 1998). Studies evaluating these devices were conducted in hospitals, clinics, doctors' private offices, and homes. Correlations among these manometers ranged from about .70 to almost 1.0 (James et al., 1988). The majority were above .85. Questions about research validity in this area were probably appropriate when coefficients were less than .75.

Measurement error attributable to patients. Many influences can affect BP. Anxiety is judged to be capable of raising pressure up to 30 mm Hg, and 20–30% of people suffer from what has been called "white-coat hypertension" (Barclay & Vega, 2006; Beevers, Lip, & O'Brien, 2001; Pickering, 1994). One study of over 400 participants found that 43% of patients displayed this condition (Helvaci & Seyhanli, 2006). The result was inappropriately high readings when BP was assessed by a professional wearing traditional white medical garb. When observations were made at home, BP tended to be normal. In addition, other factors, such as age, obesity, and alcohol usage, may affect pressure. Good practice recommends calculating the mean of multiple observations (Beevers et al., 2001).

CHAPTER 7

Intercessory Prayer

All the difficulties that gather round prayer become acute
when it takes the form of intercession.
—ELWOOD WORCESTER AND SAMUEL MCCOMB (1931, p. 310)

When we pray for others we are seeking to throw ourselves
into the Divine intention.
—ELWOOD WORCESTER AND SAMUEL MCCOMB (1931, p. 312)

A very popular hope and yet theologically complex and controversial notion is that one may be able to intercede with God to help others. This is termed "intercessory prayer" (IP). It is also termed "distant prayer," as whatever is prayed for is physically distant from the pray-er. Traditionally, family and friends who are in dire straits are the subjects, or intended beneficiaries, of such action, but, like prayer itself, IP has no limits. Something or someone requires aid or needs to be influenced, and the one to accomplish this best is God. Another common aspect of intercession implies that the more there are who pray to accomplish the same goal, the greater the likelihood that the Deity will be persuaded to change the undesirable situation. Even though the idea and activity of prayer immediately bring to mind religion and God, other explanations have been brought to bear upon this issue—most especially parapsychological reference, the idea that some power of the mind can influence the unfortunate situation. No mechanism has ever been identified for the transmission of the aspirations of those who pray and, as we further elaborate later, the claimed effects of these prayers are highly debatable from a scientific point of view.

IP is sometimes categorized as alternative medicine, a designation that covers a large number of unconventional procedures. The 2002 National Health Interview study found that 24.4% of Americans utilized IP during the year preceding this survey. This estimate seems unusually low, considering the general population's widespread use of prayer, especially petitionary prayer. A slightly earlier survey suggested that 73% believed that IP could effectuate cures (Ameling, 2000). The wide discrepancy between these survey estimates could be largely a function of how the questions were phrased.

SOME RESEARCH ISSUES

Since many of its supporters regard IP to be a researchable phenomenon, attempts have been made over the years to determine its effectiveness. The ideas underlying such efforts are not only theologically controversial but equally problematic from psychological and methodological standpoints. There are those who question whether IP can be scientifically studied, but scientific argument is commonly directed at the methodology employed in this research.

EARLY RESEARCH EFFORTS

In terms of "modern times," apparently the first investigation of the possible influence of IP was undertaken by Francis Galton, who published his findings in 1872 and 1883. He suggested that "an inquiry may be made into the longevity of persons whose lives are publicly prayed for." His example was "the public prayer for the sovereign of every state . . . which has been in the spirit of our own" (Galton, 1883, pp. 280–281). Utilizing data on longevity collected previously on 11 privileged groups of people, Galton was able to show that "the sovereigns are literally the shortest lived of all who have the advantage of affluence. The prayer therefore has no efficacy" (1883, p. 282).

The kind of prayer studied by Galton is discussed later as "background prayer," normally a rather mechanical and perfunctory exercise. Galton's comparisons are questionable since the proper statistical procedures had not yet been developed. He did, however, open a research avenue that has been extensively traveled.

This less-than-auspicious start for IP research was followed nearly a century later by the introduction of more sophisticated techniques. These were initiated by Joyce and Welldon (1965) and Collipp (1969).

A negative report on "spiritual healing" by a special committee of the British Medical Association stimulated an Archbishops' Commission to call for scientific research in the area. Joyce and Welldon (1965) responded and studied "48 patients suffering from chronic stationary or progressively deteriorating psychological or rheumatic disease" (p. 368). Two groups of 19 patients were formed and matched for sex, age, marital status, religious faith, and clinical diagnosis. The patients were not informed that they were part of any research project, but their physicians were apparently aware in a general sense of the study. Although no statistical assessment of the matchups was conducted, the experimenters deeming them "tolerable," on the surface they appeared rather good; however, neither of these assessments is scientifically acceptable. Six prayer groups were formed to pray for the treatment group. Pray-ers were given the patient's first name and condition. It was conservatively estimated that a total of 15 hours of prayer per patient was provided over a 6-month period. The prayer method was one of silent meditation, termed "the practice of the presence of God" (p. 371). Neither the patients nor their physicians knew who was targeted to receive these prayers. In other words, a rudimentary double-blind methodology was employed. At the end of the study, the two groups did not materially differ in their health outcomes. Essentially, as many patients improved as worsened in their health conditions in each of the groups.

Some 4 years later another evaluation of IP was reported by Collipp (1969). Eighteen children with leukemia participated in this study, with 10 in the experimental prayed-for group and 8 denoted as controls. Again, the doctors and patients were never informed regarding specifically who were subjects of the prayers. This study lasted for 15 months, and again no evidence was discerned that IP had had any apparent effect. Interestingly, Collipp implied that the prayer group members may have lost interest in their work. Suggesting that the children had not been healed owing to a lack of sincerity on the part of the randomly assigned pray-ers allowed Collipp's original aspirations to stand, as the pray-ers could be blamed rather than prayers.

IP AND CARDIAC PATIENTS:
GETTING SERIOUS ABOUT IP RESEARCH

The Research of Randolph C. Byrd

The door was now open to increasingly ingenious research on IP, and the challenge was taken up by a physician, Randolph C. Byrd, who published his work in the *Southern Medical Journal* in 1988. Basically, it set the pattern for most of the studies that followed by employing fairly large samples that were more exactingly selected and measured. Byrd's effort raised quite a stir in the field. Praise came primarily from those with inclinations toward religion and/ or the paranormal. Its reception by the scientific community was much cooler. Possibly because of its popularity, it was republished 9 years later in the journal *Alternative Therapies*. Since this is the most frequently cited and discussed work in the literature, it merits a thorough examination.

This project was undertaken in 1982 and 1983 on 393 coronary patients at San Francisco General Hospital. The study was explained to all potential participants, and 57 who refused to sign the informed consent form were not included in the research. Byrd's intention was to conduct a "prospective double-blind randomized protocol to assess the therapeutic effects of intercessory prayer" (Byrd, 1988, p. 826). This meant that the patients, medical staff, and Byrd were supposed to be "blinded" throughout the study, not knowing who would or would not receive prayers. The next step was to create experimental prayer-treatment and control groups. Members of the former would be the "recipients" of prayers by intercessors, who were religiously active "born-again Christians." Three to seven intercessors prayed daily for each person in the experimental group, knowing only the patient's first name, diagnosis, and physical condition. Some 192 patients constituted the prayer group and 201, the control group. Byrd's tables and reference to the use of unpaired t-tests, chi-square, and a stepwise logistic regression appear at first glance to be impressive.

Questions and Challenges

Despite Byrd's obviously hard work, this effort raises many serious questions. First, it appears that comparisons of the two groups at the beginning of the study showed no significant differences, apparently at the .05 level for 33 variables. Despite the large size of the groups, for specific variables 29 comparisons had 10 or fewer patients in one or both groups. The majority of these were composed of less than six patients, and two had none. A similar situation prevailed when group comparisons were made at the end of the study: 25 of the variables had less than 10 patients for the group to which they were assigned, 17 had five or fewer patients, and three had either a single patient or none. Assessing the significance of group differences with such numbers becomes highly problematic.

A common concern in medical trials is the effect of different treatment dosages. The amount of medication required to produce a cure is typically the central question of a study. Here IP takes on the role of the "medicine"; however, the "dosage" varied widely among the patients. This uncontrolled administration of the "treatment" would be rejected as inappropriate for a physical substance (e.g., blood pressure medication). If IP is to be evaluated in the medical context, variations in dose effects must be taken seriously.

Another major analytical issue concerns the claimed six "significant" differences between the experimental (prayed-for) group and the control group. Stated simply, when a sufficiently large number of comparisons are made, there is a high probability that some meaningless findings may appear to be important. Applying some statistical adjustments can help researchers avoid such errors,[1] a position also advanced by Sloan and Ramakrishnan (2006).

Although the analysis difficulties alone were not sufficient to totally invalidate this study, problems also existed on other fronts. Again raising the question of "blindedness," Byrd was unclear as to whether he alone or others categorized the patients in relation to the "severity score" (Roberts, Ahmed, & Hall, 2010). Tessman and Tessman (2000) believed that Byrd alone evaluated the outcome condition of the patients, using criteria he developed after the study was completed. These authors stated that Byrd did this when he was obviously "unblinded." They further indicated that this detailed analysis was undertaken only *after* Byrd's article was initially reviewed, based on a contact between Byrd and Dr. Irwin Tessman (personal communication, May 25, 2008). Someone reading the Byrd article would not be aware of such a possibility from reading the article. The study's coordinator, of course, "was completely unblinded" (p. 32), but we know nothing about the nature of her communications with Byrd. Such troublesome questions cast further doubt on

Byrd's claims that intercessory prayer is effective (Harris & Tessman, 2001).

Another measurement problem further clouds these results. Variables can be identified as simple markers that indicate whether a person has or does not have a particular characteristic or condition. When making more complex assessments (e.g., as with Byrd's severity index), different scorers might not always agree quantitatively and/ or qualitatively (despite Byrd's best efforts to develop clear criteria). If Byrd were the sole judge, interscorer agreement would not be an issue. But if there were multiple judges, we definitely would want data on their relative agreement and whether they agreed with Byrd's criteria. Without such information, the reliability of this kind of measure would not be well established.

Other difficulties concern the variables for which statistical significance was claimed between the prayer-treatment and control groups. These concern both the problem of very low numbers and whether the control group was initially sicker than the experimental group. Again, conclusions from the data supporting a constructive role for prayer are problematic.[2]

Byrd's selection of coronary patients proved popular and was adopted by a number of researchers who succeeded him. In essence, those needing help were divided into two groups, one receiving prayers and the other designated as controls. Double-blind procedures were employed, and differences appeared largely in the measures and variables selected and the data analyses performed.

The Research of William A. Harris and Associates

William A. Harris and colleagues (1999) conducted a major study that was designed to replicate Byrd's effort. It utilized 990 cardiac patients who were admitted to the Coronary Care Unit (CCU) at the Mid-America Heart Institute (MAHI). On admission to the hospital, all were randomly assigned to either a prayer-treatment group ($N = 466$) or a control group ($N = 524$). Those who spent less than one day in the CCU were subsequently eliminated from the study.

Prayer was offered daily for 28 days by four members of a prayer team for "a speedy recovery with no complications." The pray-ers were provided only with the first names of those for whom they were to offer prayers.[3] Patients were blinded to the fact that they were being prayed for—hence, they never met their intercessors. Reference is made, however, to "blinded retrospective chart review(s)." A secretary was the only person who was not blinded, and she met with the patients. In a similar manner, the data collectors and the statistician were also blinded.

Two scores were computed: a weighted MAHI-CCU score based on 35 variables and the total Byrd score. Ten of Harris's medical colleagues reviewed the patients' charts, and they agreed 96% of the time, thus evidencing good interrater agreement. Group comparisons were provided on both the weighted and the unweighted MAHI-CCU scores. Both were statistically significant, though the two scores are, in all likelihood, highly correlated.[4]

Despite prayers for a "speedy recovery," neither the length of the CCU or hospital stays attained significance. Still, for the weighted MAHI-CCU scores, p was .04 in favor of the treatment group. No significant differences were found for the Byrd scores, and yet the comments of Harris and colleagues (1999) implied that the numbers for the prayer-treatment group were better than those for the usual-care control patients. This type of statement tends to be misleading, as it subtly implies significance. The authors additionally suggested that they might have been observing the effects of IP performed by others rather than that performed by the formal intercessors employed for this work. Even though they further noted that this was "unknowable and uncontrollable" (p. 2277), to imply such influence is certainly beyond the boundaries of science. One might normally infer that this extra prayer should be the same for both groups.

Some of the critiques of Byrd's work are valid here. Cautiously, Harris and his associates accepted the stringent .005 level of significance for the 34 t-test comparisons between the prayer treatment and control groups and the .05 level for three other comparisons.[5] Simply put, no significant differences can be claimed between the usual-care and prayer-treatment groups.

To most of those who challenged Harris's assertions, the crucial position revolves around what mechanism was needed for the intercessory prayers to influence action. Was it solely God or perhaps some paranormal kinesic power? What was the nature of the therapeutic intervention that supposedly operated in such circumstances as these? First, a strong case can be made that, since there was probably no effect, no physically measurable mechanism exists (Goldstein, 2000; Hamm, 2000; Van der Does, 2000).

As Sloan (2006) has observed, Harris and colleagues' work was a marked improvement on that of Byrd; however, it still encountered many of the same critical issues that remained unresolved and that even now are the object of much debate and criticism.

The MANTRA Studies of Mitchell W. Krucoff and Colleagues

Coronary patients continued to be the subjects of choice in many subsequent studies. New research refinements were introduced, but the same basic issues plus a number of new considerations appeared. The Monitoring and Actualization of Noetic Training (MANTRA) studies, first undertaken by Mitchell W. Krucoff and coworkers (2001), illustrate some of these.

The main innovations introduced were (1) an effort to cross-validate observations by conducting both a pilot investigation and a much larger main study; (2) the utilization of four experimental conditions; and (3) a more sophisticated research design and improved data analyses. In the pilot work, 120 patients were organized into four "noetic therapy" groups: stress relaxation, imagery, touch therapy, and IP. The full course of treatment was completed by 118 patients, with 30 additional patients receiving the standard therapy. The IP condition used eight different groups and included general Christian, Catholic, Moravian, Baptist, Jewish, and Buddhist pray-ers. These participants were provided only with the patient's name and ailment. The patients, their families, and the staff were all subject to double-blind conditions in the prayer condition. All groups were compared on nine physical health variables, none of which resulted in significant differences.

Arguing that the pilot samples were small and possible trends were thus nonsignificant owing to a lack of statistical power, the researchers conducted a second but large-scale study (Krucoff et al., 2005) in which the sample numbered 748 patients. MANTRA II, however, largely confirmed MANTRA I, with nonsignificant differences again found.

While more restrained than the earlier researchers, Krucoff and colleagues (2005) engaged in an all-too-common practice that possesses an element of self-justification, namely, the discussion of nonsignificant differences and trends. The implication is that there is really something noteworthy to report that is consonant with the researchers' hypotheses, but for some unknown reason it failed to appear.

The Mayo Clinic Study

In other research with cardiac patients, Aviles and colleagues (2001) undertook an IP investigation at the Mayo Clinic in Rochester, Minnesota. Following 799 patients after discharge from the hospital, the usual IP treatment and control groups were formed. Assignment was randomized, with 400 patients subject to IP and 399 designated as controls. On the basis of medical indicators, 445 patients constituted a high-risk sample, and 315, a low-risk one. The standard double-blind procedure with respect to group placement and prayer was observed. Only Christian intercessors were employed for the 26-week study period. Five events that included as possibilities death, rehospitalization, and cardiac arrest were the prime variables studied at the end of 6 months. No significant differences between the groups were found.

The STEP Project of Herbert Benson and Colleagues

Given the popularity of studying IP in relation to cardiac patients, one could hope for a major effort to attempt some resolution on the key issue. Whether or not such an ideal was attainable, the STEP project (Study of the Therapeutic Effects of Intercessory Prayer) directed by Herbert Benson, a cardiologist at Harvard Medical School, was a prominent effort in that direction. Benson conducted this research at six major medical centers with 1,802 CABG patients (Benson et al., 2006; Dusek et al., 2002), who volunteered from an original pool of 3,295 who were eligible, with the remainder declining to participate.

Two variables were manipulated, IP versus no IP and the certainty of receiving IP versus the uncertainty of being its object. All patients were informed about the nature of the study. There were approximately 600 patients in each of three groups, resulting in a total of 1,802 participants. Those in group 1 were uncertain as to whether they would receive IP, but all were designated recipients. Group 2 patients were also uncertain; however, none received IP. These two groups undertook the same general procedure used in the previous work. Group 3 patients, by contrast, were both certain that they would be prayed for and received IP. Comparisons were made between groups 1 and 2, both of which represented uncertainty relative to IP; however, we are told that about two-thirds of these patients believed that they did receive IP (Krucoff, Crater, & Lee, 2006). This somewhat unclear indication compares fairly closely with the 73% in similar circumstances in the much smaller sample of Matthews, Marlowe, and McNutt (2000). Although objective uncertainty can be assessed, its meaning is unclear, and its subjective correlates are not easily handled. In other words, the overall uncertain condition may not be meaningfully differentiated from the state of certainty. With well over half of the participants believing they were IP targets, their expectations might have been similar to those of the patients who were assured of receiving IP.

In addition to a lack of clarity in differentiating group 1 from group 3, we further read that between 95 and 97% of those studied felt that they were the object of prayers from friends, church members, and relatives. Subjectively, uncertainty regarding IP seems to have been rare. Of course, this last factor has plagued all IP research. One may thus infer that virtually everyone in difficult health circumstances that might elicit IP receives it and is convinced that it is being offered. This issue is further discussed later in this chapter. This type of study leaves room for a fourth group whose members would be told that they would receive IP but in fact would not. A review board, however, would likely reject this option as unethical.

Another matter concerns the nature of the IP used. Although 99% of the patients in groups 1 and 3 received IP for almost 3 years, the number of intercessors ranged from 10 to 58, and IP was presented anywhere from 30 seconds to many hours per day. The chances are that considerable variability was present in practically every IP study undertaken.

When the two uncertain groups (1 vs. 2) were compared—that is, an IP group versus a non-IP group—no significant differences were found. When comparing group 1 (uncertainty) with group 3, the certain IP group, significance was observed in the direction opposite to that which might have been hypothesized. That is, the certainty of receiving IP conferred no protection and, if it had any effect, it made things worse.

What uncertainty means to those who participate in IP studies is unclear. As noted, most of the patients in this study expected to receive IP and had little personal doubt about receiving it. An uncertain condition creates a subjectively poorly defined group. We still, however, have the assigned prayers. The major variables that might be called into play appear to be cognitive, namely, the meaning of believing that one is or is not the recipient (or object) of IP. In addition, a cognitive-motivational expectancy channel was opened and might have greatly affected the psychological state of those who took part in this research (Kirsch, 1999; Matthews, Conti, & Sireci, 2001). Even though IP per se had no outward manifestations in this work, greater expectations, or expectancy, on the part of patients were observed. This inclination merits further investigation, as it might increase our understanding of what was found in the STEP project. Regardless of the lack of IP effects, we might have discovered whether expectancy can influence health outcomes. Expectancy and placebo effects do not appear to act independently of each other.

The Research of Leanne Roberts and Steve Hall

To close out this section, the work of Roberts and Hall merits our attention. Their original 1977 work was updated in 2009 (Roberts et al., 2010). The project they undertook included over 7,800 patients in 10 different studies. These researchers demonstrated great reluctance to offer a definitive conclusion, but they did observe that IP showed no "effect" relative to death or patients' clinical status; for four studies, no influence on coronary care unit readmission and, for two studies, no effects on rehospitalization rates. Still, after all of the negative findings, they termed their observations "equivocal."

IP RESEARCH ON OTHER PATIENTS

Most IP research has concentrated on cardiac patients, most likely because Byrd opened that channel so decisively and possibly also owing to the high availability of those with coronary disorders. It was only a matter of time, however, before interest was extended to other health problems, both physical and mental. As should be evident from the earlier discussions, it is virtually impossible to conduct a "perfect" study. Questions about the validity of findings may vary from the trivial to the extremely serious. For example, a number of problems trouble the findings of Byrd, and his claims of positive results for IP must be subjected to serious scrutiny. Such concerns, however, are not present in the STEP study.

A sampling of the IP research on noncardiac patients illustrates the variety of medical and psychological efforts that have been undertaken. Matthews and colleagues (2000) recruited rheumatoid arthritis patients. Sicher, Targ, Moore, and Smith (1998) investigated advanced AIDS, while Matthews and associates (2001) worked with kidney dialysis, and Green (1993) examined neurosurgical pituitary patients. While the patients in these studies all had specific medical problems, related research work focused directly on their psychological and behavioral problems. For example, Walker, Tonigan, Miller, Comer, and Kahlich (1997) dealt with alcoholism, while O'Laoire (1997) stressed self-esteem, anxiety, and depression. Similarly, Palmer, Katerndahl, and Morgan-Kidd (2004) examined prayer's effects on respondents' personal problems, while Tloczynski and Fritzsch (2002) emphasized the impact on their anxiety. Citing these studies does not mean they do not suffer from many of the difficulties already noted in this literature. It does, however, demonstrate the growing interest in IP.

Intercessory Prayer and Rheumatoid Arthritis

Matthews and colleagues (2000) conducted a relatively small study (involving only 40 rheumatoid arthritis patients) that employed both in-person prayer and IP. Relatively sophisticated univariate and multivariate statistical analyses were applied to the data, but no significant changes were observed for the IP group. In their defense, the authors note, among a number of possible confounds, the likely influence of placebo effects.

Intercessory Prayer and Kidney Dialysis Patients

Matthews and colleagues (2001) carried out a well-controlled study on 95 kidney dialysis end-stage renal disease patients. In addition, they further applied the most sophisticated statistical analyses that had so far been employed in this area. For all practical purposes, no IP or visualization effects were observed for the medical variables, although for the psychological ones a slight bias in favor of IP was shown.[6] This finding is best explained as attributable to expectancy effects. The researchers concluded that neither IP nor visualization could be "convincingly" said to have gained traction.

Intercessory Prayer and AIDS

During the mid-1990s, Sicher and colleagues (1998) conducted a small sample study of IP with advanced AIDS patients ($N = 40$). Their enthusiasm for positive findings resulted in their overinterpreting the data, with the defined group differences yielding a probability of .20 as "near" significant. Although six of the 11 comparisons were presented as having low p levels, none of the comparisons was significant at the .05 level.[7]

Intercessory Prayer with Neurosurgical Pituitary Patients

In 1993, Green completed an unpublished doctoral dissertation in which 57 patients suffering from abnormal growth of the pituitary gland were subjected to IP and expectancy conditions. Although Green demonstrated much thoughtfulness and research sophistication, what little he observed is marred by his failure to reject the null hypothesis that accompanies repeated significance testing. In the few instances where statistical significance was observed, it appeared only because of the expectancy effects. Moreover, he expended much energy talking about "near-significant" results or "approaching" significance and complaining about the "large variability" of state anxiety scores, with his small sample as possibly causing the negative results. In sum, IP did not gain any noteworthy support from this research effort.

O'Laoire (1997) assessed the possible influence of IP and "directed prayer" on a variety of self-report measures such as esteem, anxiety, and depression. These were, in all likelihood, moderately to strongly correlated.[8] The fact that no differences were observed between the experimental and control groups was perhaps the most stable of the findings.

Another investigation of IP's effects on psychological well-being was undertaken by Tlocyznski and Fritzsch (2002). A total of eight undergraduate students constituted the sample and were prayed for by one of the experimenters for 7 weeks. Five objective scales were administered, and the claim was advanced that those prayed for showed a significant reduction in anxiety relative to the non-IP participants. The lack of controls or a blinded methodology renders these findings highly dubious.

Palmer and colleagues (2004) attempted to resolve a unique personal life problem that 86 participants individually identified. A total of six dependent outcome variables was assessed.[9] Small samples made the exhaustive evaluation undertaken quite risky. The researchers even analyzed group differences for individual choices with single items, usually an unreliable procedure. Even though this study did not support the efficacy of IP, on the basis of theorizing by others, the authors cautiously suggested that prayer might be influential owing to some thus far undiscovered mental "quantum reality."

Shifting from psychological beliefs to behavior, Walker and associates (1997) undertook a study intended to influence alcoholism through IP. Studying 40 alcoholic patients in a substance abuse facility, they failed to demonstrate any IP effects.

The research on IP presented above essentially covers the field from a scientific vantage point. We have sought to demonstrate the problems that typically plague research on IP as briefly as possible. Despite Dossey's (2000) reference to "scores of controlled studies" (p. 1735) on mental healing, like other reviewers of the work on IP, we have directed our attention to the most commonly cited IP research on humans. About 20 studies fall into this category. Granted that there is additional research available on animals, plants, microorganisms, and physiological processes, its critical evaluation must be left to others.

A number of rather extensive reviews of "distant healing" were also surveyed (Astin et al., 2000; Ernst, 2003; Hodge, 2007; Masters, Spielman, & Goodson, 2006; Roberts et al., 2010; Targ, 1997), many of which did not involve IP. Some dealt with "noncontact therapeutic touch" and such paranormal phenomena as psychokinesis, for example. Reviewers were quite selective in what they chose. For example, papers where subjects were not randomized or blinded or articles that offered only anecdotal reports of a single or a few individuals were not collected. Roberts and colleagues (2010) began their analysis with 206 studies, only 10 of which ended up meeting their criteria. Hodge's (2007) survey encompassed 17 studies. Astin, Harkness, and Ernst (2000) found what they termed "100 clinical trials of distant healing" (p. 904) but ultimately reduced this number to 23 on the basis of their scientific indices. Masters and associates (2006) chose to focus only on 14 studies, most of which were subsequently shown to possess serious errors, particularly in data analysis. The intent of reviewers was not to be exhaustive but to present work that attempted to employ rigorous methods. A growing sophistication in experimental design, methodology, and analysis was developed and applied. The result, in general, has been mostly negative findings but an increased understanding of the flaws that commonly occur in attempts to validate IP experimentally.

COMMENTS AND CRITIQUES

There is no dearth of advocates for and critics of the research on intercessory prayer. These groups have generally split into various subgroups. Some of the proponents employ religious arguments, whereas others seek explanations through parapsychology. Recognizing the complexity of the problems encountered in this research, Dossey (1998) has taken positions on both sides of the issue. The rapidity with which the most up-to-date knowledge has been applied suggests that papers written a decade ago may be largely passé. As demonstrated earlier, much of what has passed for research would never have gotten into print based on contemporary standards. Without question, controversy reigns and is likely to continue.

Dossey and Hufford (2005) have offered 20 criticisms of prayer experiments, and yet they strongly supported the value of prayer, asserting that "prayer need not be dishonored or degraded through research" (p. 115). Lawrence (2002) included IP in his assessment that took the religious perspective, highlighting "four fatal flaws in recent spirituality research" (p. 125). The arguments he employed were basically theological, not scientific, but they demonstrated that the fundamental conceptualizations of prayer in most of these studies were inaccurate reflections of the actual practice. Adopting a more erudite religious–theological stance, Matthews and Clark (1999) argued for a broader scientific perspective on prayer research including IP, but what this means is never clarified. Both Dossey and Hufford and Matthews and Clark made a number of telling points, but one is hard-put not to view their commentary as attempts to counter the prevalence of negative results in this research. Dossey and Hufford, in particular, raised a variety of religious, moral, and scientific issues that are intended to stop prayer research in toto. Their negative views toward "testing God" were complemented by impressively offered parapsychological possibilities with scientific-sounding yet nebulous concepts proffered such as "quantum non-locality" (p. 113). Some of Dossey and Hufford's points, however, are worth debating and developing further. No one denies that there are serious problems conducting scientific research on IP. Still, the past 20–30 years has witnessed a growing sophistication in experimental design, methodology, and data analysis. In many instances, the more advanced the procedures employed, the more the outcome fails to reject the null hypothesis (Ernst, 2003).

Marcello Truzzi's (1987) famous dictum "Extraordinary claims require extraordinary evidence (or proof)" should not be taken lightly. Conceptually, the effectiveness of IP is an extraordinary claim. The notion that IP can be scientifically studied has, as noted, been challenged (Dossey & Hufford, 2005; Lawrence, 2002). A major exercise by those who want to believe their IP hypotheses are correct is to indicate all of the possible shortcomings in their research that may have interfered with obtaining positive results. The possibility of chance findings is simply ignored. Some data analyses that resulted in negative findings were done so well that readers might well ask why the researchers refused to accept the outcomes. Various thinkers, after the fact, imply the correctness of faith in IP but add that there are so many possible errors and difficulties that the best counsel is simply to believe and not trouble oneself about negative findings (Dossey, 2000; Dossey & Hufford, 2005; Lawrence, 2002). Because prayer brings religion and God into the picture, efforts are made to avoid this orientation by invoking parapsychology and more specifically psychokinesis. Regardless of the justification adopted, the specific mechanism that is operative, if any, remains scientifically unknown and undefined—an issue we return to shortly.

The Nature of Intercessors and IP

Research on IP immediately confronts an insurmountable problem, namely, that the attempted controls on IP ignore many if not most of its manifestations. Sloan and Ramakrishnan (2006) pointed to three forms, two of which were disregarded in the work they conducted. Attention is directed only toward the intercessors and their prayers that are part of the IP studies. Concurrently, uncontrollable supplemental prayer (SP) is present, namely, the prayers undertaken independently by relatives, associates, and friends. Finally, a generalized background prayer (BP) is identified, referring to those broad standard appeals to deities anywhere in the world. Experimental IP therefore becomes special to those who undertake research in this area. Although these other forms are recognized, researchers unavoidably stay concerned with their own IP manipulations, and nothing more is said. Given this framework, we might characterize the research groups as follows:

Prayer treatment group: IP + SP + BP + usual expectancy
Control group: SP + BP + usual expectancy

Sloan and Ramakrishnan (2006) theorized that the effects of IP may be a function of the ratio of SP to IP, and in order to detect IP effects the numbers of participants in IP groups might have to be very large. Even the potential for threshold effects has been suggested, whereby IP must really make a difference above the SP that is offered. The question of how SP is to be assessed is not discussed. The object (or presumed beneficiary) of the IP may be either one person or a number of individuals with problems.

Intercessors further vary in their identification with different faiths. Some are narrowly defined, such as Catholics, Baptists, Moravians, and so on. Protestantism covers over 200 separate denominations that are rarely specified. Similarly, the complexities of the Buddhist, Jewish, and Muslim traditions are rarely discussed in detail. The same lack of specificity holds for the prayers offered: they might be quite vague or tightly focused on specific results, vary in length from less than 5 minutes to at least 15 minutes, and might be offered only once or every day for many months. Some variation is also found in the nature of the descriptive and identifying information about the object or presumed beneficiary of the prayers. The physical distance between the latter and pray-ers is regarded as irrelevant. Those who believe in the efficacy of prayer may readily accept such diversity in approaches; however, considering the issue of scientific rigor, all of the foregoing possibilities merit consideration. Even though it is obvious from our earlier discussion of prayer's multidimensionality, all of the work on IP is concerned only with petitionary prayer. An argument can be advanced that there may well be a place for other prayer forms—though this possibility seems to have been totally ignored.

A truly critical issue concerns the necessity of cross-validating findings, something that is rarely done. It is also not enough to just talk about randomization, although that is critical in any study of this nature. Important research needs to be repeated and its findings confirmed or rejected. Large samples may be randomly subdivided. Unfortunately, there is no way of claiming that enough is enough. Believers will never close the door on certain possibilities, and no one can deny that someday a mechanism may not be discovered. Science always keeps an infinite sequence of doors open to the potential of new knowledge, no matter how fruitless something appears at a given time. Failure to reject the null hypothesis is not the same as accepting it as truth, although we may be inclined to think this way without sufficient reflection.[10] Statistical analysis does not "prove" the null hypothesis, nor does its rejection absolutely "prove" the opposite. Obviously, at this point in our search, "extraordinary evidence" has not been obtained. The antithesis describes more adequately the various research findings in this area. Despite the lack of standardization in studies of intercessory prayer and failure to establish it as a clear scientific construct, the litany continues.

Problems of Fraud and Cheating in IP Research

A Case of Potential Fraud

A pall was cast over one of the earliest of these investigations by the problems of the chief investigator, Daniel P. Wirth. His involvement for 20 years in fraudulent activities unrelated to his research ultimately resulted in his serving a prison term. Doubt, however, has arisen regarding the validity of his publications (Solfvin, Leskowitz, & Benor, 2005). No specific questions have been raised concerning Wirth's application of IP to the healing of skin wounds. Suffice it to say that the results were in the opposite direction to that hypothesized—in other words, the IP healing treatment group did worse than the controls (Wirth, 1994).

The problem became more acute in the last study involving Wirth (Cha, Wirth, & Lobo, 2001). A sample of 199 women undergoing in vitro fertilization in Korea was split into IP and control groups. Flamm (2005) indicates that the practice of informed consent was not properly implemented, and this oversight resulted in an investigation by the U.S. Department of Health and Human Services. Dr. Wang Cha, the first author, claimed that informed consent was not required in Korea, and that, had it been employed, it would have introduced bias into the study (a claim that is not further explained). Flamm countered that, since the research was double-blinded, bias would have been introduced but expectancy issues might have arisen. An interesting twist is that the patients studied were in Korea but the IP took place in the United States, Australia, and Canada. Then, again, no distance limits have ever been placed on the unknown influencing mechanisms underlying IP. According to the data, those in the IP group became pregnant twice as often as the controls. Sloan and Ramakrishnan (2006) considered "these dramatic results . . . extremely unlikely" (p. 509), implying the likelihood of fraud. In a like manner, Flamm (2004) explicitly described the research as fraudulent, flawed, and absurd, and further asserted that it could not be replicated. Probably related to the uproar this study created, Dr. Cha left Columbia University and refused to be interviewed regarding the study. Moreover, he subsequently claimed that the findings were valid. The third author, Rogerio Lobo, resigned his position as Chair of Obstetrics and Gynecology at Columbia and removed his name from the study (Lyons, 2005).

This particular work was a sad diversion from serious scientific efforts to understand research on intercessory prayer.

The More General Situation

Criticism and disbelief can cut two ways. Those who embrace IP may suspect fraud in the research of denigrators, while the latter can similarly mistrust the work of questioners who refuse to accept notions of IP's validity. A recent survey of over 2,200 primarily biomedical researchers suggested that some 9% had observed instances of misconduct and more than one-third of these did not report what they witnessed (Titus, Wells, & Rhoades, 2008). Great concern has also been regularly expressed by those working in parapsychology about purported wrongdoing by members of their own community (Hansen, 1990; Kennedy, 2005). Mainstream organizations such as the American Psychological Association have for over a century repeatedly expressed abhorrence of research fraud. To date, as far as we can determine, even though inferred, no validated charges of cheating have been directed at scientific efforts to research the possible effects of IP. Suspicions have, however, been voiced about specific research projects (Flamm, 2005; Sloan & Ramakrishnan, 2006; Solfvin et al., 2005). Even though a recommendation for cross-validated work by other than the original researcher holds for all of psychology, the character of paranormal/parapsychological research suggests that it should be particularly applied in this realm.

The Question of Mechanism: How Might IP Be Understood?

Science is not congenial to research involving cause and effect that fails to denote the influencing mechanisms. The fundamental principle is that scientific investigation must be premised upon action in the natural world. Supernatural assumptions and themes are treated as solely matters of personal belief. If they cannot be objectively evaluated, there is no place for them in science. Theories must be formulated that eventuate in testable hypotheses. Such evaluation must involve operationally defined variables that demonstrably interact in research. The outcomes of testing must not include indefinable concepts, for the data must be made public and be reproducible.

If there is one basic problem in IP research, it is that possible mechanisms for IP are simply not specified. To cite God or some parapsychological factor, neither of which can be scientifically identified, is simply not acceptable. Schermer (2004) confronted the matter of God involvement and considered the characteristics of omnipotence and omniscience that we impute to the Deity. If these characteristics are real, he asserts, IP should really be totally irrelevant. From a theological viewpoint, our experimental designs could be regarded as insulting. Another indignity might be the application of statistics to IP outcomes. For, under these circumstances, God becomes an entity that conforms to the laws of probability, and IP is relegated to the status of a manipulable commodity. One may, however, contend that these views are oversimplifications.

Considering such issues and the need or desire to be scientific, some researchers have embraced the paranormal, searching for mechanisms that might emanate from physical law. Leder (2005) proposed four possibilities that associate physics with conscious intention, specifically: (1) some undefined energy transmission; (2) a mental warping of the physical nature of space and time; (3) a quantum entanglement that transforms ideas into objective changes that disregard time and distance, and (4) a process that negates probability so that only one outcome is produced. Leder claimed that these possibilities deserve to be further researched but are not really explanations, a distinction that is rather obscure. How such research would be better handled in the future is not specified. His use of fuzzy, mysterious, and yet impressive-sounding scientific language such as "quantum" also added nothing of substantive value.

Sloan and Ramakrishnan (2006) indicated that the four known natural physical forces appear to be unrelated to IP. Sloan (2006) and Haas (2007) noted that electrochemical impulses from brain action are exceedingly weak and can only be measured under special conditions with exceptionally sensitive equipment. This was demonstrated by Volegov, Matlachov, Mosher, Espy, and Kraus (2004), using a shielding helmet. Ambient noise beyond the helmet apparently interfered with and obscured signals from the brain. Considering this plus the potential of similar transmissions unique to each person, Haas concluded that understanding and utilizing such physical messages from individual brains might even be more powerful than any potential supernatural skills. The mechanisms for such communication may exist in some extraterrestrial form or domain, but providing evidence for this speculation seems far-fetched if not impossible. Seeking their informed consent and providing instructions to the study participants in IP research probably create unmeasured psychological expectations. We have cited numerous studies where these expectations both explicitly and possibly implicitly influenced the research results. More attention needs to be directed at measuring these effects.

Another fascinating avenue that merits further exploration relates to neuropsychology. Schjoedt and colleagues' (2010) interesting and sophisticated research effort utilized fMRI and focused on the frontal cortex and the temporal lobe. Significant differences were claimed for the brain regions concerned with "executive and social cognitive networks" (p. 6). Apparently these were "deactivated" (implying an element of trust) when the Christian subjects received supportive Christian messages that were a function of intercessory prayer. A less kindly interpretation is that when God's "charisma" is introduced, analytic executive thinking processes appear to be suspended and belief in intercessory prayer is accepted. Some recent research on cognitive style (Shenhav, Rand, & Greene, in press) favors this interpretation.

Where To? What Next?

Currently there appears to be a growing consensus that (1) negative findings characterize the bulk of IP research and (2) even what is regarded as positive usually falls by the wayside owing to defective methods and data analyses. Masters and colleagues (2006) stated the obvious, namely that "there is no scientifically discernible effect that differentiates . . . individuals who are the recipients of IP from those who are not" (p. 24).

Halperin (2001) suggested that medicine can't explain everything, and hence we refer to "miraculous cures" and unexpected occurrences of all sorts. Without modifying standard medical routines, Halperin, referring to "harmless complementary forms of healing" (p. 796), asserted that the use of such alternative methods as IP should be employed. A similar position was advanced by Harris and colleagues (1999) and Matthews and colleagues (2000), who were all associated with the view that the scientific method is inappropriately applied to matters such as IP that involve religion (Halperin, 2001). The recommendation has been made, instead, to add spiritual faith to the medical armamentarium and just leave it at that (Matthews & Clark, 1999). This is obviously present with supplemental and background prayer. Anything beyond this might best be left to the patient, his own local clergy, and hospital chaplains.

Lastly, one possible and still unexplored realm in IP research concerns a shift in focus. Rather than concentrating on how IP changes a specific patient's health outcomes, perhaps it might be more fruitful to explore its effects on those who practice it (i.e., the pray-ers).

SUMMARY

This chapter has dealt with an extremely controversial subject, intercessory prayer. Although its supporters offer arguments in favor of its validity, as popular as these ideas are, they may well demean faith by implying its manipulability. In addition, the best scientific research to date challenges the claims of IP's success from both the paranormal and religion viewpoints. If proof of IP's efficacy is to be produced, further pursuit of the research avenues thus far chosen would appear to be unpromising. As we have previously observed, if ever a scholarly realm needed cross-validation by researchers other than the original ones, this is it.

NOTES

1. Byrd (1988) recognized that setting the probability (p) value for statistical significance at .05 was questionable since a large number of comparisons were being made; and even though statistical adjustments could be employed, they were not. Since he conducted 29 tests, in technical terms he was faced with the likelihood of committing a Type I (or alpha) error—namely, rejection of the true hypothesis, in this instance the null hypothesis of no difference. To circumvent this problem, Byrd constructed a severity score and stated that his outcome data were subjected to a "multivariant analysis" (p. 828) that yielded an overall significance less than .0001. When appropriately applying two versions of the Bonferroni adjustment, the .05 level he claimed for his original findings became .0017, raising the likelihood that none of the claimed significant differences would be valid. At best, only one comparison is reported to have reached the .002 level. Additional doubts could arise since, chances are, the assessed variables were not independent of one another (though they were treated as if they were). Application of a multivariate analysis of variance might have been appropriate in a best-case scenario. Given the variations in sample sizes for the various measures, especially since some were zero or one, this seemed unrealistic. Analytically, one can logically infer that the results of this effort yielded little of value.

2. Byrd alluded to the use of stepwise logistic regression to circumvent the matter of multiple t-tests. This approach implied a significantly better overall outcome for the prayer group ($p < .0001$), primarily on the basis of three predictor variables—antibiotics, diuretic use, and intubation/ventilation. Wright (1995) stressed the fact that logistic regression requires an extremely high subjects-to-variables ratio. Overall, Byrd's 393 patients to 29 variables is probably passable; however, the three significant variables pose a problem in that the treatment-control group sizes for these measures are rather small. For diuretics, there are, respectively, 5 and 15 patients; there are no patients in the prayed-for group versus 12 controls for intubation/ventilation. The antibiotic numbers are 3 and 17. A personally known physician who was consulted regarding these variables indicated that the use of antibiotics, even if employed prophylactically, suggests that the controls were sicker to begin with since antibiotics are, in general, expected to be quite independent of coronary problems. Interestingly, no data are provided regarding antibiotics when the patients entered the study. Given these considerations, inferring a role for intercessory prayer from such results would appear to be serious overkill. Kennedy (2002) applied the Bonferroni adjustment to the data and confirmed the antibiotic and intubation/ventilation results. He then employed Fisher's exact t-test, obtaining p values that further indicated significance for these two variables. The questioning of antibiotics' pertinence still holds if the controls were sicker

than those in the treatment group. In other words, only one of the 29 variables resulted in a meaningful finding. Normally with 29 variables, even at the .05 level of significance, one to two chance results might be expected. The intubation/ventilation variable is highly relevant and maintains its special position at a much more stringent level of significance. Given a statistical sampling of 29 comparisons, the likelihood for one rather consequential procedure could be a function of random selection.

3. Mention was made that "at least 95% of the patients" received the entire prayer regime, the rest presumably reflecting death or leaving the hospital before the full prayer time was completed. Some 5% of the patients were excluded because they were in the hospital less than 24 hours. In addition, 46 of the usual care patients and 42 in the prayer group died during their 28-day CCU stay. In other words, respectively, 8.8 and 9.0% of those studied were lost owing to death or not receiving the full course of treatment. The groups did not differ materially on this probably most important of all of the variables.

4. Sloan (2000) warns against confusing interrater reliability with construct validity. The important question is whether the MAHI-CCU scale measures what it is supposed to measure. It is surprising that no analysis was done on the correlations among the 34 items of the scale. Factor analysis might have demonstrated that this instrument is actually multidimensional, and different weighting systems might also have resulted. Even with indications of high interscorer agreement, indices of internal consistency reliability would have enhanced readers' understanding more. We suspect, of course, that some of the 35 individual indicators might be of little or no consequence.

5. Bonferroni analyses of the former reduced the chosen significance levels to, respectively, .00015 and .017.

6. The positive visualization condition featured six predoctoral psychology interns visualizing improvement in both the medical and psychological conditions of the patients.

7. Even though these ranged from .01 to .04, a Bonferroni adjustment indicates nonsignificance.

8. Unfortunately, the "significant" findings may be questioned. Multivariate analyses of variance such as multiple regression and multivariate covariance procedures should have been used rather than the analysis that yielded the reported findings.

9. Utilizing Bonferroni adjustments, no significant treatment differences were evidenced.

10. For instance, in personal relationships, not rejecting someone (tolerance) is not the same as accepting that person as a dear friend.

CHAPTER 8

Concluding Perspectives and Possibilities

Prayer is where the action is.
—attributed to JOHN WESLEY

*I*n this final chapter, our intention is not to offer a simple review and summary of what has been said, but rather to focus on the future. Having reminded readers of the many problems encountered in research on prayer, as presented in the previous chapters, we now desire to provide some constructive recommendations. These chiefly concern the development and application of theory as well as a variety of design and analysis issues. Although we have been critical of much of the research on prayer, we believe that the widespread practice of praying among the general population merits our attempting to thoroughly understand prayer's potentials and pitfalls. If prayer did not meet human needs rather well, it would not have survived for millennia or be expressed so strongly worldwide today.

EVALUATION ISSUES

We have presented a scientific view of prayer, largely by reviewing the research previously undertaken in the specific areas treated in the preceding chapters. Canvassing the many studies in this field, we encountered a variety of difficulties, such as inadequate statistical controls, issues of design and analysis, and overinterpretation of data. However, we have also endeavored to give credit where we feel researchers made creative and noteworthy contributions to this literature. Many practitioners in the psychology of religion find it difficult to be dispassionate, not only about their own work but also, more importantly, about science and religion in general. Those of us who attend conventions of the Society for the Scientific Study of Religion, the Religious Research Association and Division 36 of APA (Psychology of Religion) fully appreciate that religion is personally important to many of our colleagues. Without question, many if not most of the members of Division 36 are themselves religiously and spiritually active. Not a few have been trained to be or are currently serving as clergy.[1] Kirkpatrick and Hood (1990) argue that these personal positions can subtly influence research in a number of ways, including what the authors term "good" and "bad" religion in researchers' works. It is no small task to strive for objectivity and not express biases, but that is an explicit goal of the scientific method. Psychologists of religion must work particularly hard to avoid simply serving institutionalized faith and theology. We are all products of an extensive history in which religion has played central and sometimes controversial roles, and these influences inevitably affect our work in the psychology of religion.

APPLYING SCIENCE TO PRAYER

The Initial Step: Theory

To make research meaningful while employing the classic scientific method, one must begin with theory and work toward either its further development or at least the creation of useful conceptual models. In other words, one needs a specific framework to comprehend why a project is undertaken. Even those who claim their research is exploratory because it has no particular theory need to make explicit the reasons why they are undertaking that project (Bade & Cook, 2008; Richards, 1991). This requirement necessarily involves describing a theoretical basis for one's choice of variables and methodologies. The eclectic approach embodied in "Let's see what will happen if we do such and so" often reflects an unwillingness to make the necessary mental commitments to learn about the phenomenon in question, that is, what it is and what it might involve. There is an implicit theory, and the researcher is simply trying out ideas with a small sample or suggestive tests or manipulations. It is also a fine opportunity to assess effect size and power. In other words, first one should consult the appropriate literature and think through why certain factors need to be considered.

The counterargument is that the word *theory* is often loosely employed (Wilkinson & American Psychological Association, Task Force on Statistical Inference, 1999), making the research project more difficult to realize for both the author and the reader. We are not suggesting that all exploratory studies are without merit. Individual researchers, however, do need to give careful consideration to the effect on the field of simply doing exploratory work without ever following up the initial research with more full-bodied theory-directed investigations. Sustained programs of research are critical to the development of meaningful theory, and journal editors appear to be increasingly more demanding by insisting on substantive efforts.

This may seem like simplistic advice. However, as the psychology of religion hits its professional stride, there is a danger of missing out on a great deal of information because so many pertinent investigations appear in publications outside of mainstream psychology. Frequently, habit seems to take over and dictate one's choice of indices such as gender, socioeconomic status, age, and so on. Rarely is much thought given to these measures, although it is common to partial them out. In many instances where this occurs, the distinction between part and partial correlations is overlooked. The removal of variables that may not attain the .05 level of statistical significance simply increases the odds of showing that everything is more or less correlated with everything else. For example, nonsignificant correlation coefficients are of some magnitude and possible influence (Cohen, 1990). Such insights may be gleaned through the computation of partial and multiple correlations. Many findings are at a borderline level—hence, considerations such as these should not be ignored. Meehl (1990) picturesquely refers to this dilemma as the "crud factor" in social science research.

Communication Theory and Prayer

The theories explored in the preceding chapters range from very specific ones to quite broad formulations. For example, do they concern prayer in general or *specific types* of prayers? In Chapter 1, the latter possibility was briefly examined with respect to prayer as communication. This opened a pathway to the understanding and application of communication theory, which Capps (1982) explored through a psycho-theological approach that focused on meanings conveyed through communication. Acknowledging her theological perspective, Sylvia Crocker (1984) pursued such ideas in relation to five types of prayer, namely, confession, petition, praise, thanksgiving, and contemplation. Harold Ellens (1977) further extended this approach to other aspects of the psychology of religion. In a somewhat unusual treatment, Howard (2005) conducted a communication analysis of "the Sinner's prayer" through his "theory of vernacular rhetoric." This work has been greatly expanded by Grossoehme and his associates (2010). They carried out an extensive linguistic analysis of 800 prayers written in the chapel of a pediatric hospital. Although these had the potential of disclosing emotions, the researchers concluded that this did not occur. The analyses undertaken examined variables relating to causality, insight, and positive and negative emotions. Such work demonstrates considerable potential for similar studies on prayer as it relates to a variety of issues and contexts. Unfortunately, this potential has not yet motivated scholars to delve into this area. Since communication theory is infrequently found in the mainstream psychological literature, one is left to suspect that psychologists of religion are simply not fully acquainted with its possibilities. This unfortunate state of affairs has been detailed by Baesler (2003), who noted that only 11 publications have related prayer to communication. After discussing this problem, he undertook to develop a theoretical framework and an empirical research program in this area, aspects of which will be treated later in this chapter.

One productive way to connect communication to prayer may be through the concept of cognition. Our brief foray into this topic in Chapter 2 indicated that some excellent thinking has gone into various possibilities (Barrett, 2001, 2004; Koenig, 1995; Ladd & Spilka, 2002; McIntosh, 1995; Meraviglia, 1999; Ozorak, 1992; Wuthnow, 2008a, 2008b). Prayer, cognition, and communication theory thus designate one area worthy of considerably more research than has been afforded it. Communication is central to the presumed effects of inferred interaction with the Deity (Pargament, 1987, 1988). We believe that it might be fruitful to combine coping with communication theory.

The Issue of Control

In Chapter 1, the idea that prayer might enhance one's sense of control was proposed, but the idea was not given its due, either in general or in relation to specific types of prayer. A fair amount of control research has been reported for many aspects of faith but relatively little for prayer specifically (Furnham, 1982; Jackson & Coursey, 1988; McIntosh, Kojetin, & Spilka, 1985; Sexton, Leak, & Toenies, 1980; Shrauger & Silverman, 1971; Silvestri, 1979; Spilka & Schmidt, 1983; Tipton, Harrison, & Mahoney, 1980). Also the results have often been mixed and/or contradictory.

Even though a study of support immediately prior to cardiac surgery found that a scale measuring the helpfulness of prayer proved to be independent of the health locus of control (Saudia et al., 1991), some 96% of the patients prayed and 70% gave it their highest rating with regard to helpfulness. Working also with coronary patients before surgery, Ai, Peterson, Rodgers, and Tice (2005) noted that private prayer related positively to a sense of internal control. Williams (2009), however, found the locus of control to be independent of attendance at a cardiac rehabilitation program. Lastly, Mitchell (1989) discussed the use of prayer as an adjunct to psychotherapy.

In a series of creative studies designed to assess a theory of compensatory control, Aaron C. Kay and his coworkers (Kay, Gaucher, McGregor, & Nash, 2010; Kay, Gaucher, Napier, Callan, & Laurin, 2008; Kay, Moscovitch, & Laurin, 2010) researched the effects of a sense of personal control. They found that situations stressing randomness and low personal control eventuated in increased belief in a controlling God. Although prayer was not directly implicated in this work, its use was implied as part of the resources available to those having to confront their own weaknesses and distress in disadvantageous circumstances.

The general literature on control locus and its various expressions is extremely complex (Lazarus & Folkman, 1984; Thompson, 1981). We believe that this fact has not been appreciated sufficiently well by those few researchers who have worked with prayer—despite efforts by Pargament (1997) to show its role in the coping process.

Multidimensionality Revisited

If there is one aspect of prayer that merits greater theoretical and research understanding, it is that prayer is multifaceted. Scholars have repeatedly selected a few forms for study, and we have observed that the same or similar names may actually identify different item composites. As a first step, this problem needs to be resolved (Breslin et al., 2010). Invariably, little effort has gone into understanding the role of such measures in the larger prayer context. Generally, there is relatively little overlap as we go from one researcher to the next. The case can be made that slowly the simple single variable of prayer frequency is being put aside in favor of selected kinds of prayer that are usually operationalized through scales and other indices. Petitionary prayer seems to be getting the most attention, but it too is more complicated than the initial view of it might imply. One needs to know why it has been chosen, in what contexts it reflects various needs, and how its expression varies. In addition its limits are poorly specified. Although personal aggrandizement through prayer comes first to mind, prayers for the alleviation of others' difficulties possess a petitionary quality, and this was evidenced in extensive factor-analytic work accomplished by Luckow and her associates (1996).

Applying Theoretical Perspectives

Meehl's (1978) lengthy, respected, and repeated (also repeatedly ignored) observations about the difficulty of developing proper theories within the "soft" portion of the discipline (e.g., the psychology of religion) should be taken seriously. Chief among Meehl's concerns is that theories are rarely subjected to "risky" tests that could discredit their underlying premises. He notes that, instead, they are typically insulated from doubts by complex (usually post hoc) caveats, including specific experimental conditions. Because of this, nonsignificant results do not speak directly to the status of the conceptualization in question but rather to a highly contextualized framework. Faced with potentially disconfirming evidence, researchers conveniently blame the caveats and experimental conditions for the resulting nonsignificant findings while the underlying theory remains intact. All of these shortcomings (e.g., nature of tests, sample, analysis, etc.) should have been known prior to the study's being undertaken. Simply put, these excuses are no justification for conducting questionable work. We have seen many examples of this in the preceding chapters as researchers struggled to support their hopes in the face of negative or, at best, tentative research findings confirming their views. In other words, serious scholars may never get close to proving their theories when they focus their efforts too much on purifying the testing conditions (Meehl, 1978).

Mindful of Meehl's admonitions, we present in the remainder of this chapter one model of how best to understand the practice of prayer. While we primarily use the language of theory, we realize that our proposal is unlikely to meet Meehl's stringent requirements about levels of precision and risky testing methods. Moreover, we do not claim that this is necessarily the right or the only way to conceive of prayer, but we do believe that these ideas should stimulate readers either to test their own formulations additionally or to systematically develop more powerful alternatives to guide the research process.

The Variety of Theories in the Psychology of Prayer

The Levin Scheme

Of the various models advanced by serious researchers, Levin's (1996, 2009) choice is probably the most engaging one. His conception of prayer consists of local versus nonlocal and physical versus nonphysical axes, an observation partially echoed by Breslin and Lewis in both their initial work (2008) and their more extensive follow-up study (Breslin et al., 2010). Using the two axes, Levin describes prayers as uniquely different in each of the four quadrants of his 2 × 2 typology. He insists, for example, that scientists must be willing to acknowledge the distinctly nonscientific possibility that prayer operates "as advertised" in a realm that is both nonlocal and nonphysical. Although some may argue that explanations involving invisible, unmeasurable actions of a supraphysical Deity are equivalent to no explanation at all, we have to ask whether this perspective accords with any scientific criteria. Levin's rejoinder is that science is only one particular way of knowing, and as such it carries certain limitations of its own (see Watts & Williams, 1988). Levin correctly reminds us that, no matter how deeply we are committed to some version of the scientific paradigm, such a steadfast commitment might actually represent a potential bias. Levin's call for greater awareness is a helpful contribution to the literature, but we believe it requires further theoretical backing and empirical testing in order to understand where it might take us in developing a defensible scientific psychology of prayer.

An Entrée into Communication

Other attempts to delineate the boundaries of prayer have been made by Beach and colleagues (2008a) and Lambert, Fincham, Stillman, Graham, and Beach (2010). Their studies of the effects of intentional praying resulted in a model of prayer that may be viewed in terms of communication. They assert that one of the ways prayer "works" is by shifting the attention of a couple away from themselves as individuals and toward their partner; in that way, prayer recontextualizes the relationship as other-centered. This approach is wholly in accord with Baesler's (2003) "Relational Prayer Model," which points in much the same direction. Baesler's first few chapters cast prayer in a formal communications model, complete with senders and receivers of messages. This approach includes a heavy emphasis on the context in which prayer occurs (whether in small or large groups). Baesler also insists that prayer is best studied while it is being engaged in. This creates a less reductionistic impression that concurs with Levin's call to leave room for purely transcendent mechanisms. What the latter are "scientifically" remains undefined.

Characteristics of and Contexts for Prayer

Both Bänziger and colleagues (2008) and Janssen and colleagues (1990) have referenced the multiple features of prayer, as praying involves both bodily action and language. For instance, they are concerned with the direction, time, and place of prayer as well as how it addresses need, coordinates action, and has some manifest effect. In so doing, they effectively agree with Baesler's (2003) insistence that prayer is best studied in situ as opposed to ex situ. Janssen and colleagues' work explores the nature and function of prayer in a predominately secular country (the Netherlands), producing findings that mirror those of others in a less secular setting such as the United States. Contexts may vary greatly and should always be taken into account.

Back to the Pray-er: Self and Personality

Our own work (Ladd & Spilka, 2002, 2006) has sought to integrate three lines of thinking. First, we adopted the classic ideas advanced by William James (1902/1985), who viewed prayer as a way of establishing a broader sense of the self's role in the universe. Second, we accepted the position of Anna Louise Strong (1909), who in the first book devoted to the psychology of prayer described the discipline as a social activity. Third, we perceived that James's (1907) early formulations and framework could be instrumental in coordinating these and other topics. Although Leuba (1907, 1912) originally presented his ideas as a guide to the psychology of religion in general, they are particularly helpful in dealing specifically with prayer. Four components are critical for Leuba: motivations, conceptual understandings, practices, and results. James's pragmatism speaks to motivation and cognition, while Strong's functionalism emphasizes the practice aspect of prayer. Since in this volume we have attempted a broad survey of empirical materials in order to explore the underlying concepts and subsequent outcomes related to prayer, we believe that Leuba's concerns and emphases have been covered. The final and continuing task is to assemble these pieces into a coherent whole.

We contend that prayer is an attempt to establish or maintain a sense of connectivity with the self, others, and the supraphysical (Ladd & McIntosh, 2008). This permits one to explore the quadrants suggested by Levin (1996), the communication perspective provided by Baesler (2003), and the various dimensions described by Janssen and colleagues (1990; Bänziger et al., 2008).

Particularly in American society, not only are people encouraged to pray about content relevant to the three directions just cited (self, others, the supraphysical), but also they do so normally. Prayer, however, takes place in real contexts, not hypothetical ones; hence, the classic theological directions for prayer have to be relevant to context-specific themes. Three relatively consistent motivational constructs that help us think about the psychological role of praying have been identified: (1) mutual internal concerns (the self–other relationship), (2) the embracing paradox (e.g., "The first shall be last," "Why do bad things happen to good people?"), and (3) bold assertion (challenging the status quo).

First, a theme centering on mutual internal concerns of both the self and others describes praying in which individuals try to perceive their own personal condition as an avenue to understanding the inner life of other people. The goal, in a cognitive sense, is to find out how to connect with others through self-reflection.

The second way of combining directions suggests that people turn to prayer in order to embrace paradoxes of faith such as the simultaneous experience of prayer as inclusive of both turmoil and relief. It is not necessary that practitioners believe that prayer will eradicate all their problems, but they do find in prayer at least some respite from life's most pressing issues and, of course, an enhanced sense of personal control. A portion of the motivation to pray is that the process can represent a kind of "offloading" troublesome matters in the form of "turning them over to God." This is psychologically relevant because it reduces one's overall cognitive load. When a situation becomes intractable, it lessens one's ability to think flexibly and induces a state of cognitive exhaustion, as described by Sedek and colleagues (Sedek & Kofta, 1990; Sedek, Kofta, & Tyszka, 1993). This depletion of mental energy exacerbates whatever dilemma the person may be facing. With prayer, one is more or less able to isolate the disturbing component and hopefully remove it from consideration, at least temporarily, allowing for psychological rejuvenation.

Less common but nonetheless important is a third practical impetus for praying: bold assertion. For example, one may feel unfairly treated and thus take up that complaint through prayer. These prayers possess a sense of entitlement; it takes a strong-willed individual to challenge the manner in which their omnipotent Deity operates. Conceivably, prayers of this sort fall along a continuum from a healthy self-regard to a not-so-healthy narcissism.

Over a number of investigations we have been able to see how these approaches to prayer align with personality traits (Ladd, Ladd, Harner, 2007), character development (Ladd, Ladd, Ashbaugh, 2007), issues of health (M. L. Ladd, Cook, Becker, & Ladd, 2009), physiological ramifications (Ladd & McIntosh, 2008; Ladd & Ladd, 2010), forgiveness and theodicy (Ladd, Hvidt, & Ladd, 2007), and other variables. Some of this work has been directed toward establishing the convergent and divergent validity of pertinent measures (Ladd & Spilka, 2006). Other research projects have employed experimental or quasi-experimental designs (Ladd et al., in press; Ladd & Ladd, 2010) to handle causal links. Although certain approaches to the research suggest a common consensus, questions may be posed about the adequacy of models for the practice of prayer. Much of what currently exists in the literature is documented here, including the foregoing models. The focus is either on the content or function of prayer or the failure to capture the fullness of prayer activity. The difficulty in considering content is that the words and phrases used in prayer do not necessarily shed light on why they were selected. Beyond these concerns, the overall social context, as noted long ago by Strong (1909), is an additional influence that must be taken into account.

The premise that prayer occurs in response to needs of some sort (e.g., Strong, 1909) is not fully compelling, for while it reflects people's actual experiences, it cannot tell us why these needs generate a prayer response as opposed to some other form of behavior. We could trace backwards from behavior to intentional decision in standard social-psychological fashion, but the answer is often based on social learning constructs; that is, people pray because they think it works, and they believe it works as well as it does simply because they prayed. If one engages in a particular activity, the person must think he is capable of justifying it logically—a basic premise underlying cognitive dissonance.

What is needed is a way of thinking about prayer that does not border on circular reasoning and captures both "why" and "how" aspects in a manner that is not reductionist. To fill this need, we have come to think of prayer in terms of its relation to a Platonic understanding of human nature (Book 4, *The Republic*; Lorenz, 2008). In Plato's text, the force driving human thought and action (the soul, broadly conceived) consists of three components: passion, rationality, and spirit. The first characterizes base features needed to perpetuate control, well-being, and survival. The second represents a reflective component that is somewhat of a luxury, presupposing adequate time and interest to engage in the task. The third element expresses a sense of discipline and honor that variously supports passion or reason, depending on the situation.

People are not just motivated by needs originating in these three interwoven factors. This is similar to the proposition of Strong (1909) as well as Janssen and colleagues (1990), but neither takes us inexorably to an understanding of why prayer might be the specified response. One way to make the connection is to consider that any response is heavily dependent on how the individual perceives the surrounding environment.

Drawing on recent work in cognitive science (for summaries, see Barrett, 2004; Tremlin, 2006), one may contend that humans normally see events not only as they actually transpire but also as they are colored with one's needs and biases. In addition, people have an equally natural tendency to infer patterns of intentionality in dealing with ambiguous stimuli (Epley, Akalis, Waytz, & Cacioppo, 2008; Guthrie, 1993). This tendency is, of course, reminiscent of earlier

Gestalt psychological propositions or even older systems that articulated ways in which human beliefs are both helped and hindered by malleable perceptions.

One interpretation suggests that the perception of mysteriously operating unseen agents can lead quite naturally to postulating the existence of "spirits" or "gods" in the world (Boyer, 2001; McCauley & Lawson, 2002). This suggests that when needs motivate people to action, whether mental or physical, they will employ solutions of either a tangible or intangible nature. In other words, if there are visible and invisible options for problem solving, it makes sense to avail oneself of both modes with the expectation that one or the other may meet with success. Searches occurring simultaneously at these two levels address the lingering question inherent in Janssen and colleagues' (1990) model by specifying that prayer is generated as part of a "package" response to perceived needs, whatever their features. Anna Louise Strong (1909) cogently argued this point over a century ago. What she did not have access to were cognitive psychology data that could support her well-honed intuition.

Prayer, then, could be propagated among people as a default condition of information seeking alongside naturalistic endeavors. While this model explains prayers in private and spontaneous contexts fairly well, it does not satisfy the emphases of Baesler (2003) or Beach and colleagues (2008a) regarding the social facets of praying. Why should such behavior continue in highly social contexts? Others have argued that prayer persists socially because it helps form a "common moral community" (Azar, 2010, p. 56) or similar types of social support. We consider the likelihood that the mechanism may simply be part of the human condition.

Mimicry Theory

What we might term "mimicry theory" possesses evolutionary–genetic potential. Still, on the assessable level of behavior with its motivational and cognitive potential, it merits consideration for future research.

Lakin, Jefferis, Cheng, and Chartrand (2003) propose that the process of spontaneous imitation of the behavior of others works to augment group cohesion. Since there are clear benefits such as safety and the sharing of resources within groups, it is advantageous to belong; learning and imitating the activities of members is a way of increasing the odds of acceptance. Again, this idea was offered by Strong (1909); what we are adding is new only in the sense of assimilating more recent developments in the literature that validate her keen insights.

Cursory observation reveals that there is a large amount of mimicked behavior inherent in prayer sessions (Lakin et al., 2003). Often this imitative behavior is initiated by a leader, whether official or ad hoc, but the replication of action often appears spontaneous. This implies that prayer behavior in group settings can persist on the basis of its mimetic power to facilitate social cohesion and signal in-group or out-group status. Even if any given individual has doubts concerning prayer's ability to provide information helpful to navigate the shoals of life, that person's impetus to sustain social benefits may be strong enough to perpetuate the behavior. Justification of this action, in all likelihood, would be post hoc. The principle of intermittent or partial reinforcement suggests that if, during the course of this group-motivated responsivity, a single instance of prayer provides high-quality information, then the practice may continue on its own merits. Supplemented as it is by group-level social reinforcement, it can gain additional motivational strength. Once begun, such praying may carry with it physiologically rewarding side effects (Ladd & McIntosh, 2008). To the extent that prayer has these unintended positive ramifications, it should continue, even during periods when it is not perceived as being especially helpful or appropriate with regard to the amount and kind of information obtained. The danger here is that Levin's (1996) point concerning the avoidance of reductionism could be lost, but such a limitation may simply be unnecessary.

Attribution Theory

It is surprising that attribution theory and concepts (Spilka et al., 1985) have been so little used in prayer research. Appeals to either physical or supraphysical entities (the latter corresponding to prayer) are fundamentally attempts to discern meaning, establish control, or heighten esteem. These outcomes may seem rather far removed from the immediacy of prayerful actions. Meaning, control, and esteem are higher-order activation constructs that for prayer circumstances imply reflection even though the prayer itself may appear to be a habitual response. To pray implies conscious or unconscious evaluation of oneself, and also the reasons for, and the object of, prayer.

Schieman and colleagues (2010) asked whether the pray-er matters to God (see Chapter 5). This judgment requires both self and deity assessment. "Mattering" is an aspect of meaning that reflects the degree of control the supplicant feels when praying, possibly in general or simply in a specific prayer situation. This sense of control moreover mirrors the value one places on the self. That extensive attributional analyses of prayer have not yet been forthcoming leaves a considerable gap in our understanding of the what, how, and why of prayer.

Coping and Attribution

Designating prayer as a coping strategy involves attribution. Different forms of prayer imply variety in self, God, and process attributions. On one level prayer is a mechanism. Its activation takes us back to the necessity of meeting needs. Felt needs cause the person to explore both self and environment, evaluating available resources (i.e., a primary appraisal; see Lazarus & Folkman, 1984). Note how the deferring, collaborative, and self-directive coping modes of Pargament and colleagues (1988) make attributions to self, the situation, and the Deity.

The role of prayer, then, is not exclusively coping per se but also includes the additional role of facilitating the search for adequate coping mechanisms. The one who starts to pray is in the midst of a quest: How do I connect to this particular event or feeling? How do I articulate my situation? What we are contending is that prayer is so often referred to as the quintessential act of faith because it represents an early step toward gathering information about how best to respond to life. It may also serve as a final step, after which the pray-er awaits an answer.

DESIGN AND ANALYSIS
CONSIDERATIONS AND QUESTIONS

The Problematic Aspect

Science demands rigorous conceptualizations of problems and the impersonal application of methods to whatever is studied. This observation holds for both the passionate religionist and the skeptical challenger. Feelings must be held in check during all phases of the scientific process. These phases should typically begin with theory and are most likely to end with numbers. Unhappily, this course is not without its problems.

Issues in Design and Analysis

In essence, research is shaped by theory and the language selected, and the hypotheses formulated may be subtly affected by unexamined preconceptions. Much of the work cited here on prayer may be challenged at every level—in the selection of samples, information collection, presentation of the data, analyses conducted, and finally the interpretations offered. Unfortunately, shortcomings are not difficult to find. For example, categories may be devised and percentages within these supplied without, however, providing a solid grasp of the data. To illustrate, a "low," "medium," and "high" breakdown does not indicate why three as opposed to four or two groups were chosen. Such group cutoff points may also pose important issues. Without more explicit information, readers may wonder about the degree to which inferences reflect the personal dispositions of the researchers. Qualitative studies are equally if not even more prone to raise such questions.

Statistics and Data Analysis[2]

Alhough we do not intend to write a volume on research design and statistics, we cannot avoid some obvious problems students of prayer have repeatedly confronted and overwhelmingly ignored.

Statistics may create as much ambiguity as they alleviate. One is not required to go as far as Earnest Rutherford, who is often credited with saying that if an experiment needs statistics you need a better experiment.[3] Cobb (1990), however, reminds us that Nobel prize–winning material is often backed by simple statistics. Our data require statistics, but throughout this volume, regardless of the complexity of analysis, many findings are technically supportive of hypotheses at a borderline level without connoting any practical or meaningful significance.[4] Although some researchers have been tentative in their inferences, many, if not most, have exercised too little caution. In addition, where .05 or .01 indices usually end the treatment of data, consideration might be productively given to taking additional steps. These probabilities often seem to have acquired a semisacred quality when, as Cohen (1990) has indicated, "All this means is that the effect is not nil and nothing more" (p. 1307).[5] Instead of responding as if the necessary information has been provided, the researcher might, at that point, be better advised to begin further meaningful treatment of the data. We would therefore like to recommend an important and highly enlightening paper by Jacob Cohen that addresses common shortcomings found in so many of the studies cited in this volume.

In accordance with the demands made by journal editors for positive results, the majority of the studies reported findings that accorded with a constructive role for prayer. Indications of only weak effects, however, were commonly reported, along with relatively low correlations or regression coefficients when such were employed; thus, while there may be slight statistical differences, substantive ones are generally not apparent. In addition, while large samples were frequently collected, replication that could be quite easily accomplished by randomly splitting such samples was rarely performed. Nelson, Rosenthal, and Rosnow (1986) pointed out that, even though psychologists "place greater confidence in results from larger samples . . . and successful replication" (p. 1300), there are additional considerations. Replication, of course, poses a number of problems, chiefly among them the erosion of noteworthy findings over time (Lehrer, 2010). Nonetheless, researchers should split large initial random samples whenever possible to extract more information.

Despite such concerns, the importance of replication has gained official recognition in psychology through a new organization, the Open Science Collaboration, which is attempting "to systematically replicate psychological experiments recently published in leading journals" (Carpenter, 2012).

The Fisher Heritage

Tradition in data analysis has emphasized Fisher's approach of seeking statistical significance at the .05 or .01 level. Usually these levels are equated by researchers as the minimum threshold for "good" findings. Apparently, Fisher originally selected these points based on their convenience (Rosenthal, Rosnow, & Rubin, 2000). When large samples are employed, t- or F-tests and correlation coefficients utilizing these levels must be examined with caution. For instance, Francis and Robbins (2008) utilized 1,476 respondents to assess relationships between Jungian approaches to personality and also to prayer. With this sizable sample, coefficients significant at the .05 level can be as low as .051. While statistically suggestive, a correlation of .051 explains less than one-half of one percent of the variance, making its practical meaning ambiguous. Large samples have both advantages and disadvantages. Most researchers will opt for large samples over small ones, for they increase the power of the statistical tests. While the additional power helps avoid a Type I error, overemphasizing power only augments the probability of a Type II error. With enough power, every difference will appear statistically significant; without enough power, every difference will be nonsignificant. Clearly, neither extreme is helpful, and employing power analyses prior to designing and executing studies is one way to address the issue.

Many of the studies cited in this volume compare experimental and control groups or contrast different groups in cross-sectional designs. The resulting t's or F's are again judged relative to the .05 or .01 level of significance. What we really need to know is the size of an observed effect, the magnitude of the finding that the .05 or .01 level of significance signifies. Cohen (1990) notes that it is "ridiculous to try to develop theories about human behavior with p values from Fisherian hypothesis testing (with) no more than a primitive sense of effect size" (p. 1309). This tells us what our result means in a potentially practical or applied sense. As we have repeatedly noted, particularly with large samples, the outcome frequently appears minimal. The larger the effect, the greater the power of our test and the more likely we have rejected a false hypothesis (Cohen, 1977; Cohen & Cohen, 1983). We strongly recommend that scholars in the psychology of prayer take this next step and follow the extensive guidelines of the APA Task Force concerned with this topic (Wilkinson & American Psychological Association, Task Force on Statistical Inference, 1999). These guidelines cover far more territory than we can here. The general message we would like to convey is that research ingenuity is not limited to theory construction and research design but also extends to the statistical procedures we employ to answer questions in this field. In sum, we agree with Cohen (1990) that "failure to subject your research plans to power analysis is simply irrational" (p. 1310).

SUMMARY

There can be no question about the existence of serious gaps in the psychology of prayer. Some of these likely derive from selective and incomplete examination of the mainstream literature for cues and directions that might be applied to the study of prayer. We have only touched on a few of these. Particular attention has been directed toward the labors of some scholars who have produced work that is theoretically and methodologically noteworthy.

In part, because of the immense amount of research in contemporary psychology and the rapidity with which modern-day psychologists of religion are emulating mainstream emphases and productivity, we approached prayer from many different vantage points. Our position is that prayer is practiced because it establishes a broad and satisfying range of coping resources, stretching from the basic biological level to perceived supraphysical ones. The conceptual structure of this field is best understood in terms of the basic directions and themes of prayer. This emphasis includes a central component of mimicry that facilitates the social aspects of prayer. Conscious and unconscious attributions, usually unanalyzed, structure the comprehension and utilization of prayer and represent a rich potential for future research. We strongly recommend that readers take note of Baesler's (2003) formulations regarding communication, as his well-conceptualized theoretical approach presents a wealth of future research possibilities.

Finally, we note that efficacy for those who pray is a question asked and answered in the supraphysical realm as it is conceived by the pray-er. Scientific investigations of prayer should take seriously prayer's theological underpinnings, as these may be a source for theory and hypotheses regarding the nature and practice of prayer. Of all the possible individual and group religious expressions, prayer is truly the *action* dimension. The complexity of belief and experience cannot match this pattern of behavioral expression. It is, in an important sense, a rich end point that merits a full appreciation of its motivational, cognitive, and social underpinnings. The study of these is a daunting task for present and future researchers.

Our viewpoint has, however, helped uncover a variety of theory-oriented research possibilities in the various domains surveyed. We hope these efforts will provide a starting point for others to take up the many research opportunities suggested throughout this volume.

NOTES

1. The brief background information contained in the Directory of the American Psychological Association reveals the religious training and experience of many members as well as their current and/or former job affiliations with religious organizations.
2. This section is written for the researcher and may be more technical than other readers wish to deal with.
3. Numerous times in the preceding chapters we have noted that studies yielded only extremely low correlations that suggested meaningfulness. Squaring the correlation coefficient indicates the proportion of variance accounted for, and the larger the proportion, the better the predictability of the correlation. With a very large sample, a low coefficient may result in a trivial reduction in variance.
4. Unless otherwise specified, in the great majority of cases we are dealing with linear relationships. Examination of the graph from which the coefficient is computed may suggest that the relationship is curvilinear and that the association in question is therefore slightly stronger than originally believed.
5. This statement is widely attributed to British physicist/chemist Ernest Rutherford, though its original source is unknown. Here it is retrieved from *http://thinkexist.com/quotation/if_your_experiment_needs_statistics-you_ought_to/338030.html.*

References

Abramowitz, L. (1993). Prayer as therapy among the frail Jewish elderly. *Journal of Gerontological Social Work, 19*(3/4), 69–75.

Acevedo, G. A. (2010). Collective rituals or private practice in Texas: Assessing the impact of religious factors on mental health. *Review of Religious Research, 52*, 188–206.

Achterberg, J., Dossey, B., & Kolkmeier, L. (1994). *Rituals of healing: Using imagery for health and wellness.* New York: Bantam Books.

Adams, T. (2008). Impact of prayer on the relationship between supervisory support and employee's perception of workplace equity. *Emerging Leadership Journeys, 1*, 3–13.

Ai, A. L., Bolling, S. F., & Peterson, C. (2000). The use of prayer by coronary artery bypass patients. *International Journal for the Psychology of Religion, 10*, 205–219.

Ai, A. L., Dunkle, R. E., Peterson, C., & Bolling, S. F. (1998). The role of private prayer in psychological recovery among midlife and aged patients following cardiac surgery. *The Gerontologist, 38*, 591–691.

Ai, A. L., Dunkle, R. E., Peterson, C., & Bolling, S. F. (2000). Spiritual well-being, private prayer, and adjustment of older cardiac patients. In J. A. Thorson (Ed.), *Perspectives on spiritual well-being and aging* (pp. 98–119). Springfield, IL: Charles C Thomas.

Ai, A. L., Ladd, K. L., Peterson, C., Cook, C. A., Shearer, M., & Koenig, H. G. (2010). Long-term adjustment after surviving open heart surgery: The effect of using prayer for coping replicated in a prospective design. *The Gerontologist, 50*(6), 798–809.

Ai, A. L., Peterson, C., Bolling, S. F., & Rodgers, W. (2006). Depression, faith-based coping, and short-term functioning in adult and older patients undergoing cardiac surgery. *Journal of Psychosomatic Research, 60*, 21–28.

Ai, A. L., Peterson, C., Rodgers, W. L., & Tice, T. N. (2005). Faith factors and internal locus of control in patients prior to open-heart surgery. *Journal of Health Psychology, 10,* 669–676.

Ai, A. L., Peterson, C., Saunders, D. G., Bolling, S. F., & Dunkle, R. E. (1996, August). *Psychosocial adjustment and health care practices following CABG (coronary artery graft bypass surgery).* Poster session paper presented at the annual meeting of the American Psychological Association, Toronto.

Ai, A. L., Peterson, C., Tice, T. N., Huang, B., Rodgers, W., & Bolling, S. F. (2007). The influence of prayer coping on mental health among cardiac surgery patients: The role of optimism and acute distress. *Journal of Health Psychology, 12,* 580–596.

Ali, S., & Rouse, A. (2002). Practice audits: Reliability of sphygmomanometers and blood pressure recording bias. *Hypertension, 16,* 359–361.

Alexander, C. N., Schneider, R. H., Staggers, F., Sheppard, W., Clayborne, B. M., Raingorth, M., et al. (1996). Trial of stress reduction for hypertension in older African Americans: II. Sex and risk subgroup analysis. *Hypertension, 28,* 228–237.

Al-Kandari, Y. Y. (2003). Religiosity and its relation to blood pressure among selected Kuwaitis. *Journal of Biosocial Science, 35,* 463–472.

Alvarado, K. A., Templer, D. I., Bresler, C., & Thomas-Dobbins, S. (1995). The relationship of religious variables to death depression and death anxiety. *Journal of Clinical Psychology, 51,* 202–204.

Ameling, A. (2000). Prayer: An ancient healing practice becomes new again. *Holistic Nursing, 14*(3), 40–48.

American Psychological Association. (2008, October 7). Stress in America. Retrieved from *www.apa.org/news/press/releases/2008/10/stress-in-america.pdf.*

Andersson, G. (2008). Chronic pain and praying to a higher power: Useful or useless. *Journal of Religion and Health, 47,* 176–187.

Andresen, J. (2000). Meditation meets behavioral medicine. *Journal of Consciousness Studies, 7,* 17–73.

Antoni, M. H., Cruess, S., Cruess, D. G., Kumar, M., Lutgendorf, S., Ironson, G., et al. (2000). Cognitive-behavioral stress management reduces distress and 24-hour urinary free cortisol output among symptomatic HIV infected gay men. *Annals of Behavioral Medicine, 22,* 29–37.

Antoni, M. H., Ironson, G., & Schneiderman, N. (2007). *Cognitive-behavioral stress management for individuals living with HIV.* New York: Oxford University Press.

Argyle, M., & Beit-Hallahmi, B. (1975). *The social psychology of religion.* London: Routledge & Kegan Paul.

Arredondo, J. (1978, December). *La salud mental de la raza: Curanderas and mental health centers in two Mexican-American communities.* Unpublished doctoral dissertation, University of Denver.

Ashby, J. S., & Lenhart, R. S. (1994). Prayer as a coping strategy for chronic pain patients. *Rehabilitation Psychology, 39*, 205–209.

Astin, J. A. (1998). Why patients use alternative medicine: Results of a national study. *Journal of the American Medical Association, 279*, 1548–1553.

Astin, J. A., Harkness, E., & Ernst, E. (2000). The efficacy of distant healing: A systematic review of randomized trials. *Annals of Internal Medicine, 132*, 903–910.

Atran, S. (2002). *In Gods we trust.* New York: Oxford University Press.

Atran, S., & Norenzayan, A. (2004). Religion's evolutionary landscape: Counterintuition, commitment, compassion, communion. *Behavioral and Brain Sciences, 27*, 713–770.

Aviles, J. M., Whelan, S. E., Hernke, D. A., Williams, B. A., Kenny, K. E., O'Fallon, W. M., et al. (2001). Intercessory prayer and cardiovascular disease progression in a coronary care unit population: A randomized controlled trial. *Mayo Clinic Proceedings, 76*, 1192–1198.

Azar, B. (2010, December). A reason to believe. *Monitor on Psychology*, pp. 52–56.

Bade, M. K., & Cook, S. W. (2008). Functions of Christian prayer in the coping process. *Journal for the Scientific Study of Religion, 47*, 123–133.

Bader, C., Dougherty, K., Froese, P., Johnson, B., Mencken, F. C., Park, J. Z., et al. (2006). *American piety in the 21st century: New insights to the depth and complexity of religion in the U.S.* Waco, TX: Baylor University Institute for Studies of Religion.

Baesler, E. J. (2003). *Theoretical explorations and empirical investigations of communication and prayer.* Lewiston, NY: Edwin Mellen Press.

Bailey, R. H., Knaus, V. L., & Bauer, J. H. (1991). Aneroid sphygmomanometers: An assessment of accuracy at a university hospital. *Archives of Internal Medicine, 151*, 1409–1412.

Ballantyne, C. (2009, March 16). Can traffic up your heart attack risk? Retrieved from *www.scientificamerican.com/blog/post.cfm?id=traffic-triggers-heart-attacks-2009-03-13.*

Bänziger, S., Janssen, J., & Scheepers, P. (2008). Praying in a secularized society: An empirical study of praying practices and varieties of prayer. *International Journal for the Psychology of Religion, 18*, 256–265.

Bänziger, S., Van Uden, M., & Janssen, J. (2008). Praying and coping: The relation between varieties of praying and religious coping styles. *Mental Health, Religion, and Culture, 1*, 101–118.

Barclay, L., & Vega, C. (2006). American Heart Association updates: Recommendation for blood pressure measurements. Retrieved from *www.medscape.com/viewarticle/496270.*

Barclay, W. (1962). *A guide to daily prayer.* New York: Harper & Row.

Barefoot, J. C., Brummett, B. H., Williams, R. B., Siegler, I. C., Helms, M. J., Boyle, S. H., et al. (2011). Recovery expectations and long-term prognosis of patients with coronary heart disease. *Archives of Internal Medicine, 171*(10), 929–935.

Barnes, P. M., Powell-Griner, E., McFann, K., & Nahin, R. L. (2004). Complementary and alternative medicine use among adults: United States. *Seminars in Integrative Medicine, 2*, 54–71.

Barrett, J. L. (2001). How ordinary cognition informs petitionary prayer. *Journal of Cognition and Culture, 1*, 259–269.

Barrett, J. L. (2004). *Why would anyone believe in God?* Walnut Creek, CA: Altamira Press.

Barrett, J. L., & Keil, F. C. (1996). Conceptualizing a nonnatural entity: Anthropomorphism in God concepts. *Cognitive Psychology, 31*, 219–247.

Barrett, J. L., & Lawson, E. T. (2001). Ritual intuitions: Cognitive contributions to judgments of ritual efficacy. *Journal of Cognition and Culture, 1*, 183–201.

Barrett, J. L., & Malley, B. (2007). A cognitive typology of religious actions. *Journal of Cognition and Culture, 7*, 201–211.

Barrett, J. L., & Van Orman, B. (2009). The effect of image use in worship on God's concepts. *Journal of Psychology and Christianity, 15*, 38–45.

Batson, C. D., Schoenrade, P., & Ventis, W. L. (1993). *Religion and the individual.* New York: Oxford University Press.

Beach, S. R. H., Fincham, F. D., Hurt, T. R., McNair, L. M., & Stanley, S. M. (2008a). Prayer and marital intervention: A conceptual framework. *Journal of Social and Clinical Psychology, 27*, 641–669.

Beach, S. R. H., Fincham, F. D., Hurt, T. R., McNair, L. M., & Stanley, S. M. (2008b). Prayer and marital intervention: Toward an open, empirically-grounded dialogue. *Journal of Social and Clinical Psychology, 27*, 693–710.

Beck, F. O. (1906). Prayer: A study in its history and psychology. *American Journal of Religious Psychology and Education, 2*, 107–121.

Beckman, R. J. (1995). *Prayer: Beginning conversations with God.* Minneapolis, MN: Augsburg

Beevers, G., Lip, G. Y. H., & O'Brien, E. (2001). Methods of blood pressure measurement. *British Medical Journal, 322*, 981–985.

Bell, R. A., Suerken, C., Quandt, S. A., Grzywacz, J. G. Lang, W., & Acury, T. A. (2005). Prayer for health among U.S. adults. *Complementary Health Practices Review, 10*, 175–188.

Bender, C. (2008). How does God answer back? *Poetics, 36*, 476–492.

Benson, H. (1975). *The relaxation response.* New York: William Morrow.

Benson, H., Dusek, J. A., Sherwood, J. B., Lam, P., Bethea, C. F., Carpenter, W., et al. (2006). Study of the Therapeutic Effects of Intercessory Prayer (STEP) in cardiac bypass patients: A multicenter randomized trial of uncertainty and certainty of receiving intercessory prayer. *American Heart Journal, 151*, 934–942.

Berk, L. E. (1993). *Infants, children, and adolescents*. Boston: Allyn & Bacon.

Berkowitz, L. (1978). *Cognitive theories in social psychology*. New York: Academic Press.

Bill-Harvey, D., Rippey, R. M., Abeles, M., & Pfeiffer, C. A.(1989). Methods used by urban, low-income minorities to care for their arthritis. *Arthritis Care and Research, 2*, 60–64.

Blumenthal, J. A., Babyak, M. A., Ironson, G., Thoresen, C., Powell, L., Czajkowski, S., et al. (2007). Spirituality, religion, and clinical outcomes in patients recovering from an acute myocardial infarction. *Psychosomatic Medicine, 69*, 502–508.

Bouchard, T. J., Jr. (2004). Genetic influence on human psychological traits: A survey. *Psychological Science, 13*, 148–151.

Bower, G. H., & Hilgard, E. R. (1981). *Theories of learning* (5th ed.). Englewood Cliffs, NJ: Prentice-Hall.

Bowne, B. P. (1910). *The essence of religion*. Boston: Houghton Mifflin.

Boyer, P. (2001). *Religion explained*. New York: Basic Books.

Boyer, P. (2003). Religious thought and behavior as by-products of brain function. *Trends in Cognitive Science, 7*, 119–124.

Bradshaw, M., Ellison, C. G., & Flannelly, K. J. (2008). Prayer, God imagery, and symptoms of psychopathology. *Journal for the Scientific Study of Religion, 47*, 644–659.

Bremner, R. H., Koole, S. L., & Bushman, B. J. (2011). "Pray for those who mistreat you": Effects of prayer on anger and aggression. *Personality and Social Psychology Bulletin, 37*, 830–837.

Breslin, M. J., & Lewis, C. A. (2008). Theoretical models of the nature of prayer and health: A review. *Mental Health, Religion, and Culture, 11*(1), 9–21.

Breslin, M. J., Lewis, C. A., & Shevlin, A. (2010). A psychometric evaluation of Poloma and Pendleton's (1991) and Ladd and Spilka's (2002, 2006) measures of prayer. *Journal for the Scientific Study of Religion, 49*, 710–723.

Brown, L. B. (1966). Egocentric thought in petitionary prayer: A cross-cultural study. *Journal of Social Psychology, 68*, 197–210.

Brown, L. B. (1968). Some attitudes underlying petitionary prayer. In A. Godin (Ed.), *From cry to word* (pp. 65–84). Brussels, Belgium: Lumen Vitae Press.

Brown, L. B. (1987). *The psychology of religious belief*. London: Academic Press.

Brown, L. B. (1994). *The human side of prayer*. Birmingham, AL: Religious Education Press.

Browning, R. (1895). Pippa passes. In H. E. Scudder (Ed.), *The complete poetical works of Browning*. Cambridge, MA: Riverside Press. (Original work published 1841)

Brummett, B. H., Barefoot, J. C., Siegler, I. C., Clapp-Channing, N. E.,

Lytle, B. L., Bosworth, H. B., et al. (2001). Characteristics of socially isolated patients with coronary artery disease at elevated risk for mortality. *Psychosomatic Medicine, 63*, 273–274.

Buck, A. C., Williams, D. R., Musick, M. A., & Sternthal, M. J. (2009). An examination of the relationship between multiple dimensions of religiosity, blood pressure, and hypertension. *Social Science and Medicine, 68*, 314–322.

Bukato, D., & Daehler, M. W. (1992). *Child development*. Boston: Houghton Mifflin.

Burazeri, G., Goda, A., & Kark, J. D. (2008). Religious observance and acute coronary syndrome in predominantly Muslim Albania: A population-based case-control study in Tirana. *Annals of Epidemiology, 18*, 937–945.

Burke, M. J., Towers, H. M., O'Malley, Fitzgerald, D. J., & O'Brien, E. T. (1982). Sphygmomanometers in hospital and family practice: Problems and recommendations. *British Medical Journal, 285*, 469–471.

Butler, M. H., Gardner, B. C., & Bird, M. H. (1998). Not just a time-out: Change dynamics of prayer for religious couples in conflict situations. *Family Process, 37*, 451–475.

Butler, M. H., & Harper, J. M. (1994). The divine triangle: Deity in the marital system of religious couples. *Family Process, 33*, 277–286.

Butler, M. H., Stout, J. A., & Gardner, B. C. (2002). Prayer as a conflict resolution ritual: Clinical implications of a religious couples' report of relationship softening, healing perspective, and change responsibility. *The American Journal of Family Therapy, 30*, 19–37.

Buttrick, G. A. (1942). *Prayer*. New York: Abingdon-Cokesbury.

Buttrick, G. A. (1970). *The power of prayer today*. New York: World.

Byrd, R. C. (1988). Positive therapeutic effects of intercessory prayer in a coronary care unit population. *Southern Medical Journal, 81*, 826–829.

Cabrol, R. P. D. F. (1900). *Le livre de la prière antique*. Paris: Librairie Réligieuse H. Oudin.

Calkins, M. W. (1911). The nature of prayer. *Harvard Theological Review, 4*, 489–500.

Canter, P. M. (2003). The therapeutic effects of meditation. *British Medical Journal, 326*, 1049–1050.

Canzanello, V. J., Jensen, P. L., & Schwartz, G. I. (2001). Are aneroid sphygmomanometers accurate in hospital and clinic settings? *Archives of Internal Medicine, 161*, 729–731.

Capps, D. (1982). The psychology of petitionary prayer. *Theology Today, 39*, 130–141.

Carlson, C. R., Bacaseta, P. E., & Simanton, D. A. (1988). A controlled evaluation of devotional meditation and progressive relaxation. *Journal of Psychology and Theology, 16*, 362–368.

Carlson, C. R., Friedman, S., & Spilka, B. (1991). *The structure of prayer and well-being.* Paper presented at the annual meeting of the Rocky Mountain Psychological Association, Denver, CO.

Carney, R. M., Rich, M. W., Freedland, K. E., Saini, J., teVelde, A., Simeone, C., et al. (1988). Major depressive disorder predicts cardiac events in patients with coronary artery disease. *Psychosomatic Medicine, 50,* 627–633.

Carney, S. I., Gillies, A., Green, S. I., Patterson, O., Taylor, M. S., & Smith, A. J. (2002). Hospital blood pressure measurement: Staff and device assessment. *Journal of Quality in Clinical Practice, 19*(2), 95–98.

Carpenter, S. (2012). Psychology's bold initiative. *Science, 335,* 1558–1561.

Carroll, S. B. (2005). *Endless forms most beautiful.* New York: Norton.

Carson, V. B. (1993). Prayer, meditation, exercise, and special diets: Behaviors of the hardy person with HIV/AIDS. *Journal of the Association of Nurses in AIDS Care, 4,* 18–28.

Carson, V. B., & Green, H. (1992). Spiritual well being: A predictor of hardiness in patients with Acquired Immunodeficiency Syndrome. *Journal of Professional Nursing, 8,* 209–220.

Carson, V. B., & Huss, K. (1979, March). Prayer—an effective therapeutic and teaching tool. *JPN and Mental Health Services, 17,* 34–37.

Cha, K. W., Wirth, D. P., & Lobo, R. A. (2001). Does prayer influence the success of in vitro fertilization–embryo transfer? *Journal of Reproductive Medicine, 46,* 781–787.

Chang, B-H., Noonan, A. E., & Tennstedt, S. L. (1998). The role of religion/spirituality in coping with caregiving for disabled elders. *The Gerontologist, 38,* 463–470.

Charney, D. S. (2004). Psychobiological mechanisms of resilience and vulnerability. *Focus, 11,* 368–391.

Childs, B. H. (1983). The possible connection between "private speech" and prayer. *Pastoral Psychology, 32,* 24–33.

Childs, E. (2010). Religious attendance and happiness: Examining gaps in the current literature—a research note. *Journal for the Scientific Study of Religion, 49,* 550–560.

Clark, W. H. (1958). *The psychology of religion.* New York: Macmillan.

Clarke, T. E. (1983). Jungian types and forms of prayer. *Review for Religious, 42,* 661–676.

Clift, W. B. (1982). *Jung and Christianity.* New York: Crossroad.

Coan, R. W. (1978). The Myers–Briggs Type Indicator. In O. K. Buros Jr. (Ed.), *The eighth mental measurements yearbook* (Vol. 1, pp. 970–975). Highland Park, NJ: Gryphon Press.

Cobb, L. (1990). Top-down research design. Retrieved from *www.aetheling.com/docs.*

Coe, G. A. (1916). *The psychology of religion.* Chicago: University of Chicago Press.

Cohen, J. (1977). *Statistical power analysis for the behavioral siences* (rev. ed.). New York: Academic Press.

Cohen, J. (1990). Things I have learned (so far). *American Psychologist, 45*, 1304–1312.

Cohen, J., & Cohen, P. (1983). *Applied multiple regression/correlation analysis for the behavioral sciences.* Hillsdale, NJ: Erlbaum.

Coleman, C. L., Holzemer, W. L., Eller, L. S., Corless, I., Reynolds, N., Nokes, K. M., et al. (2006). Gender differences in use of prayer as a self-care strategy for managing symptoms in African Americans living with HIV/AIDS. *Journal of the Association of Nurses in AIDS Care, 17*, 16–23.

Cole, B. S., & Pargament, K. I. (1999). Spiritual surrender: A paradoxical path to control. In W. R. Miller (Ed.), *Integrating spirituality into treatment* (pp. 170–198). Washington, DC: American Psychological Association.

Coles, R. (1990). *The spiritual life of children.* Boston: Houghton Mifflin.

Collipp, P. J. (1969). The efficacy of prayer: A triple-blind study. *Medical Times, 97*, 201–204.

Cook, C. A., Ladd, K. L., Ritter, E. A., Foreman, K. M., & Mertes, S. C. (2010, March). *Experimental prayer research: Contextual and content artifacts of fMRI investigations.* Paper presented at the Division 36, American Psychological Association Mid-Winter Conference on Religion and Spirituality, Columbia, MD.

Cotton, S., TseVat, J., Szaflarski, M., Kudel, I., Sherman, S. N., Feinberg, J., et al. (2006). Changes in religiousness and spirituality attributed to HIV/AIDS. *Journal of General Internal Medicine, 21*, S14–S20.

Cox, T. (1988). Psychobiological factors in stress and health. In S. Fisher & J. Reason (Eds.), *Handbook of life stress, cognition and health* (pp. 603–627). New York: Wiley.

Crocker, S. F. (1984). Prayer as a model of communication. *Pastoral Psychology, 33*, 83–92.

Cronan, T. A., Kaplan, R. M., Posner, L., Blumberg, E., & Kozin, F. (1989). Prevalence of the use of unconventional remedies for arthritis in a metropolitan community. *Arthritis and Rheumatism, 32*, 1604–1607.

Cruess, D. G., Antoni, M. H., McGregor, B. A., Kilbourn, K. M., Boyers, A. E., Aalferi, S. M., et al. (2000). Cognitive-behavioral stress management reduces serum cortisol by enhancing benefit finding among women being treated for early stage breast cancer. *Psychosomatic Medicine, 62*, 304–308.

Cummings, N., O'Donohue, W., & Cummings, J. (Eds.). (2009). *Psychology's war on religion.* Phoeniz, AZ: Zeig, Tucker & Thiesen.

Cunningham, W. R., & Brookband, J. W. (1988). *Gerontology.* New York: Harper & Row.

Curtis, B. M., & O'Keefe, J. H. (2002). Autonomic atone as a cardiovascular risk factor: The dangers of chronic fight or flight. *Mayo Clinic Proceedings, 77*, 45–54.

D'Aquili, E. G. (1978). The neurobiological bases of myth and concepts of deity. *Zygon, 13*, 257–275.

D'Aquili, E. G., & Newberg, A. B. (1999). *The mystical mind.* Minneapolis, MN: Fortress.

David, J., Ladd, K., & Spilka, B. (1992, August). *The multidimensionality of prayer and its role as a source of secondary control.* Paper presented at the annual meeting of the American Psychological Association, Washington, DC.

Deardorff, J. (2009, January 14). Doctors going alternative. Retrieved from *http://articles.chicagotribune.com/2009-01-14/news/0901130339_1_alternative-medicine-integrative-medicine-acupuncture.*

Dedert, E. A., Studts, J. L., Weissbeckera, I., Salmon, P. G., Banis, P. L., & Sephton, S. E. (2004). Religion may help preserve the cortisol rhythm in women with stress-related illness. *International Journal of Psychiatry in Medicine, 34*, 61–77.

Delany, H. D., Miller, W. R., & Bisono, A. M. (2007). Religiosity and spirituality among psychologists: A study of clinician members of the American Psychological Association. *Professional Psychology: Research and Practice, 38*, 538–546.

DeNoon, D. J. (2009, March 13). Traffic triples heart attack risk. Retrieved from *www.medicinenet.com/scripts/;main/art.asp?articlekey.*

De Vogli, R., Tarani, C., & Marmot, M. G. (2007). Negative aspects of close relationships and heart disease. *Archives of Internal Medicine, 167*, 1951–1957.

Diener, E., & Chan, M. Y. (2011). Happy people live longer: Subjective well-being contributes to health and longevity. *Applied Psychology: Health and Well Being, 3*, 1–43.

Dittes, J. E. (1969). The psychology of religion. In G. Lindzey & E. Aronson (Eds.), *The handbook of social psychology* (Vol. 5, pp. 602–659). Reading, MA: Addison-Wesley.

D'Onofrio, B., Eaves, L. J., Murrelle, L., Maes, H. H., & Spilka, B. (1999). Understanding biological and social influences on religious affiliation, attitudes, and behaviors: A behavior–genetic perspective. *Journal of Personality, 67*, 953–984.

Dossey, L. (1993). *Healing words: The power of prayer and the practice of medicine.* New York: HarperSanFrancisco.

Dossey, L. (1996). *Prayer is good medicine.* New York: HarperSanFrancisco.

Dossey, L. (1998). Prayer, medicine, and science: The new dialogue. *Journal of Health Care Chaplaincy, 7*(1–2), 7–37.

Dossey, L. (2000). Prayer and medical science: A commentary on the prayer study by Harris et al. and a response to critics. *Archives of Internal Medicine, 160*, 1735–1738.

Dossey, L., & Hufford, D. J. (2005, March). Are prayer experiments legitimate?: Twenty criticisms. *Explore, 1*(2), 109–117.

Dresser, H. W. (1929). *Outlines of the psychology of religion*. New York: Crowell.

Dubois-Dumee, J.-P. (1989). *Becoming prayer*. Boston: St. Paul Publications.

Dudley, M. G., & Kosinski, F. A. (1990). Religiosity and marital satisfaction: A research note. *Review of Religious Research, 32*, 78–86.

Dunn, K. S., & Horgas, A. L. (2000). The prevalence of prayer as a spiritual self-care modality in elders. *Journal of Holistic Nursing, 18*, 337–351.

Dusek, J. A., Sherwood, J. B., Friedman, R., Myers, P., Bethea, C. F., Levitsky, S., et al. (2002). Study of the therapeutic effects of intercessory prayer (STEP): Study design and research methods. *American Heart Journal, 143*, 577–584.

Eisdorfer, C., & Lawton, M. P. (Eds.). (1973). *The psychology of adult development and aging*. Washington, DC: American Psychological Association.

Eisenberg, D. M., Kessler, R. C., Foster, C., Norlock, F. E., Calkins, D. R., & Delbanco, T. L. (1993). Unconventional medicine in the United States—prevalence, costs, and patterns of use. *New England Journal of Medicine, 328*(4), 246–252.

Elkins, D., Anchor, K. N., & Sandler, H. M. (1979). Relaxation training and prayer behavior as tension reduction techniques. *Behavioral Engineering, 5*(3), 81–87.

Ellens, J. H. (1977). Communication theory and petitionary prayer. *Journal of Psychology and Theology, 5*, 48–54.

Eller, E. (1937). *Das Gebet: Religionspspsychologische studien*. Paderborn, Germany: Schoningh.

Ellison, C., Burdette, A. M., & Wilcox, W. B. (2010). The couple that prays together: Race and ethnicity, religion, and relationship quality among working-age adults. *Journal of Marriage and Family, 72*, 963–975.

Ellison, C. G., Boardman, J. D., Williams, D. R., & Jackson, J. S. (2001). Religious involvement, stress and mental health: Findings from the 1995 Detroit Area Study. *Social Forces, 80*, 215–249.

Ellison, C. G., & George, L. K. (1994). Religious involvement, social ties, and social support in a southeastern community. *Journal for the Scientific Study of Religion, 33*, 46–61.

Ellison, C. G., & Taylor, R. J. (1996). Turning to prayer: Social and situational antecedents of religious coping among African-Americans. *Review of Religious Research, 38*, 111–131.

Ellison, C. W., & Smith, J. (1991). Toward an integrative measure of health and well-being. *Journal of Psychology and Theology, 19*, 35–48.

Enstrom, J. E. (1989). Health practices and cancer mortality among active California Mormons. *Journal of the National Cancer Institute, 81*, 1807–1814.

Epel, E. S., Blackburn, E. H., Lin, J., Dhabnar, F. S., Adler, N. E., Morrow, J. A., et al. (2004). Accelerated telomere shortening in response to life stress. *Proceedings of the National Academy of Sciences. 101,* 17312–17315.

Epley, N., Akalis, S., Waytz, A., & Caccioppo, J. T. (2008). Creating social connection through inferential reproduction: Loneliness and perceived agency in gadgets, Gods, and greyhounds. *Psychological Science, 19,* 14–20.

Erikson, E. H. (1959). Identity and the life cycle. *Psychological Issues, 1,* Monograph 1.

Erikson, E. H. (1963). *Childhood and society.* New York: Norton.

Ernst, E. (2003). Distant healing—an "update" of a systematic review. *Wien Klin Wochenschrift, 115*(7–8), 241–245.

Eysenck, H. J., & Eysenck, S. B. G. (1975). *Manual of the Eysenck Personality Questionnaire.* London: Hodder & Stoughton.

Eysenck, H. J., & Eysenck, S. B. G. (1976). *Psychoticism as a dimension of personality.* London: Hodder & Stoughton.

Farberow, N. L. (1963). *Taboo topics.* New York: Atherton.

Fairchild, D., Roth, H., Milmoe, S., Gotthard, C., Fehrmann, L., Richards, S., et al. (1993). *God images and prayer behavior: Consonance in the psychology of religion.* Paper presented at the joint annual meeting of the Rocky Mountain and Western Psychological Associations, Phoenix, AZ.

Feher, S., & Maly, R. C. (1999). Coping with breast cancer in late life: The role of religious faith. *Psycho-Oncology, 8,* 408–416.

Feierman, J. R. (Ed.). (2009). *The biology of religious behavior.* Santa Barbara, CA: Praeger.

Festinger, L., Riecken, H. W., & Schachter, S. (1956). *When prophecy fails.* Minneapolis: University of Minnesota Press.

Fincham, F. D., Beach, S. R. H., Lambert, Stillman, T., & Braithwaite, S. (2008). Spiritual behaviors and relationship satisfaction: A critical analysis of the role of prayer. *Journal of Social and Clinical Psychology, 27,* 362–388.

Fincham, F. D., Lambert, N. M., & Beach, S. R. H. (2010). Faith and unfaithfulness: Can praying for your partner reduce infidelity? *Journal of Personality and Social Psychology, 99,* 649–659.

Finney, J. R., & Malony, H. N. (1985a). Contemplative prayer and its use in psychotherapy: A theoretical model. *Journal of Psychology and Theology, 13,* 172–181.

Finney, J. R., & Malony, H. N. (1985b). Empirical studies of Christian prayer: A review of the literature. *Journal of Psychology and Theology, 13,* 104–115.

Finney, J. R., & Malony, H. N. (1985c). An empirical study of contemplative prayer as an adjunct to psychotherapy. *Journal of Psychology and Theology, 13,* 284–290.

Fiske, S. T., & Taylor, S. E. (1991). *Social cognition* (2nd ed.). New York: McGraw-Hill.

Flamm, B. (2004). The Columbia University "miracle" study: Flawed and fraud. *Skeptical Inquirer, 28*(5), 25–31.

Flamm, B. L. (2005). Prayer and the success of IVF. *Journal of Reproductive Medicine, 50,* 71.

Foster, R. J. (1992). *Prayer: Finding the heart's true home.* San Francisco: Harper.

Fowler, J. W. (1981). *Stages of faith: The psychology of human development and the quest for meaning.* New York: Harper & Row.

Francis, L. J. (1996). Personality and prayer among adult churchgoers. *Irish Journal of Psychology, 17,* 282–289.

Francis, L. J. (1997). Personality, prayer and church attendance among undergraduate students. *International Journal for the Psychology of Religion, 7,* 127–132.

Francis, L. J., & Bolger, J. (1997). Personality, prayer and church attendance in later life. *Social Behaviour and Personality, 25,* 335–338.

Francis, L. J., & Brown, L. B. (1991). The influence of home, church and school on prayer among sixteen-year-old adolescents in England. *Review of Religious Research, 33*(2), 112–122.

Francis, L. J., & Burton, L. (1994). The influence of personal prayer on purpose in life among Catholic adolescents. *Journal of Beliefs and Values, 15,* 6–9.

Francis, L. J., & Daniel, E. D. (1997). Personality and prayer among church going Methodists in England. *Journal of Beliefs and Values, 18,* 235–237.

Francis, L. J., & Evans, T. E. (1995). The psychology of Christian prayer: A review of empirical research. *Religion, 25,* 371–388.

Francis, L. J., & Gibbs, D. (1996). Prayer and self-esteem among 8-11 year olds in the United Kingdom. *Journal of Social Psychology, 136,* 791–793.

Francis, L. J., & Robbins, M. (2008). Psychological type and prayer preferences among Anglican clergy in the United Kingdom. *Mental Health, Religion and Culture, 11,* 67–84.

Frankl, V. (1963). *Man's search for meaning.* New York: Washington Square Press.

Frankl, V. (1969). *The will to meaning: Foundations and applications of logotherapy.* New York: New American Library.

Freud, S. (1928). *The future of an illusion.* New York: Liveright.

Fry, P. S. (1990). A factor-analytic investigation of home-bound elderly individuals' concerns about death and dying, and their coping responses. *Journal of Clinical Psychology, 46,* 737–748.

Fuller, R. B. (1975). *Synergetics.* New York: Macmillan.

Fuller, R. C. (1989). *Alternative medicine and American religious life.* New York: Oxford University Press.

Furnham, A. F. (1982). Locus of control and theological beliefs. *Journal of Psychology and Theology, 10,* 130–136.

Gallo, W. T., Bradley, E. H., Falba, T. A., Dubin, J. A. Cramer, L. D., Bogardus, S. T., et al. (2004). Involuntary job loss as a risk factor for subsequent myocardial infarction and stroke: Findings from the Health and Retirement Survey. *American Journal of Industrial Medicine, 45,* 408–416.

Galton, F. (1883). *Inquiries into human faculty and its development.* New York: Macmillan

Gansler, T., Kaw, C., Crammer, C., & Smith, T. (2008). A population-based study of prevalence of complementary methods use by cancer survivors. *Cancer, 113,* 1048–1057.

Garbarini, N. (2005). Single neuron speaks. *Scientific American Mind, 16*(3), 10.

Gazzaniga, M. S. (1985). *The social brain.* New York: Basic Books.

General Social Survey. (2008). GSS cumulative datafile, 1972–2006. Retrieved July 25, 2008, from *sda.berkeley.edu/archive.htm.*

Glaser, B., & Strauss, A. L. (1967). *The discovery of grounded theory: Strategies for qualitative research.* New York: Walter de Gruyter.

Gloss, T. (2009). Symposium: Faith in a higher power: The study of religion in psychology. *Observer, 22*(6), 43.

Godin, A. (1958). Psychological growth and Christian prayer. *Lumen Vitae, 13,* 517–530.

Godin, A. (1971). Some developmental tasks in Christian education. In M. P. Strommen (Ed.), *Research on religious development* (pp. 109–154). New York: Hawthorn Books.

Godin, A. (1985). *The psychological dynamics of religious experience.* Birmingham, AL: Religious Education Press.

Goldberger, L., & Breznitz, S. (Eds.). (1982). *Handbook of stress: Theoretical and clinical aspects.* New York: Free Press.

Goldhaber, D. (1985). *Life-span human development.* New York: Harcourt Brace Jovanovich.

Goldman, R. (1964). *Religious thinking from childhood to adolescence.* London: Routledge & Kegan Paul.

Goldstein, J. (2000). Waiving informed consent for research on spiritual matters? *Archives of Internal Medicine, 160,* 1870–1871.

Goodall, J. (1988). *In the shadow of man* (rev. ed.). Boston: Houghton Mifflin.

Gorsuch, R. L. (1968). The conceptualization of God as seen in adjective ratings. *Journal for the Scientific Study of Religion, 7,* 56–64.

Gorsuch, R. L., & McPherson, S. E. (1989). Intrinsic/extrinsic measurement: I/E revised and single item scales. *Journal for the Scientific Study of Religion, 28,* 348–354.

Gotay, C. C. (1984). The experience of cancer during early and advanced stages: The views of patients and their mates. *Social Science and Medicine, 18,* 605–613.

Gould, J., & Kolb, W. L. (Eds.). (1964). *A dictionary of the social sciences.* New York: Free Press.

Grayson, A. (2009, March 28). For many, Hurricane Katrina meant heart ills. Retrieved from *http://abcnews.go.com*.

Greeley, A. (1974). *Ecstasy: A way of knowing*. Englewood Cliffs, NJ: Prentice-Hall.

Green, W. M. (1993). *The therapeutic effects of distant intercessory prayer and patients' enhanced positive expectations on recovery rates and anxiety levels of hospitalized neurosurgical pituitary patients: A double blind study*. Unpublished doctoral dissertation, California Institute of Integral Studies, San Francisco.

Griffith, E. E. H., English, T., & Mayfield, V. (1980). Possession, prayer, and testimony: Therapeutic aspects of the Wednesday night meeting in a Black church. *Psychiatry, 43*, 120–128.

Gross, R. M. (2002). Meditation and prayer: A comparative analysis. *Christian–Buddhist Studies, 22*, 77–86.

Grossoehme, D. H., VanDyke, R., Jacobson, C. J., Cotton, S., Ragsdale, J. R., & Seid, M. (2010). Written prayers in a pediatric hospital: Linguistic analysis. *Psychology of Religion and Spirituality, 2*, 227–233.

Gruner, L. (1985). The correlation of private, religious devotional practices and marital adjustment. *Journal of Comparative Family Studies, 16*, 47–59.

Gurin, G., Veroff, J., & Feld, S. (1960). *Americans view their mental health: A nationwide interview study*. New York: Basic Books.

Guthrie, S. E. (1993). *Faces in the clouds: A new theory of religion*. New York: Oxford University Press.

Haan, N. (1982). The assessment of coping, defense, and stress. In L. Goldberger & S. Breznitz (Eds.), *Handbook of stress: Theoretical and clinical aspects* (pp. 254–269). New York: Free Press.

Haas, D. C. (2007). Prayer: A neurological inquiry. *Skeptical Inquirer, 31*, 51–53.

Hackney, C. H., & Sanders, G. S. (2003). Religiosity and mental health. *Journal for the Scientific Study of Religion, 42*, 43–55.

Hall, C. S., & Lindzey, G. (1978). *Theories of personality* (3rd ed.). New York: Wiley.

Hallesby, O. (1975). *Prayer*. Minneapolis, MN: Augsburg. (Original work published 1931)

Halperin, E. C. (2001). Should academic medical centers conduct clinical trials of the efficacy of intercessory prayer? *Academic Medicine, 76*, 791–797.

Hamm, E. M. (2000, June 26). No effect of intercessory prayer has been proven. *Archives of Internal Medicine, 160*, 1872–1873.

Hammerfald, K., Eberle, M., Grau, A., Kinsperger, A., Zimmerman, U. E., & Gaab, J. (2005). Persistent effects of cognitive-behavioral stress management on cortisol responses to acute stress in healthy subjects—a randomized controlled trial. *Psychoneuroendocrinology, 31*, 333–339.

Hansen, G. P. (1990). Deception by subjects in psi research. *Journal of the American Society for Psychical Research, 84*, 25–80.

Hardy, A. (1976). *The biology of God.* New York: Taplinger.

Hardy, A. (1979). *The spiritual nature of man: A study of contemporary religious experience.* Oxford, UK: Clarendon.

Harkness, G. (1948). *Prayer and the common life.* New York: Abingdon-Cokesbury.

Harris, S., Kaplan, J. T., Curiel, A., Brookheimer, S. Y., Iacoboni, M., & Cohen, M. S. (2009). The neural correlates of religious and nonreligious belief. *PLoS ONE* [online journal], *4*(10), e7272.

Harris, J. I., Schoneman, S. W., & Carrera, S. R. (2005). Preferred prayer styles and anxiety control. *Journal of Religion and Health, 44*, 403–412.

Harris, W. A., & Tessman, I. (2001, March 13). *Is there scientific evidence that intercessory prayer speeds medical recovery?: A debate.* Transcript of debate, University of Missouri–Columbia.

Harris, W. S., Gowda, M., Kolb, J. W., Strychacz, C. P., Vacek, J. L., Jones, P. G., et al. (1999). A randomized, controlled trial of the effects of remote, intercessory prayer on outcomes in patients admitted to the coronary care unit. *Archives of Internal Medicine, 159*(19), 2273–2278.

Hay, D. (1994). "The biology of God": What is the current status of Hardy's hypothesis? *International Journal for the Psychology of Religion, 4*, 1–23.

Heiler, F. (1958). *Prayer: A study in the history and psychology of religion.* New York: Oxford University Press. (Original work published 1932)

Helminiak, D. A. (1982, September/October). How is meditation prayer? *Review for Religious*, pp. 774–782.

Helvaci, M. R., & Seyhanli, M. (2006). What a high prevalence of white coat hypertension in society! *Internal Medicine, 45*, 671–674.

Hendry, G. S. (1972). The life line of theology. *Princeton Seminary Bulletin, 65*, 22–30.

Herman, E. (1921). *Creative prayer.* London: James Clarke

Hettler, T. R., & Cohen, L. H. (1998). Intrinsic religiousness as a stress moderator for adult Protestant churchgoers. *Journal of Community Psychology, 26*, 597–609.

Hill, P. C., & Pargament, K. I. (2003). Advances in the conceptualization and measurement of religion and spirituality. *American Psychologist, 58*, 64–74.

Hinnebusch, P. (1969). *Prayer: The search for authenticity.* New York: Sheed & Ward.

Hinson, E. G. (1979). *The reaffirmation of prayer.* Nashville, TN: Broadman Press.

Hodge, A. (1931). *Prayer and its psychology.* New York: Macmillan.

Hodge, D. R. (2007). A systematic review of the empirical literature on intercessory prayer. *Research on Social Work Practice, 17*, 174–187.

Hoff, A., Johannessen-Henry, C. T., Ross, L., Hvidt, N. C., & Johansen, C. (2008). Religion and reduced cancer risk—what is the explanation? *European Journal of Cancer, 44,* 2573–2579.

Hoffman, S. J. (1992). *Prayers, piety and pigskins: Religion in modern sports.* Paper presented at the annual meeting of the Society for the Scientific Study of Religion, Washington, DC.

Hofstadter, D. R. (1979). *Godel, Escher, Bach: An eternal golden braid.* New York: Basic Books.

Holahan, C. J., & Moos, R. H. (1987). Personal and contextual determinants of coping strategies. *Journal of Personality and Social Psychology, 52,* 946–955.

Hollywell, C., & Walker, J. (2008). Private prayer as a suitable intervention for hospitalized patients: A critical review of the literature. *Journal of Clinical Nursing, 18,* 637–651.

Hood, R. W., Jr., Hill, P. C., & Spilka, B. (2009). *The psychology of religion: An empirical approach* (4th ed.). New York: Guilford Press.

Hood, R. W., Jr., Morris, R. J., & Harvey, D. K. (1993, October). *Religiosity, prayer and their relationship to religious experience.* Paper presented at the annual meeting of the Religious Research Association, Raleigh, NC.

Hood, R. W., Jr., Morris, R. J., & Watson, P. J. (1989). Prayer experience and religious orientation. *Review of Religious Research, 31,* 39–45.

Houston, B. K. (1972). Control over stress, locus of control, and response to stress. *Journal of Personality and Social Psychology, 21,* 249–255.

Howard, G. S., Hill, T. L., Maxwell, S. E., Baptista, T. M., Farias, M. H., Coelho, C., et al. (2009). What's wrong with research literatures? And how to make them right. *Review of General Psychology, 13,* 146–166.

Howard, R. G. (2005). A theory of vernacular rhetoric: The case of the "Sinner's Prayer." *Folklore, 116,* 172–188.

Hulme, W. E., (1990). Prayer in pastoral care. In R. J. Hunter (Ed.), *Dictionary of pastoral care and counseling* (pp. 940–942). Nashville, TN: Abingdon.

Ikedo, F., Gangahar, D. M., Quader, M. A., & Smith, L. M. (2007). The effects of prayer, relaxation technique during general anesthesia on recovery outcomes following cardiac surgery. *Complementary Therapies in Clinical Practice, 13,* 85–94.

Ironson, G., Stuetzle, R., & Fletcher, M. A. (2006). An increase in religiousness/spirituality occurs after HIV diagnosis and predicts slower disease progression over 4 years in people with HIV. *Journal of General Internal Medicine, 21,* 562–568.

Jackson, L. E., & Coursey, R. D. (1988). The relationship of God control and internal locus of control to intrinsic religious motivation, coping and purpose in life. *Journal for the Scientific Study of Religion, 27,* 399–410.

Jalowiec, A. (2003). The Jalowiec Coping Scale. In O. L. Strickland & C. Dilorio (Eds.), *Measurement of coping and outcomes* (2nd ed., pp. 71–87). New York: Springer.

James, G. D., Pickering, T. G., Yee, L. S., Harshfield, G. A., Riva, S., & Laragh, J. H. (1988). The reproducibility of average ambulatory, home and clinic pressures. *Hypertension, 11,* 545–549.

James, W. (1907). *Pragmatism: A new name for some old ways of thinking.* New York: Longmans, Green.

James, W. (1985). *Varieties of religious experience.* Cambridge, MA: Harvard University Press. (Original work published 1902)

Janssen, J., De Hart, J., & Den Draak, C. (1989). Praying practices. *Journal of Empirical Theology 2,* 28–39.

Janssen, J., De Hart, J., & Den Draak, C. (1990). A content analysis of the praying practices of Dutch youth. *Journal for the Scientific Study of Religion, 29,* 99–107.

Janssen, J. A., Prins, M. H., Van Der Lans, J. M., & Baerveldt, C. (2000). The structure and variety of prayer: An empirical study of Dutch youth. *Journal of Empirical Theology, 13,* 29–54.

Jantos, M., & Kiat, H. (2007). Prayer as medicine: How much have we learned? *Medical Journal of Australia, 186*(10), S51–S53.

Johnston, L. (n.d.). The science of prayer and healing. Retrieved November 11, 2008, from *http://healingtherapies.info/prayer_and_healing.htm.*

Jonas, W. (2005). *Mosby's dictionary of complementary and alternative medicine.* New York: Elsevier.

Jones, D. W., Appel, L. J., Sheps, S. G., Rocella, F. J., & Lenfant, C. (2003). Measuring blood pressure accurately: New and persistent challenges. *Journal of Hypertension, 6,* 177–185.

Jones, E. E. (1964). *Ingratiation: A social psychological analysis.* New York: Appleton-Century-Crofts.

Joris, C. (2008, August). Why is it comforting to discuss problems with others? Retrieved from *www.sciam.com/article.cfm?id=ask-the-brains-aug-08&print=true.*

Joyce, C. R. B., & Welldon, R. M. C. (1965). The objective efficacy of prayer: A double-blind clinical trial. *Journal of Chronic Diseases, 18,* 367–377.

Jung, C. G. (1933). *Modern man in search of a soul.* New York: Harcourt, Brace & World.

Kaldjian, L. C., Jekel, J. F., & Friedland, G. (1998). End-of-life decisions in HIV-positive patients: The role of spiritual beliefs. *AIDS, 12,* 103–107.

Kaplan, B. H. (1976). A note on religious beliefs and coronary heart disease. *Journal of the South Carolina Medical Association, 72,* 60–64.

Katkin, E. S., Dermit, S., & Wine, S. K. F. (1993). Psychophysiological assessment of stress. In L. Goldberger & S. Breznitz (Eds.), *Handbook of stress: Theoretical and clinical aspects* (2nd ed., pp. 142–157). New York: Free Press.

Katz, J., Weiner, H., Gallagher, T., & Hellman, I. (1970). Stress, distress, and ego defenses. *Archives of General Psychiatry, 23*, 131–142.

Kay, A. C., Gaucher, D., McGregor, I., & Nash, K. (2010). Religious belief as compensatory control. *Personality and Social Psychology Review, 14*, 37–48.

Kay, A. C., Gaucher, D., Napier, J. L., Callan, M. J., & Laurin, K. (2008). God and the government: Testing a compensatory control mechanism for the support of external systems. *Journal of Personality and Social Psychology, 95*, 18–35.

Kay, A. C., Moscovitch, D. A., & Laurin, K. (2010). Randomness, attributions of arousal and belief in God. *Psychological Science, 21*, 216–218.

Kay, A. C., Whitson, J. A., Gaucher, D., & Galinsky, A. D. (2009). Compensatory control: Achieving order through the mind, our institutions, and the heavens. *Current Directions in Psychological Science, 18*, 264–268.

Keating, D. P. (1980). Thinking processes in adolescence. In J. Adelson (Ed.), *Handbook of adolescent psychology* (pp. 211–246). New York: Wiley.

Keating, T. (1999). *Open mind, open heart: The contemplative dimension of the Gospel.* New York: Continuum.

Kelemen, D. (2004). Are children "intuitive theists"? *Psychological Science, 15*, 295–301.

Kendall, P. C., & Bemis, K. M. (1983), Thought and action in psychotherapy: The cognitive-behavioral approaches. In M. Herson, A. E. Kazdin, & A. S. Bellack (Eds.), *The clinical psychology handbook* (pp. 565–592). New York: Pergamon.

Kennedy, J. E. (2002). Commentary on "experiments on distant intercessory prayer" in *Archives of Internal Medicine. Journal of Parapsychology, 66*, 177–182.

Kennedy, J. E. (2005). Notes on a case of scientific fraud. Retrieved from *http://jeksite.org.*

Kennedy, L. (1974). *Pursuit.* New York: Viking.

Kierkegaard, S. (2006). *Fear and trembling* (S. Walsh, Trans.; C. S. Evans & S. Walsh, Eds.). New York: Cambridge University Press.

Kirkendall, W. M., Burton, A. C., Epstein, F. H., & Fries, E. D. (1967). Recommendations for human blood pressure determinations by sphygmomanometer. *Circulation, 36*, 980–988.

Kirkpatrick, L. A. (2005). *Attachment, evolution, and the psychology of religion.* New York: Guilford Press.

Kirkpatrick, L. A., & Hood, R. W., Jr. (1990). Intrinsic–extrinsic religious orientation: The boon or bane of contemporary psychology of religion. *Journal for the Scientific Study of Religion, 29*, 442–462.

Kirkwood, N. A. (2002). *Pastoral care to Muslims: Building bridges.* New York: Haworth Pastoral Press.

Kirsch, I. (1999). *How expectancies shape experience.* Washington, DC: American Psychological Association.

Kluger, J. (2008). *Simplexity: Why simple things become complex (and how complex things can be made simple)*. New York: Hyperion.

Koenig, H. G. (1995). Religion as cognitive schema. *International Journal for the Psychology of Religion, 5*, 31–37.

Koenig, H. G., George, L. K., Blazer, D. G., Pritchett, J. T., & Meador, K. G. (1993). The relationship between religion and anxiety in a sample of community dwelling older adults. *Journal of Geriatric Psychiatry, 26*, 65–93.

Koenig, H. G., George, L. K., Hays, J. C., Larson, D. B., Cohen, H. J., & Blazer, D. G. (1998). The relationship between religious activities and blood pressure in older adults. *International Journal of Psychiatry in Medicine, 28*(2), 189–213.

Koenig, H. G., George, L. K., & Siegler, I. C. (1988). The use of religion and other emotion-regulating coping strategies among older adults. *The Gerontologist, 28*, 303–310.

Koenig, H. G., Kvale, J. N., & Ferrel, C. (1988). Religion and well-being in later life. *The Gerontologist, 28*, 18–28.

Koenig, H. G., McCullough, M. E., & Larson, D. B. (2001). *Handbook of religion and health*. New York: Oxford University Press.

Koppe, W. A. (1973). *How persons grow in Christian community*. Philadelphia: Fortress Press.

Kopplin, D. (1976, August). *Religious orientations of college students and related personality characteristics*. Paper presented at the annual meeting of the American Psychological Association, Washington, DC.

Krause, N. L. (2000). Aging. In H. R. Ebaugh (Ed.), *Handbook of religion and social institutions* (pp. 139–160). New York: Springer.

Krause, N. L. (2004). Assessing the relationships among prayer expectancies, race, and self-esteem in late life. *Journal for the Scientific Study of Religion, 43*, 395–408.

Krause, N. L., Chatters, M., Meltzer, T., & Morgan, D. L. (2000). Using focus groups to explore the nature of prayer in late life. *Journal of Aging Studies, 14*, 194–212.

Krause, N. L., & Tran, T. V. (1989). Stress and religious involvement among older blacks. *Journal of Gerontology: Social Sciences, 44*, S4–S13.

Krucoff, M. W., Crater, S. W., Gallup, D., Blankenship, J. C., Cuffe, M., Guarneri, M., et al. (2005, July 16). Music, imagery, touch, and prayer as adjuncts to interventional cardiac care: The Monitoring and Actualisation of Noetic Training (MANTRA) II randomised study. *Lancet, 366*, 211–217.

Krucoff, M. W., Crater, S. W., Green, C. L., Maas, A. C., Seskevich, J. E., Lane, J. D., et al. (2001). Integrative noetic therapies as adjuncts to percutaneous intervention during unstable coronary syndromes: Monitoring and Actualization of Noetic Training (MANTRA) feasibility pilot. *American Heart Journal, 142*, 760–767.

Krucoff, M. W., Crater, S. W., & Lee, K. L. (2006). From efficacy to safety concerns: A STEP forward or a step back for clinical research and intercessory prayer?: The study of therapeutic effects of intercessory prayer (STEP). *American Heart Journal, 151*, 762–764.

Ladd, K. L., Cook, C. A., Foreman, K. M., Ritter, E. A., & Cora, J. (2010, March). *The influence of posture on prayer experience: Preliminary findings.* Paper presented at the Division 36, American Psychological Association Mid-Winter Conference on Religion and Spirituality, Columbia, MD.

Ladd, K. L., Hvidt, N. C., & Ladd, M. L. (2007, September). *Measuring core practice and concern: Prayer and theodicy.* Paper presented at the International Conference on Spirituality, Prague, Czech Republic.

Ladd, K. L., & Ladd, M. L. (2010). Book review of A. Newberg and M. R. Waldman. How God changes your brain: Breakthrough findings from a leading neuroscientist. *International Journal for the Psychology of Religion, 20*, 219–222.

Ladd, K. L., & Ladd, M. L. (2012, January). *Prayer and personality: Virtues and vices.* Presentation at the Psychology of Religion and Spirituality pre-conference meeting of the Society for Personality and Social Psychology, San Diego, CA.

Ladd, K. L., Ladd, M. L., Ashbaugh, P., Trnka, D., Harner, J., St. Pierre, K., et al. (2007). Inward, outward, upward prayer and personal character. *Research in the Social Scientific Study of Religion* [Special issue *Positive Psychology, Religion, and Spirituality*], *18*, 209–231.

Ladd, K. L., Ladd, M. L., Harner, J., Swanson, T., Metz, T., St. Pierre, K., et al. (2007). Inward, outward, upward prayer: Links to personality (Big Five). *Archiv für Religionspychologie, 49*, 151–175.

Ladd, K. L., & McIntosh, D. N. (2008). Meaning, God, and prayer: Physical and metaphysical aspects of social support. *Mental Health, Religion and Culture, 11*, 23–38.

Ladd, K. L., & Spilka, B. (2002). Inward, outward, and upward: Cognitive aspects of prayer. *Journal for the Scientific Study of Religion, 41*, 475–484.

Ladd, K. L., & Spilka, B. (2006). Inward, outward, and upward: Scale reliability and validation. *Journal for the Scientific Study of Religion, 45*, 233–251.

Ladd, K. L., Spilka, B., McIntosh, D. N., & Luckow, A. (1996). *The distilled essence of prayer.* Paper presented at the annual meeting of the Society for the Scientific Study of Religion, Nashville, TN.

Ladd, K. L., Vreugdenhil, S., Ladd, M. L., & Cook, C. (in press). Interpersonal conversations and prayers: Differences of content and attachment functions. *Journal of Communication and Religion.*

Ladd, M. L., Cook, C. A., Becker, B. L., & Ladd, K. L. (2009, August). *Prayers of the* St. Joseph Daily Missal: *Comparing human and computer coding strategies.* Paper presented at the annual meeting of the

International Association for the Psychology of Religion, Vienna, Austria.

Laird, S. P. (1991). *A preliminary investigation into the role of prayer as a coping technique for adult patients with arthritis.* Unpublished doctoral dissertation, University of Kansas, Lawrence.

Laird, S. P., Snyder, C. R., Rapoff, M. A., & Green, S. (2004). Measuring private prayer: Development, validation, and clinical application of the multidimensional prayer inventory. *International Journal for the Psychology of Religion, 14*, 251–272.

Lakin, J. L., Jefferis, V. E., Cheng, C. M., & Chartrand, T. L. (2003). The Chameleon Effect as social glue: Evidence for the evolutionary significance of nonconscious mimicry. *Journal of Nonverbal Behavior, 27*, 145–162.

Lambert, N. M., Fincham, F. D., Braithwaite, S. R., Graham, S. M., & Beach, S. R. H. (2009). Can prayer increase gratitude? *Psychology of Religion and Spirituality, 1*, 139–149.

Lambert, N. M., Fincham, F. D., & Graham, S. M. (2011). Understanding the layperson's perception of prayer: A prototype analysis. *Psychology of Religion and Spirituality, 3*, 55–65.

Lambert, N. M., Fincham, F. D., Marks, L. D., & Stillman, T. F. (2010). Invocation and intoxication: Does prayer decrease alcohol consumption? *Journal of Addictive Behaviors, 24*, 209–219.

Lambert, N. M., Fincham, F. D., Stillman, T. F., Graham, S. M., & Beach, S. R. M. (2010). Motivating change in relationships: Can prayer increase forgiveness? *Psychological Science, 21*, 126–132.

Lange, M. A. (1983). Prayer and psychotherapy: Beliefs and practice. *Journal of Psychology and Christianity, 2*, 36–49.

Larson, D. B., Koenig, H. G., Kaplan, B. H., Greenberg, R. S., Logue, E., & Taylor, H. A. (1989). The impact of religion on men's blood pressure. *Journal of Religion and Health, 28*, 265–277.

Lartey, E. Y. (2003). *An intercultural approach to pastoral care and counseling* (2nd ed.). New York: Jessica Kingsley.

Last, J. (2009). Psychotherapy and prayer. Retrieved November 8, 2009, from *www.aish.com/sp/pr/68843407.html*.

Lawrence, R. L. (2002). Four fatal flaws in recent spirituality research. *Journal of Health Care Chaplaincy, 12*(1–2). 125–130.

Lawson, E. T., & McCauley, R. N. (1990). *Rethinking religion: Connecting cognition and culture.* Cambridge, UK: Cambridge University Press.

Lawson, E. T., & McCauley, R. N. (2002). The cognitive representation of religious ritual form: A theory of participants' competence with religious ritual systems. In I. Pyysiainen & V. Anttonen (Eds.), *Cognitive approaches in the cognitive science of religion* (pp. 153–176). New York: Continuum.

Lazarus, R. (1981, July). Little hassles can be hazardous to your health. *Psychology Today*, pp. 58–62.

Lazarus, R. S. (1966). *Psychological stress and the coping process.* New York: McGraw-Hill.

Lazarus, R. S., & Folkman, S. (1984). *Stress, appraisal, and coping.* New York: Springer.

Leder, D. (2005). "Spooky actions at a distance": Physics, psi, and distant healing. *Journal of Alternative and Complementary Medicine, 11,* 923–930.

Lee, R. S. (1963). *Your growing child and religion.* New York: Macmillan.

Lehrer, J. (2010, December 13). The truth wears off. *The New Yorker,* pp. 52–55.

Lerner, M. J. (1980). *The belief in a just world.* New York: Plenum Press.

Leuba, J. H. (1907). Religion as a factor in the struggle for life. *American Journal of Religious Psychology and Education, 2,* 307–343.

Leuba, J. H. (1912). *A psychological study of religion: Its origin, function and future.* New York: Macmillan.

Levenson, H. (1973). Multidimensional locus of control in psychiatric patients. *Journal of Consulting and Clinical Psychology, 41,* 397–404.

Levin, J. (2001). *God, faith, and health.* New York: Wiley.

Levin, J. S. (1996). How prayer heals: A theoretical model. *Alternative Therapies, 2,* 66–73.

Levin, J. S. (2009). How faith heals: A theoretical model. *Explore, 5,* 77–96.

Levin, J. S., Lyons, J. S., & Larson, D. B. (1993). Prayer and health during pregnancy: Findings from the Galveston low birthweight survey. *Southern Medical Journal, 86,* 1022–1027.

Levin, J. S., & Markides, K. S. (1986). Religious attendance and subjective health. *Journal of Religion and Health, 25,* 31–39.

Levin, J. S., & Taylor, R. J. (1997). Age differences in patterns and correlates of the frequency of prayer. *The Gerontologist, 37,* 75–88.

Levin, J. S., & Vanderpool, H. Y. (1989). Is religion therapeutically significant for hypertension? *Social Sciences and Medicine, 29,* 69–78.

Lewin, K. (1951). *Field theory in social science.* New York: Harper & Brothers.

Lewis, H. D. (1959). *Our experience of God.* London: George Allen Unwin.

Lim, C., & Putnam, R. D. (2010). Religion, social networks and life satisfaction. *American Sociological Review, 75,* 914–933.

Lindenthal, J. J., Myers, J. K., Pepper, M. P., & Stern, M. S. (1970). Mental status and religious behavior. *Journal for the Scientific Study of Religion, 9,* 143–149.

Liu, C-Y., Wei, C-C., & Lo, P-C. (2009). Variation analysis of sphygmogram to assess cardiovascular system under meditation. *Evidence-Based Complementary and Alternative Medicine, 6,* 107–112.

Long, D., Elkind, D., & Spilka, B. (1967). The child's conception of prayer. *Journal for the Scientific Study of Religion, 6,* 101–109.

Lorenz, H. (2008). Plato on the soul. In G. Fine (Ed.), *The Oxford handbook of Plato*. New York: Oxford University Press.

Loveland, M. T., Sikkink, D., Myers, D. J., & Radcliff, B. (2005). Private prayer and a civic involvement. *Journal for the Scientific Study of Religion, 44*, 1–14.

Luckow, A. (1997). *The structure of prayer: Exploratory and confirmatory analyses*. Unpublished master's thesis, University of Denver, Denver, CO.

Luckow, A., Ladd, K. L., Spilka, B., McIntosh, D. N., Poloma, M., Parks, C., et al. (1996, August 11). *The structure of prayer: Explorations and confirmations*. Paper presented at the annual convention of the American Psychological Association, Toronto.

Luo, M. (2010, February 25). At closing plant, ordeal included heart attacks. *New York Times*. Retrieved from *www.nytimes.com/2010/02/25/us/25stress.html*.

Luskin, F. (2000). Review of the effects of spiritual and religious factors on mortality and morbidity with a focus on cardiovascular and pulmonary disease. *Journal of Cardiopulmonary Rehabilitation, 20*, 8–15.

Lutgendorf, S. K., Antoni, M. H., Ironson, G., Klimas N., Kumar, M., Starr, K., et al. (1997). Cognitive-behavioral stress management decreases dysphoric mood and herpes simplex virus-Type 2 antibody titers in symptomatic HIV-seropositive gay men. *Journal of Consulting and Clinical Psychology, 65*, 31–43.

Lyons, J. S., (2005, January 3). Research into prayer, fertility link now doubted. *San Jose Mercury News*.

Magaletta, P. R., & Brawer, P. A. (1996, August 11). *The use of prayer in psychotherapy: Ethical considerations*. Paper presented at the annual meeting of the American Psychological Association, Toronto.

Mahboubeh Rezael, M., Adib-Hajbaghery, N. S., & Fatemeh, H. (2008). Prayer in Iranian cancer patients undergoing chemotherapy. *Complementary Therapies in Clinical Practice, 14*, 90–97.

Mahoney, A. (2005). Religion and conflict in marital and parent–child relationships. *Journal of Social Issues, 61*, 689–706.

Mahoney, A., Pargament, K. I., Murray-Swank, A. B., & Murray-Swank, A. N. (2003). Sanctification of family relationships. *Review of Religious Research, 44*, 220–236.

Mahoney, A., Pargament, K. L., Tarakeshwar, N., & Swank, A. B. (2001). Religion in the home in the 1980s and 1990s: A meta-analytic review and conceptual analysis of links between religion, marriage, and parenting. *Journal of Family Psychology, 15*, 559–596.

Mahoney, A., & Tarakeshwar, N. (2005). Religion's role in marriage and parenting in daily life and during family crises. In R. F. Paloutzian & C. L. Park (Eds.), *Handbook of the psychology of religion and spirituality* (pp. 171–198). New York: Guilford Press.

Makros, J., & McCabe, M. (2003). The relationship between religion, spirituality, psychological adjustment and quality of life among people with multiple sclerosis. *Journal of Religion and Health, 42*, 143–159.

Maloney, G. A. (1976). *TM and Christian meditation.* Pecos, NM: Dove.

Maltby, J. (1995). Personality, prayer, and church attendance among U.S. female adults. *Journal of Social Psychology, 135*, 529–531.

Maltby, J., & Lewis, C. A. (1999). Religious orientation and psychological well-being: The role of the frequency of personal prayer. *British Journal of Health Psychology, 4*, 363–378.

Maltby, J., Lewis, C. A., & Day, L. (2008). Prayer and subjective well-being: The application of a cognitive-behavioural framework. *Mental Health, Religion and Culture, 11*, 119–129.

Manfredi, C., & Pickett, M. (1987). Perceived stressful situations and coping strategies utilized by the elderly. *Journal of Community Health Nursing, 4*, 99–110.

Marcia, J. E. (1980). Identity in adolescence. In J. Adelson (Ed.), *Handbook of adolescent psychology* (pp. 159–207). New York: Wiley.

Markandu, N. D., Whitcher, F., Arnold, A., & Carney, C. (2000). The mercury sphygmomanometer should be abandoned before it is proscribed. *Journal of Human Hypertension, 14*, 31–36.

Markides, K. (1983). Aging, religiosity, and adjustment: A longitudinal analysis. *Journal of Gerontology, 38*, 621–625.

Marks, L. D. (2008). Prayer and marital intervention: Asking for divine help . . . or professional trouble? *Journal of Social and Clinical Psychology, 27*, 678–685.

Marsden, P., Karagianni, E., & Morgan, J. F. (2007). Spirituality and clinical care in eating disorders: A qualitative study. *International Journal of Eating Disorders, 40*, 7–12.

Martin, J. C., & Sachse, D. S. (2002). Spirituality characteristics of women following renal transplantation. *Nephrology Nursing Journal, 29*, 577–581.

Maslow, A. H. (1954). *Motivation and personality.* New York: Harper & Brothers.

Maslow, A. H. (1964). *Religions, values, and peak-experiences.* Columbus: Ohio State University Press.

Masters, K. S., Spielman, G. I., & Goodson, J. T. (2006). Are there demonstrable effects of distant intercessory prayer?: A meta-analytic review. *Annals of Behavioral Medicine, 32*, 21–26.

Matthews, D. A., & Clark, C. (1999). *The faith factor: Proof of the healing power of prayer.* Baltimore: Penguin.

Matthews, D. A., Marlowe, S. M., & McNutt, F. S. (2000). Effects of intercessory prayer on patients with rheumatoid arthritis. *Southern Medical Journal, 93*, 1177–1186.

Matthews, W. J., Conti, J. M., & Sireci, S. G. (2001, September/October). The effects of intercessory prayer, positive visualization, and expectancy on the well-being of kidney dialysis patients. *Alternative Therapies, 7*(5), 42–52.

Maugans, T. A., & Wadland, W. C. (1991). Religion and family medicine: A survey of physicians and patients. *Journal of Family Practice, 32,* 210–214.

May, P. R. (1977). Religious judgments in children and adolescents: A research report. *Learning for Living: The British Journal of Religion in Education, 16,* 115–122.

McBrien, R. P. (Ed.). (1995). *The HarperCollins encyclopedia of Catholicism.* New York: HarperCollins.

McCaffrey, A. M., Eisenberg, D. M., Legedza, A. T. R., Davis, R. B., & Phillips, R. S. (2004). Prayer for health concerns: Results of a national survey on prevalence and patterns of use. *Archives of Internal Medicine, 164,* 858–862.

McCauley, R. N., & Lawson, E. T. (2002). *Bringing ritual to mind.* Cambridge, UK: Cambridge University Press.

McConnaughy, J. (2009, March 27). Katrina stress still causing heart attacks. Retrieved from *www.google.com/hostednews/AP/aleqmshm2p68.*

McCullough, M. E. (1995). Prayer and health: Conceptual issues, research review, and research agenda. *Journal of Psychology and Theology, 23,* 15–29.

McCullough, M. E., Hoyt, W. T., Larson, D. B., Koenig, H. G., & Thoresen, C. (2000). Religious involvement and mortality: A meta-analytic review. *Health Psychology, 19,* 211–222.

McCullough, M. E., & Larson, D. B. (1999). Prayer. In W. R. Miller (Ed.), *Integrating spirituality into treatment* (pp. 85–110). Washington, DC: American Psychological Association.

McCullough, M. E., & Willoughby, B. L. B. (2009). Religion, self-regulation, and self-control: Associations, explanations, and implications. *Psychological Bulletin, 135,* 69–93.

McGregor, B. A., Antoni, M. H., Boyers, A., Alferi, S. M., Blomberg, B. B., & Carver, C. S. (2004). Cognitive-behavioral stress management increases benefit finding and immune function among women with early-stage breast cancer. *Journal of Psychosomatic Research, 56,* 1–8.

McGuire, M. (1988). *Ritual healing in suburban America.* New Brunswick, NJ: Rutgers University Press.

McIntosh, D. N. (1995). Religion as schema with implications for the relation between religion and coping. *International Journal for the Psychology of Religion, 5,* 1–16.

McIntosh, D. N., Kojetin, B. A., & Spilka, B. (1985). *Form of personal faith and general and specific locus of control.* Paper presented at the annual convention of the Rocky Mountain Psychological Association, Tucson, AZ.

McKay, D. W., Campbell, N. R., Parab, L. S., Chockalingam, A., & Fodor, J. G. (1990). Clinical assessment of blood pressure. *Journal of Human Hypertension, 4*(6), 639–645.

McKay, R., & Dennett, D. (2009). The evolution of misbelief. *Brain and Behavioral Sciences, 32*, 493–510.

McKinney, J. P., & McKinney, K. G. (1999). Prayer in the lives of adolescents. *Journal of Adolescence, 22*, 279–290.

McKinney, L. O. (1994). *Neurotheology: Virtual religion in the 21st century.* Arlington, MA: American Institute for Mindfulness.

McNulty, K., Livneh, H., & Wilson, L. M. (2004). Perceived uncertainty, spiritual well-being and psychosocial adaptation in individuals with multiple sclerosis. *Rehabilitation Psychology, 49*, 91–99.

Meehl, P. (1978). Theoretical risks and tabular asterisks: Sir Karl, Sir Ronald, and the slow progress of soft psychology. *Journal of Consulting and Clinical Psychology, 46*, 806–834.

Meehl, P. E. (1990). Appraising and amending theories: The strategy of Lakatosian defense and two principles that warrant it. *Psychological Inquiry, 1*, 108–141.

Meisenhelder, J. B., & Chandler, E. N. (2000a). Prayer and health outcomes in church lay leaders. *Western Journal of Nursing Research, 22*, 706–716.

Meisenhelder, J. B., & Chandler, E. N. (2000b). Prayer and health outcomes in church members. *Alternative Therapies in Health and Medicine, 6*, 56–60.

Meissner, W. W. (1961). *Annotated bibliography in religion and psychology.* New York: Academy of Religion and Health.

Mendelsohn, G. A., & Sundberg, N. D. (1965). Myers–Briggs Type Indicator. In O. K. Buros (Ed.), *The sixth mental measurements yearbook* (p. 147). Highland Park, NJ: Gryphon Press.

Meraviglia, M. G. (1999). Critical analysis of spirituality and its empirical indicators: Prayer and meaning in life. *Journal of Holistic Nursing, 17*, 18–33.

Meredith, K. L., Jeffe, D. B., Mundy, L. M., & Fraser, V. J. (2001). Sources influencing patients in their HIV medication decisions. *Health Education and Behavior, 28*, 40–50.

Michael, C. P., & Norrisey, M. C. (1984). *Prayer and temperament: Different prayer forms for different personality types.* Charlottesville, VA: Open Door.

Mion, D., & Pierin, A. M. G. (1998). How accurate are sphygmomanometers? *Journal of Human Hypertension, 12*, 245–248.

Mitchell, C. E. (1989). Internal locus of control for expectation, perception and management of answered prayer. *Journal of Psychology and Theology, 17*, 21–26.

Moore, T. V. (1959). *Heroic sanctity and insanity.* New York: Grune & Stratton.

Mountain, V. (2005). Prayer is a positive activity for children—a report on recent research. *International Journal of Children's Spirituality, 10*, 291–305.

Mozes, A. (2009, March 13). Traffic jams the heart. Retrieved from *http://*

*us.rd.yahoo.com/health/news/rss/search/healthday/trafficjamsharms
theheart.html.*

Navrot, A., Richardson, A., Marrocco, C., Dashosh, D., Kvern, K., Yang, J., et al. (1995, April). *Prayer and the sense of control: A multidimensional approach.* Paper presented at the annual meeting of the Rocky Mountain Psychological Association, Boulder, CO.

Nayak, S., Matheis, R. J., Schoenberger, N. E., & Shiflett, S. C. (2003). Use of unconventional therapies by individuals with multiple sclerosis. *Clinical Rehabilitation, 17,* 181–191.

Nelson, N., Rosenthal, R., & Rosnow, R. I. (1986). Interpretation of significance levels and effect sizes by psychological researchers. *American Psychologist, 41,* 1299–1301.

Neufeld, P. D. (1986). Observer error in blood pressure measurement. *Canadian Medical Association Journal, 135,* 633–637.

Newberg, A., d'Aquili, E., & Rause, V. (2001). *Why God won't go away.* New York: Ballantine Books.

Newberg A., & Waldman, M. R. (2001). *How God changes your brain.* New York: Ballantine Books.

Nichols, T. E., & Poline, J.-B. (2009). Commentary on Vul et al.'s (2009) "Puzzlingly high correlations in fMRI studies of emotion, personality, and social cognition." *Psychological Science, 4,* 291–293.

Nicholson, C. (2010, December 25). The strongest predictor for low stress. Retrieved February 28, 2011, from *www.scientificamerican.com/podcast/episode.cf,?id=the-strongest-predictor-for-low-stress.*

O'Connor, P. J., Pronk, N. P., Tan, A., & Whitehead, R. R. (2005). Characteristics of adults who use prayer as an alternative therapy. *American Journal of Health Promotion, 19,* 369–375.

O'Keefe, J. H., Poston, W. S. C., Haddock, C. K., & Harris, W. (2004). Psychosocial stress and cardiovascular disease: How to heal a broken heart. *Mayo Clinic Proceedings, 30,* 37–43.

O'Laoire, S. (1997). An experimental study of the effects of distant, intercessory prayer on self-esteem, anxiety, and depression. *Alternative Therapies in Health and Medicine, 3*(6), 38–53.

Oser, F., & Gmunder, P. (1991). *Religious judgment: A developmental approach.* Birmingham, AL: Religious Education Press.

Oxman, T. E., Freeman, D. H., Jr., & Manheimer, E. D. (1995). Lack of social participation or religious strength and comfort as risk factors for death after cardiac surgery in the elderly. *Psychosomatic Medicine, 57,* 5–15.

Ozorak, E. W. (1992, November). *In the eye of the beholder: A social-cognitive model of religious belief development.* Paper presented at the annual convention of the Society for the Scientific Study of Religion, Washington, DC.

Ozorak, E. W. (2005). Cognitive approaches to religion. In R. F. Paloutzian

& C. L. Park (Eds.), *Handbook of the psychology of religion and spirituality* (pp. 216–234). New York: Guilford Press.

Page, S. A., Verhoef, M. A., Stebbins, R. A., Metz, L. M., & Levy, C., (2003). The use of complementary and alternative therapies by people with multiple sclerosis. *Chronic Diseases and Injuries in Canada, 24(2/3)*.

Palmer, R. F., Katerndahl, D., & Morgan-Kidd, J. (2004). A randomized trial of the effects of remote intercessory prayer: Interactions with personal beliefs on problem-specific outcomes and functional status. *Journal of Alternative and Complementary Medicine, 10*, 438–448.

Pargament, K. I. (1987, August). *God help me: Towards a theoretical framework of coping for the psychology of religion.* William James Award Address, American Psychological Association convention, New York.

Pargament, K. I. (1988). Religion and the problem-solving process: Three styles of coping. *Journal for the Scientific Study of Religion, 27*, 90–104.

Pargament, K. I. (1992). Of means and ends: Religion and the search for significance. *International Journal for the Psychology of Religion, 2*, 201–229.

Pargament, K. I. (1995). Merely a defense?: The variety of religious means and ends. *Journal of Social Issues, 51*, 13–32.

Pargament, K. I. (1997). *The psychology of religion and coping: Theory, research, practice.* New York: Guilford Press.

Pargament, K. I., Ano, G. G., & Wachholtz, A. B. (2005). The religious dimension of coping: Advances in theory, research, and practice. In R. F. Paloutzian & C. L. Park (Eds.), *Handbook of the psychology of religion and spirituality* (pp. 479–495). New York: Guilford Press.

Pargament, K. I., & Hahn, J. (1986). God and the just world: Causal and coping attributions to God in health situations. *Journal for the Scientific Study of Religion, 25*, 193–207.

Pargament, K. I., Kennell, J., Hathaway, W., Grevengoed, N., Newman, J., & Jones, W. (1988). Religion and the problem-solving process: Three styles of coping. *Journal for the Scientific Study of Religion, 27*, 90–104.

Pargament, K. I., Koenig, H. G., & Perez, L. M. (2000). The many methods of religious coping: Development and initial validation of the RCOPE. *Journal of Clinical Psychology, 56*, 519–543.

Pargament, K. I., McCarthy, S., Shah, P., Ano, G., Tarakeshwar, N., Wachholtz, A., et al. (2004). Religion and HIV: A review of the literature and clinical implications. *Southern Medical Journal, 97*, 1201–1209.

Pargament, K. I., & Park, C. L. (1995). Merely a defense?: The variety of religious means and ends. *Journal of Social Issues, 51*, 13–32.

Park, D. C., & Schwarz, N. (2000). *Cognitive aging.* Philadelphia: Psychology Press.

Parker, G. B., & Brown, L. B. (1986). Coping behaviors as predictors of the course of clinical depression. *Archives of General Psychiatry, 43,* 561–565.

Peacock, J. R., & Poloma, M. M. (1999). Religiosity and life satisfaction across the life course. *Social Indicators Research, 48,* 321–345.

Pearce, M. J. (2005). A critical review of the forms and value of religious coping among informal caregivers. *Journal of Religion and Health, 44,* 81–118.

Pendleton, S. M., Cavalli, K. S., Pargament, K. I., & Nasr, S. Z. (2002). Religious/spiritual coping in childhood cystic fibrosis: A qualitative study. *Pediatrics, 109,* 134.

Pennington, M. B. (1986). *Centered living: The way of centering prayer.* New York: Doubleday.

Perloff, D., Grim, C., Flack, J., Frohlich, E. D., McDonald, M., & Morgenstern, B. Z. (1993). Human blood pressure determination by sphygmomanometer. *Circulation, 88,* 2460–2470.

Petrovski, L. (1996, October 2). Divine silence. *The Denver Post,* p. 1G.

Pew Forum. (2010, April 22). Prayer in America. Retrieved from *http:// pewforum.org/docs/?DocID=179.*

Phillips, D. Z. (1981). *The concept of prayer.* New York: Seabury.

Piaget, J. (1958). *The growth of logical thinking from childhood to adolescence.* London: Routledge & Kegan Paul.

Pickering, T. G. (1994). Blood pressure measurement and detection of hypertension. *Lancet, 344,* 31–35.

Poloma, M. M., & Gallup, G. H., Jr. (1990, November). *Religiosity, forgiveness and life satisfaction: An exploratory study.* Paper presented at the annual meeting of the Society for the Scientific Study of Religion, Virginia Beach, VA.

Poloma, M. M., & Gallup, G. H., Jr. (1991). *Varieties of prayer: A survey report.* Philadelphia: Trinity Press International.

Poloma, M. M., & Pendleton, B. F. (1989). Exploring types of prayer and quality of life: A research note. *Religious Research, 31,* 46–53.

Poloma, M. M., & Pendleton, B. F. (1991a). The effects of prayer and prayer experiences on measures of general well-being. *Journal of Psychology and Theology, 19,* 71–83.

Poloma, M. M., & Pendleton, B. F. (1991b). Prayer, prayer experience and measures of well-being. In M. M. Poloma & B. Pendleton (Eds.), *Exploring neglected dimensions of religion in quality of life research* (pp. 43–64). Lewiston, NY: Edwin Mellen Press.

Pope, A. (1948). *Alexander Pope: Selected works* (L. Kronenberger, Ed.). New York: Modern Library.

Powell, L. H., Shahabi, L., & Thoresen, C. E. (2003). Religion and spirituality: Linkages to physical health. *American Psychologist, 58,* 36–52.

Pratt, J. B. (1910). An empirical study of prayer. *American Journal of Religious Psychology and Education, 4,* 48–67.

Pratt, J. B. (1927). *The religious consciousness.* New York: Macmillan.

Pruyser, P. (1968). *A dynamic psychology of religion.* New York: Harper & Row.

Puglisi, M. (1929). *Prayer.* New York: Macmillan.

Rabin, B. S. (1999). *Stress, immune function, and health.* New York: Wiley-Liss.

Randall, J. H. (1911). *New philosophy of life.* New York: Dodge.

Raymond, G. L. (1907). *The psychology of inspiration.* New York: Funk & Wagnalls.

Rehman, H. U., & Asfour, N. A. (2010, January 12). Prayer nodules. *Canadian Medical Association Journal-Journal de L'Association Médicale Canadienne, 182*(1), E19. Retrieved December 22, 2010, from *www.ncbi.nlm.nih.gov/pmc/articles/PMC2802629.*

Rew, L., Wong, Y. J., & Sternglanz, R. W. (2004). The relationship between prayer, health behaviors, and protective resources in school-age children. *Issues in Comprehensive Pediatric Nursing, 27,* 245–255.

Richards, D. G. (1991). The phenomenology and psychological correlates of verbal prayer. *Journal of Psychology and Theology, 19,* 354–363.

Richards, T. A., Wrubel, J., Grant, J., & Folkman, S. (2003). Subjective experiences of prayer among women who care for children. *Journal of Religion and Health, 42,* 201–219.

Robbins, M., Francis, L. J., & Edwards, B. (2008). Prayer, personality and happiness: A study among undergraduate students in Wales. *Mental Health, Religion and Culture, 11,* 93–99.

Roberts, L., Ahmed, I., Hall, S., & Davidson, A. (2010). Intercessory prayer for the alleviation of ill health. *Cochrane Database of Systematic Reviews, Issue 1* (Article No. CD000368), DOI: 10.1002/14651858.CD000368.pub3.

Roberts, M. K., & Davidson, J. D. (1984). The nature and sources of religious involvement. *Review of Religious Research, 25,* 334–350.

Robinson-Smith, G. (2002). Prayer after stroke: Its relationship to quality of life. *Journal of Holistic Nursing, 20,* 352–366.

Roehlkepartain, E. C., Benson, P. L., Scales, P. C., Kimball, L., & King, P. E. (2008). *With their own voices.* Minneapolis, MN: Search Institute.

Roehlkepartain, E. C., King, P. E., Wagener, L., & Benson, P. L. (Eds.). (2006). *The handbook of spiritual development in childhood and adolescence.* Thousand Oaks, CA: Sage.

Rosenberg, R. (1990). The development of the concept of prayer in Jewish–Israeli children and adolescents. *Studies in Jewish Education, 5,* 91–129.

Rosenthal, R., Rosnow, R. L., & Rubin, D. B. (2000). *Contrasts and effect sizes in behavioral research.* New York: Cambridge University Press.

Ross, E. J., Weiss, D., & Jackson, L. (1996). The relation of Jungian psychological type to religious attitudes and practices. *International Journal for the Psychology of Religion, 6,* 263–279.

Ross, L. E., Hall, I. J., Fairley, T. L., Yhenneko, J. T., & Howard, D. L.

(2008). Prayer and self-reported health among cancer survivors in the United States, National Health Interview Survey, 2002. *Journal of Alternative and Complementary Medicine, 14,* 931–938.

Ross, M. G. (1950). *Religious beliefs of youth.* New York: Association Press.

Rotter, J. B. (1966). Generalized expectancies for internal versus external control of reinforcement. *Psychological Monographs, 80*(1, Whole No. 609), 1–28.

Rubin, Z., & Peplau, A. (1973). Belief in a just world and reactions to another's lot: A study of participants in the National Draft Lottery. *Journal of Social Issues, 29,* 73–93.

Sabatier, A. (1897). *Outlines of a philosophy of religion based on psychology and history.* New York: James Pott.

Safavi, M., Sabuhl, F., & Mahmoudi, M. (2007). The effect of prayer on blood pressure. *Iranian Journal of Nursing and Midwifery Research, 12,* 35–39.

Saudia, T. L., Kinney, M. R., Brown, K. C., & Young-Ward, L. (1991). Health locus of control and helpfulness of prayer. *Heart and Lung, 20,* 60–65.

Saver, J. L., & Rabin, J. (1997). The neural substrate of religious experience. *Journal of Neuropsychiatry and Clinical Neurosciences, 9,* 498–510.

Saxe, R., Tenenbaum, J. B., & Carey, S. (2005). Secret agents: Inferences about hidden causes by 1- and 12-month-old infants. *Psychological Science, 16,* 995–1001.

Schermer, M. (2004). Flying carpets and scientific prayers. *Scientific American, 291*(5), 34.

Schieman, S., Bierman, A., & Ellison, C. G. (2010). Religious involvement, beliefs about God, and the sense of mattering among older adults. *Journal for the Scientific Study of Religion, 49,* 517–535.

Schjoedt, U. (2009). The religious brain: A general introduction to the experimental neuroscience of religion. *Method and Theory in the Study of Religion, 21,* 310–339.

Schjoedt, U., Stodkilde-Jorgensen, H., Geertz, A. W., & Roepstorff, A. (2008). Reward prayers. *Neuroscience Letters, 443,* 165–168.

Schjoedt, U., Stodkilde-Jorgensen, H., Geertz, A. W., & Roepstorff, A. (2009). Highly religious participants recruit areas of social cognition in personal prayer. *Social, Cognitive and Affective Neuroscience, 4,* 199–207

Schjoedt, U., Stodkilde-Jorgensen, H., Geertz, A. W., Lund, T. E., & Roepstorff, A. (2010, March 12). The power of charisma—Perceived charisma inhibits the frontal executive network of believers in intercessory prayer. *Social Cognitive and Affective Neuroscience Advance Access, 6,* 119–127.

Schnall, E. (2008). The relationship between religion and cardiovascular outcomes and all-cause mortality in the women's health initiative observational study. *Psychology and Health* [online journal], pp. 1–15.

Search Institute. (1990). *Effective Christian education: A national study of Protestant denominations.* Minneapolis, MN: Author.

Sedek, G., & Kofta, M. (1990). When cognitive exertion does not yield cognitive gain: Toward an informational explanation of learned helplessness. *Journal of Personality and Social Psychology, 58*, 729–743.

Sedek, G., Kofta, M., & Tyszka, T. (1993). Effects of uncontrollability on subsequent decision making: Testing the cognitive exhaustion hypothesis. *Journal of Personality and Social Psychology, 65*, 1270–1281.

Seeman, T. E., Dubin, L. F., & Seeman, M. (2003). Religiosity/spirituality and health. *American Psychologist, 58*, 53–63.

Seligman, M. E. P. (1975). *Helplessness: On depression, development, and death*. San Francisco: Freeman.

Seventh annual black church week of prayer for the healing of AIDS March 5–11. (2006, March 9). *Westside Gazette*. Retrieved from *www.encyclopedia.com/doc/1P3-1054629731.html*.

Sexton, P., Leak, G., & Toenies, F. (1980). Relationship of locus of control and modernity to certainty of religious beliefs. *Psychological Reports, 46*, 1285–1286.

Shapiro, D. H. (1982). Overview: Clinical and physiological comparisons of meditation and other self-control strategies. *American Journal of Psychiatry, 139*, 267–274.

Sharp, S. (2010). How does prayer help manage emotions? *Social Psychology Quarterly, 73*, 417–437.

Shenhav, A., Rand, D. G., & Greene, J. D. (in press). Divine intuition: Cognitive style influences belief in God. *Journal of Experimental Psychology: General*.

Shrauger, J. S., & Silverman, R. E. (1971). The relationship of religious background and participation to locus of control. *Journal for the Scientific Study of Religion, 10*, 11–16.

Sicher, F., Targ, E., Moore, D., & Smith, H. S. (1998). A randomized double-blind study of the effect of distant healing in a population with advanced AIDS: Report of a small scale study. *Western Journal of Medicine, 169*, 356–363.

Siegel, K., Anderman, S. J., & Schrimshaw, E. W. (2001). Religion and coping with health-related stress. *Psychology and Health, 16*, 631–653.

Silvestri, P. J. (1979). Locus of control and God-dependence. *Psychological Reports, 45*, 89–90.

Sloan, R. P. (2000, June 26). Data without a prayer. *Archives of Internal Medicine, 160*, 1870.

Sloan, R. P. (2006). *Blind faith*. New York: St. Martin's Press.

Sloan, R. P., & Bagiella, E. (2002). Claims about religious involvement and health outcomes. *Annals of Behavioral Medicine, 24*, 14–21.

Sloan, R. P., & Ramakrishnan, R. (2006). Science, medicine and intercessory prayer. *Perspectives in Biology and Medicine, 49*, 504–514.

Smart, N. (1972). *The concept of worship*. London: Macmillan.

Smith, B. W., Dalen, J., Wiggins, K. T., Christopher, P. J., Bernard, J. F., &

Shelley, B. M. (2008). Who is willing to use complementary and alternative medicine? *Explore, 4*, 359–367.

Smith, C., & Denton, M. L. (2005). *Soul searching: The religious and spiritual lives of American teenagers.* New York: Oxford University Press.

Smith, C., Faris, R., Denton, L. M., & Regnerus, M. (2003). Mapping American adolescent subjective religiosity and attitudes of alienation toward religion: A research report. *Sociology of Religion, 64*, 111–133.

Smith, C., & Snell, P. (2009). *Souls in transition: The religious and spiritual lives of emerging adults.* New York: Oxford University Press.

Solfvin, J., Leskowitz, E., & Benor, D. J. (2005). Questions concerning the work of Daniel P. Wirth. *Journal of Alternative and Complementary Medicine, 11*, 949–950.

Sood, A. K., Armaiz-Pena, G. N., Halder, J., Nick, A. M., Stone, R. L., Hu, W., et al. (2010). Adrenergic modulation of focal adhesion kinase protects human ovarian cancer cells from anoikis. *Journal of Clinical Investigation, 120*(5), 1515–1523.

Spacapan, S., & Oskamp, S. (1989). Introduction to the social psychology of aging. In S. Spacapan & S. Oskamp (Eds.), *The social psychology of aging* (pp. 9–24). Newbury Park, CA: Sage.

Spencer, F. A., Goldberg, R. J., Becker, R. C., & Gore, J. M. (1998). Seasonal distribution of acute myocardial infarction in the Second National Registry of Myocardial Infarction. *Journal of the American College of Cardiology, 31*, 1226–1233.

Spielberger, C. D. (1985). Assessment of state and trait anxiety: Conceptual and methodological issues. *Southern Psychologist, 2*, 6–16.

Spilka, B. (1976). The compleat person: Some theoretical views and research findings for a theological-psychology of religion. *Journal of Psychology and Theology, 4*, 15–24.

Spilka, B., Armatas, P., & Nussbaum, J. (1964). The concept of God: A factor analytic approach. *Review of Religious Research, 6*, 28–36.

Spilka, B., & McIntosh, D. N. (1999). Bridging religion and psychology: The Hall-James generation as transition from the "Old" to the "New" psychology. In L. J. Rector & W. Santaniello (Eds.), *Psychological perspectives and the religious quest* (pp. 7–39). Lanham, MD: University Press of America.

Spilka, B., & Reynolds, J. F. (1965). Religion and prejudice: A factor-analytic study. *Review of Religious Research, 6*, 163–168.

Spilka, B., & Schmidt, G. (1983). General attribution theory for the psychology of religion: The influence of event-character on attributions to God. *Journal for the Scientific Study of Religion, 22*, 326–339.

Spilka, B., Shaver, P., & Kirkpatrick, L. A. (1985). A general attribution theory for the psychology of religion. *Journal for the Scientific Study of Religion, 24*, 1–20.

Sprehn, G. C., Chambers, J. E., Saykin, A. J., Konski, A., & Johnstone, P.

A. S. (2009). Decreased cancer survival in individual separated at time of diagnosis. *Cancer, 115,* 5108–5116.

Stark, R. (1968). Age and faith: A changing outlook or an old process. *Sociological Analysis, 29,* 1–10.

Stein, R. (2006, March 24). Researchers look at prayer and healing. Retrieved from *www.washingtonpost.com/wp-dyn/content/article/2006/03/23.*

Sterling, P., & Eyer, J. (1988). Allostasis: A new paradigm to explain arousal pathology. In S. Fisher & J. Reason (Eds.), *Handbook of life stress, cognition and health* (pp. 629–649). New York: Wiley.

Stevens-Long, J. (1984). *Adult life: Developmental processes* (2nd ed.). Palo Alto, CA: Mayfield.

Stevens-Long, J. (1990). Adult development: Theories past present and future. In R. A. Nemiroff & C. A. Colarusso (Eds.), *New dimensions in adult development* (pp. 125–169). New York: Basic Books.

Stewart, G. S. (1939). *The lower levels of prayer.* New York: Abingdon.

Stolz, K. R. (1913). *Auto-suggestion in private prayer.* Grand Forks, ND: Author.

Stolz, K. R. (1923). *The psychology of prayer.* New York: Abingdon.

Straus, S. E., & Stoney, C. (2005). Prayer and spirituality in health: Ancient practices, modern science. *National Center for Complementary and Alternative Medicine, 12*(1).

Strawbridge, W. J., Cohen, R. D., Shema, S. J., & Kaplan, G. A. (1997). Frequent attendance at religious services and mortality over 28 years. *American Journal of Public Health, 87,* 957–961.

Strawbridge, W. J., Shema, S. J., Cohen, R. D., & Kaplan, G. A. (2001). Religious attendance increases survival by improving and maintaining good health behaviors, mental health, and social relationships. *Annals of Behavioral Medicine, 23,* 68–74.

Strickland, F. L. (1924). *Psychology of religious experience.* New York: Abingdon.

Strong, A. L. (1909). *The psychology of prayer.* Chicago: University of Chicago Press.

Sudsuang, R., Chentanez, V., & Veluvan, K. (1991). Effect of Buddhist meditation on serum cortisol and total protein levels, blood pressure, pulse rate, lung volume and reaction time. *Physiology of Behavior, 50,* 543–548.

Sullivan, K. T., & Karney, B. R. (2008). Incorporating religious practice in marital interventions: To pray or not to pray? *Journal of Social and Clinical Psychology, 27,* 670–677.

Surwillo, W. W., & Hobson, D. P. (1978). Brain electrical activity during prayer. *Psychological Reports, 43,* 135–143.

Sutton, T. D., & Murphy, S. P. (1989). Stressors and patterns of coping in renal transplant patients. *Nursing Research, 38*(1), 46–49.

Tamminen, K. (1991). *Religious development in childhood and youth.* Helsinki, Finland: Suomalainen Tiedeakatemia.

Tan, S.-Y. (1996). Practicing the presence of God: The work of Richard J.

Foster and its applications to psychotherapeutic practice. *Journal of Psychology and Christianity, 15*, 17–28.

Targ, E. (1997). Evaluating distant healing: A research review. *Alternative Therapies, 3*, 74–78.

Tartaro, J., Luecken, L. J., & Gunn, H. E. (2005). Exploring heart and soul: Effects of religiosity/spirituality and gender on blood pressure and cortisol stress responses. *Journal of Health Psychology, 10*, 753–766.

Tatala, M. (2009). Development of prayer in adolescence and youth. *Journal of Psychology and Counseling, 17*, 113–116.

Tennen, H., Affleck, G., Urrows, S., Higgins, P., & Mendola, R. (1992). Perceiving control, construing benefits, and daily processes in rheumatoid arthritis. *Canadian Journal of Behavioral Science, 24*, 186–203.

Tessman, I., & Tessman, J. (2000). Efficacy of prayer: A critical evaluation of claims. *Skeptical Inquirer, 24*(2), 31–33.

Tholl, U., Forstner, K., & Anlauf, M. (2004). Measuring blood pressure: Pitfalls and recommendations. *Nephrology Dialysis Transplantation, 19*, 766–770.

Thompson, S. C. (1981). Will it hurt less if I can control it?: A complex answer to a simple question. *Psychological Bulletin, 90*, 89–101.

Thune-Boyle, I. C., Stygall, J. A., Keshtgar, M. R., & Newman, S. P. (2006). Do religious/spiritual coping strategies affect illness adjustment in patients with cancer?: A systematic review of the literature. *Social Science and Medicine, 63*, 151–164.

Tillett, W. F. (1926). *Providence, prayer, and power: Studies in the philosophy, psychology, and dynamics of the Christian religion.* Nashville, TN: Cokesbury.

Timio, M., Verdecchia, P., Venanzi, S., Gentili, S., Ronconi, M., Francucci, B., et al. (1988). Age and blood pressure changes: A 20-year follow-up study in nuns in a secluded order. *Hypertension, 12*(4), 457–461.

Tipton, R. M., Harrison, B. M., & Mahoney, J. (1980). Faith and locus of control. *Psychological Reports, 46*, 1151–1154.

Titus, S. L., Wells, J. A., & Rhoades, L. J. (2008, June 19). Commentary: Repairing research integrity. *Nature, 453*, 980–982.

Tloczynski, J., & Fritzsch, S. (2002). Intercessory prayer in psychological well-being using a multiple baseline across subjects design. *Psychological Reports, 91*, 731–741.

Tonne, C., Melle, S., Mittleman, M., Coull, B., Goldberg, R., & Schwartz, J. (2007). A case-control analysis of exposure to traffic and acute myocardial infarction. *Environmental Health Perspectives, 115*(1), 53–57.

Tremlin, T. (2006). *Minds and gods: The cognitive foundations of religion.* New York: Oxford University Press.

Truzzi, M. (1987). On pseudo-skepticism. Retrieved from *www.answers.com/topic/marcello-truzzi.*

Turner, J. A., & Clancy, S. (1986). Strategies for coping with chronic low back pain: Relationship to pain and disability. *Pain, 24,* 355–364.

Tuttle, D. H., Shutty, M. S., Jr., & DeGood, D. E. (1991). Empirical dimensions of coping in chronic pain patients: A factorial analysis. *Rehabilitation Psychology, 36,* 179–189.

Tyrrell, B. J. (1985). Christotherapy: An approach to facilitating psychospiritual healing and growth. In R. J. Wicks, R. D. Parsons, & D. Capps (Eds.), *Clinical handbook of pastoral counseling* (pp. 58–75). New York: Paulist Press.

Uchino, B. N. (2004). *Social support and physical health.* New Haven, CT: Yale University Press.

Ulanov, A., & Ulanov, B. (1982). *Primary speech: A psychology of prayer.* Atlanta: John Knox Press.

Urubshurow, V. K. (1992). Meditation and prayer (1): Creative imagination in the lives of Ignatius Loyola and Tsong Khapa: Visualization in Roman Catholic and Tibetan Buddhist practice. In A. V. Kaam (Ed.), *Studies in formative spirituality* (Vol. 14, pp. 41–56). Pittsburgh: Duquesne University.

U.S. Bureau of the Census. (2008). *Statistical abstract of the United States: 2009.* Washington, DC: U.S. Government Printing Office.

VandeCreek, L. (2001). The parish clergy's ministry of prayer with hospitalized parishioners. In L. J. Francis (Ed.), *Psychological perspectives on prayer* (pp. 207–217). Herfordshire, UK: Gracewing.

VandeCreek, L., & Cooke, B. (1996). Hospital pastoral care practices of parish clergy. In J. M. Greer, M. L. Lynn, & D. O. Moberg (Eds.), *Research in the social scientific study of religion* (pp. 253–264). Boston: Brill.

VandeCreek, L., Janus, M.-D., Pennebaker, J. W., & Binau, B. (2002). Praying about difficult experiences as self-disclosure to God. *International Journal for the Psychology of Religion, 12,* 25–39.

VandeCreek, L., Paget, S., Horton, R., Robbins, L., Oettinger, M., & Tai, K. (2004). Religious and nonreligious coping methods among persons with rheumatoid arthritis. *Arthritis and Rheumatism, 51,* 49–55.

Van der Does, W. (2000, June 26). A randomized controlled trial of prayer. *Archives of Internal Medicine, 160,* 1871–1872.

Vaux, K. (1990). Theology as the queen (bee) of the disciplines? *Zygon, 25*(3), 317–322.

Volegov, P., Matlachov, A., Mosher, J., Espy, M. A., & Kraus, R. H., Jr. (2004). Noise-free magnetoencephalography recordings of brain function. *Physics in Medicine and Biology, 49,* 2117–2128.

Vul, E., Harris, C., Winkielman, P., & Pashler, H. (2009). Puzzlingly high correlations in fMRI studies of emotion, personality, and social cognition. *Psychological Science, 4,* 274–290.

Wachholtz, A. B., & Pargament, K. I. (2005). Is spirituality a critical ingredient of meditation?: Comparing the effects of spiritual meditation, secular meditation, and relaxation on spiritual, psychological, cardiac, and pain outcomes. *Journal of Behavioral Medicine, 28,* 369–384.

Wade, N. (2010). From liability to asset: My experience with psychology's growing openness to the transcendent. *Psychology of Religion Newsletter, 34,* 3.

Walker, S. R., Tonigan, J. S., Miller, W. R., Comer, S., & Kahlich, L. (1997). Intercessory prayer in the treatment of alcohol abuse and dependence: A pilot investigation. *Alternative Therapies, 3*(6), 79–86.

Waller, N. G., Kojetin, B. A., Bouchard, T. J., Jr., Lykken, D. T., & Tellegen, A. (1990). Genetic and environmental influences on religious interests, attitudes, and values: A study of twins reared apart and together. *Psychological Science, 1,* 138–142.

Wallston, K. A. (2005). Overview of the special issue on research with the Multidimensional Health Locus of Control (MHLC) scales. *Journal of Health Psychology, 10,* 619–621.

Watts, F., & Williams, M. (1988). *The psychology of religious knowing.* Cambridge, UK: Cambridge University Press.

Webb, L. (1962). *The art of personal prayer.* New York: Abingdon.

Weisz, J. R., Rothbaum, F. M., & Blackburn, T. C. (1984). Standing out and standing in: The psychology of control in America and Japan. *American Psychologist, 39,* 955–969.

Weston, M. J., Bett, J. H. N., & Over, R. (1976). Consensus opinion and observer accuracy in electrocardiography with reference to coronary arteriographic information. *Internal Medicine Journal, 6,* 429–432.

Whittington, B. L., & Scher, S. J. (2010). Prayer and subjective well-being: An examination of six different types of prayer. *International Journal for the Psychology of Religion, 20,* 59–68.

Wilkinson, L., & American Psychological Association, Task Force on Statistical Inference. (1999). Statistical methods in psychology journals: Guidelines and explanations. *American Psychologist, 54,* 594–604.

Williams, J. W. (2009). *The relationship of private prayer and other factors to adherence to a cardiac rehabilitation regime for medical patients with cardiovascular disease.* Unpublished doctoral dissertation, Fielding Graduate University.

Williamson, W. P., Morris, R. J., & Hood, R. W., Jr. (1995, October). *Prayer as a predictor of spiritual and existential well-being.* Paper presented at the convention of the Society for the Scientific Study of Religion, St. Louis, MO.

Wirth, D. P. (1994). Complementary healing therapies. *International Journal of Psychosomatics, 41,* 61–67.

Wolfram, A. (2002). *A new kind of science.* Champaign, IL: Wolfram Media.

Wong, Y. J., Rew, L., & Slaikeu, K. D. (2006). A systematic review of recent research on adolescent religiosity/spirituality and mental health. *Issues in Mental Health Nursing, 27,* 161–183.

Woolley, J. D., & Phelps, K. E. (2001). The development of children's beliefs about prayer. *Journal of Cognition and Culture, 1,* 139–166.

Worcester, E., & McComb, S. (1931). *Body, mind and spirit.* Boston: Marshall Jones.

Worten, S. A., & Dollinger, S. J. (1986). Mother's intrinsic religious motivation, disciplinary preferences, and children's conceptions of prayer. *Psychological Reports, 58,* 118.

Worthington, E. L., Jr. (2008). Prayer and marital intervention: Can it be long and strong enough to matter? *Journal of Social and Clinical Psychology, 27,* 686–692.

Wright, R. E. (1995). Logistic regression. In L. G. Grimm & P. R. Yarnold (Eds.), *Reading and understanding multivariate statistics* (pp. 217–244). Washington, DC: American Psychological Association.

Wuthnow, R. (2008a). Prayer, cognition, and culture. *Poetics, 36,* 333–337.

Wuthnow, R. (2008b). Teach us to pray: The cognitive power of domain violations. *Poetics, 36,* 493–506.

Yates, J. W., Chalmer, B. J., Follansbee, J. P., & McKegney, M. (1981). Religion in patients with advanced cancer. *Medical and Pediatric Oncology, 9,* 121–128.

Younger, J., Finan, P., Zautra, A., Reich, J., & Davis, M. (2008). Personal control in chronic pain sufferers during acute interpersonal stress. *Psychology and Health, 23,* 515–535.

Zaleski, P. A., & Zaleski, C. (2005). *Prayer: A history.* Boston: Houghton Mifflin.

Zinnbauer, B. J., & Pargament, K. I. (2005). Religiousness and spirituality. In R. F. Paloutzian & C. L. Park (Eds.), *Handbook of the psychology of religion and spirituality* (pp. 21–42). New York: Guilford Press.

Index

Page references in *italic* refer to tables.

Acquired immune deficiency syndrome (AIDS), 131–133, 151
Acute coronary syndrome, 128
Adolescent prayer
  egocentrism and altruism in, 74–75
  formal operational logic and, 72–74
  influence of parents on, 74
  review of research on, 71–72, 76–77, 87
  structure and content, 75–76
Adolescents
  petitionary prayer and, 58
  tasks of adolescence, 72
Adrenal glands, 116
Adrenocorticotropic hormone (ACTH), 116
Adult prayer
  correlates of, 83
  early adulthood, 79–81
  midlife, 81–83
  old age, 83–84
  prayer and death, 85
  review of research on, 77–79, 85–87
  well-being and, 95
Affective experience, effect of prayer on, 42–43
African Americans
  arthritis and prayer, 134
  HIV/AIDS and prayer, 132
  prayer and well-being, 90–91
  prayer in midlife, 82
  prayer in old age, 84
AIDS, 131–133, 151
Akron Area Survey, 92
Alcoholics Anonymous, 102
Alcohol use, 102
Alternative medicine. *See* Complementary and alternative medicine
Alternative Therapies, 142
Altruism, and egocentrism in adolescent prayer, 74–75
Altruistic prayer, 67
American Psychological Association (APA), 2, 157
Angels, 28
Anger, coping with, 91
Animism, 63
Anxiety disorders, 98–99

APA Task Force, 179
Arthritis, 134–135
Attributions, 34–35
Attribution theory, 175–176
Auto-suggestion, 14

B

Background prayer, 140, 155
Behavior, effect of prayer on, 42
Benson, Herbert, 147–149
Biases, 8
Blood pressure
  sources of measurement error, 137–138n1
  studies on religion, prayer, and blood pressure, 120–123
  systolic and diastolic, 120
Bold assertion (BA), 54, 172
Brain studies. *See* Neuropsychology
British Medical Association, 141
Buddhists, prayer nodules and, 136
Byrd, Randolph C., 142–144, 161–162n2, 161n1

C

CAM. *See* Complementary and alternative medicine
Cancer, 129–131
Cardiac patients
  intercessory prayer research
    of Randolph C. Byrd, 142–144, 161–162n2, 161n1
    of William A. Harris, 144–146, 162n4
    MANTRA studies of Mitchell Krucoff, 146–147
    Mayo Clinic study, 147
    of Leanne Roberts and Steve Hall, 149
    STEP project of Herbert Benson, 147–149
  prayer and control, 167
  prayer and psychological responses to cardiac problems, 126–128
Cardiovascular health
  prayer and psychological responses to cardiac problems, 126–128
  religion, prayer, and blood pressure, 120–123